ENEMIES

ENEMiES

How America's Foes Steal Our Vital Secrets— and How We Let it Happen

Bill Gertz

CROWN
FORUM

New York

Published in the United States by Crown Forum, an imprint of the
Crown Publishing Group, a division of Random House, Inc., New York.
www.crownpublishing.com

Crown Forum and colophon are registered
trademarks of Random House, Inc.

Library of Congress Cataloging-in-Publication Data
Gertz, Bill.
Enemies: How America's foes steal our vital secrets—
and how we let it happen / Bill Gertz.
Includes index.
1. Espionage—United States. 2. Terrorism—United States.
3. War on Terrorism, 2001–
I. Title.
UB251.U5G47   2006
327.120973—dc22   2006020610

ISBN-13: 978-0-307-33805-1
ISBN-10: 0-307-33805-3

Printed in the United States of America

Design by Lauren Dong

10 9 8 7 6 5 4 3 2 1

First Edition

To the unsung heroes of American counterintelligence

There is one evil I dread, and that is their spies.

—George Washington, on British intelligence,
in a letter to Josiah Quincy, March 24, 1776

Contents

ENEMiES

THE GAPiNG HOLES iN AMERiCA'S DEFENSES

I think that if I were asked to single out one specific group of men, one type, one category, as being the most suspicious, unbelieving, unreasonable, petty, inhuman, sadistic, double-crossing set of bastards in any language, I would say without hesitation: the people who run counter-espionage departments.

—*Sign on the office wall of an FBI counterintelligence official, circa 1988 (from the 1962 Eric Ambler novel* The Light of Day*)*

On March 7, 2005, agents of the U.S. Immigration and Customs Enforcement service, known as ICE, arrested a Philippines national for overstaying his visa in New York City. That immigration violation would soon reveal a much deeper problem.

The day after the arrest, FBI intelligence analyst Leandro Aragoncillo walked into the ICE offices at Twenty-six Federal Plaza in downtown New York City. He told the agents that the man they had arrested, former Philippines police intelligence specialist Michael Aquino, was his friend, and he asked whether he could do anything to help straighten out the visa problem. The ICE agents were deferential but cautious, making no commitments to Aragoncillo. The next day, Aragoncillo called back and asked how the investigation was going. The phone call did it. The ICE agent in charge of the case smelled a rat. "Anytime somebody tries to push their weight around like that, that sets off alarm bells," one federal agent later told me of Aragoncillo's interference. The ICE agent contacted the FBI's New York field office, which in turn alerted FBI headquarters. That set off an ethics inquiry into the matter.

Within days, FBI investigators recognized that Aragoncillo's intervention was more than a matter of ethics. He was a foreign spy—a mole operating right under their noses.

Investigators discovered that Aragoncillo, who had worked in the White House for almost three years before joining the FBI, had used his top-secret security clearance at both the White House and the Bureau to pass highly classified intelligence documents to political officials in the Philippines, his native land. The Filipino officials used the documents as part of a plot to overthrow the government of the Philippines.

On September 10, 2005, the FBI arrested Aragoncillo for betraying the United States and spying for foreign officials.

Just four months after Aragoncillo's arrest, in January 2006, Michelle Van Cleave resigned from her position as head of the Office of the National Counterintelligence Executive, known by the initials NCIX. Van Cleave had been the most senior counterintelligence official in the entire U.S. government. Her resignation came quickly on the heels of the retirement of the deputy NCIX director Kenneth deGraffenreid.

Neither the arrest of Aragoncillo nor the departures of the nation's two top counterintelligence officials had much impact. True, Aragoncillo's arrest and indictment prompted a flurry of news stories in the fall of 2005; after all, it involved a mole operating in the White House itself. But the story soon faded away, to the point that when Aragoncillo pleaded guilty to espionage and other charges, in May 2006, it drew little attention. And the departures of Van Cleave and deGraffenreid barely registered at all. They seemed to be just two more small changes in the massive Washington bureaucracy.

But in fact these incidents, taken together, point to a much greater problem—one that poses a grave threat to the national security of the United States.

The Aragoncillo case highlighted the fact that foreign governments and terrorist organizations are actively spying within the United States and stealing our most vital secrets—on our nuclear weapons, missile defenses, efforts to defeat global terrorism, intelligence sources and methods, cryptographic codes, sensitive foreign policy dealings, and much more.

Today, nearly 140 nations and some 35 known and suspected terrorist groups target the United States through espionage, according to intelligence officials. And since 1985, nearly 80 Americans have been caught spying for other countries. Over the past several decades, foreign agents have penetrated every U.S. national security agency except the Coast Guard. That includes the CIA, the FBI, the National Security Agency, the Defense Intelligence Agency, the Defense Department, the State Department, and the Energy Department.

Far from getting better since the Cold War ended, the enemy spying picture seems to be getting worse.

More than anything else, the Aragoncillo case revealed that the FBI remains highly vulnerable to foreign espionage. After the 2001 arrest of FBI turncoat Robert Hanssen—a spy for Moscow, and one of the most damaging moles in U.S. history—the Bureau instituted some internal security reforms. But the Aragoncillo case highlighted how little the reforms have actually accomplished. Computer controls designed to trigger alarms when someone like Aragoncillo stole classified documents did not tip off the FBI. If it hadn't been for an ICE agent questioning whether it was proper for an FBI analyst to help out someone involved in a visa violation, the FBI would not have looked into Aragoncillo's case at all.

The intensity of foreign spying and the intelligence community's failure to prevent espionage make the disarray at the nation's top counterintelligence office—and the larger counterintelligence problems it underscored—particularly disturbing. Counterintelligence is, quite simply, the process of identifying and catching foreign spies, either to neutralize them or to exploit knowledge of their activities for one's own purposes. ("Turning" foreign agents—that is, convincing captured spies to work as double agents for the United States rather than go to jail—is one of the highest objectives of U.S. counterintelligence.)

The 1947 National Security Act defines counterintelligence as "information gathered, and activities conducted, to protect against espionage, other intelligence activities, sabotage, or assassinations conducted by or on behalf of foreign governments or elements thereof, foreign organizations, or foreign persons, or international terrorist activities." An updated definition drafted by the Bush administration, but not yet formally adopted by the U.S. government, states that counterintelligence is "information gathered and activities conducted to identify, assess, neutralize, and exploit the intelligence activities and capabilities of foreign powers, terrorist groups, and other foreign entities that harm U.S. national security at home and abroad." As the draft wording documents, foreign intelligence activities include everything from traditional espionage—human spying—to "technical collection, sabotage, influence operations, and manipulation of, or interference with, U.S. defense and intelligence activities."

In short, counterintelligence represents an absolutely essential line of defense against our enemies, including terrorist organizations. As former Senate Intelligence Committee staff member Angelo Codevilla has noted, counterintelligence is "the queen of the intelligence chessboard." Unfortunately, the U.S. government has disregarded our counterintelligence capabilities and done little to repair the long-neglected and deeply fragmented counterintelligence apparatus.

The result, as we will see, has been repeated, staggering failures to prevent our enemies from infiltrating our government and intelligence community. Counterintelligence failings receive little attention, but they leave gaping holes in America's defenses. Simply put, our enemies have been so successful at getting inside the U.S. government because the United States lets it happen.

These dangers are the great untold story of the War on Terror and the post–Cold War era.

Enemies Within

This book will provide an inside look at the intelligence-gathering, spying, and influence operations of America's most dangerous enemies, from Communist regimes like China, North Korea, and Cuba to the terrorist organizations that now represent an immediate threat to Americans and U.S. allies around the world. These enemies recognize the importance of ancient Chinese military strategist Sun Tzu's dictum: The acme of skill is defeating your enemy without firing a shot.

A close look at the shadowy world of intelligence and counterintelligence also reveals that distinctions between our enemies and our friends are sometimes not so clear. The fact is that many countries generally considered friendly to the United States have targeted our government and military with aggressive spying operations. "Friendly spies" come from France, India, Pakistan, Japan, South Korea, Taiwan, and, as the Leandro Aragoncillo case indicated, the Philippines, among other countries.

And those threats pale in comparison to the one posed by Russia. In recent years the United States has received many warnings that Russia might not be the ally to the West many observers hoped it would be after the end of the Cold War. The authoritarian tactics of Russian president Vladimir Putin (a former Soviet KGB official), Moscow's opposition to the United States within the United Nations, and especially the substantial evidence that Russia aided Saddam Hussein's Iraqi military right up to the beginning of the Iraq War—these and other developments have made U.S.-Russia relations frosty. But Russia's espionage operations against the United States should be even greater cause for alarm about Moscow. After a decade-long hiatus, Russian intelligence services are sending spies to this country in record numbers. In fact, there are as many Russian spies in the country today as there were during the Cold War.

As this book will demonstrate, it is not an accident that Russia has been responsible for the two most devastating spy cases of the past few decades—those of FBI mole Robert Hanssen and CIA turncoat Aldrich Ames. Significantly, both spy operations continued well after the collapse of the Soviet Union.

Communist China's intelligence services pose by far the greatest danger to the United States. Chinese spying operations have not simply penetrated U.S. government and intelligence agencies and stolen secrets. They have also enabled Beijing to execute extensive "disinformation" and perception-management operations, which are critical to a Communist regime intent on hiding its extensive military buildup, its repressive nature, its territorial ambitions (including, most notably, Taiwan), and its targeting of the United States. As we will see, Chinese disinformation campaigns have prevented the U.S. government from understanding, and responding to, the true threat posed by Communist China. They have also kept the United States from adequately protecting itself against future Chinese spying operations and other dangers from Beijing. Some intelligence officials say that Chinese influence operations have set back U.S. defensive and security measures against China by a decade or more.

The Chinese, along with other enemies, have fueled their significant military buildup and eaten into the U.S. military advantage by stealing sensitive dual-use and military technologies right out of America's most sensitive laboratories. The threat has become especially acute because illicit weapons proliferation makes the technology available to dangerous U.S. adversaries, including terrorists.

While the Aldrich Ames and Robert Hanssen cases have garnered the most headlines of any spy cases in recent years, Communist Chinese spies have done nearly as much damage to the United States. The most disturbing Chinese spy case is that of "Parlor Maid," a Chinese-born businesswoman named Katrina Leung. In December 2005, Leung reached a plea deal with U.S. prosecutors that spared her from the most serious espionage charges. The truth is that the failure to convict Leung as a Chinese spy reflects gross negligence and terrible bungling on the part of the FBI and federal prosecutors. The failure in that case and many others raises serious questions about whether China's intelligence penetration and influence operations have reached the highest levels of the U.S. government.

As will become apparent, the Parlor Maid affair was in many ways just as devastating as the Ames and Hanssen cases, or perhaps even more damaging. But the real story of the Katrina Leung case has never been told. It will be revealed for the first time in this book—as will numerous other instances of enemy penetration of the United States and harrowing U.S. counterintelligence failures.

The danger posed by enemy spies is not theoretical. It is very real, and if our leaders do not address the threat, Americans will be left to deal with the deadly consequences. Anyone who doubts our enemies' lethal intentions should remember their blunt threats against the United States. For example, in July 2005 Chinese Major General Zhu Chenghu declared that if the United States interfered militarily with Taiwan, "I think we will have to respond with nuclear weapons." He added, "The Americans will have to be prepared that hundreds . . . of cities will be destroyed by the Chinese."

Let there be no doubt, there are real consequences when our enemies steal the most important secrets of our military and intelligence services.

If the United States does not answer the intelligence threat, the success of foreign intelligence operations could, as Michelle Van Cleave put it, "come at dear cost, putting in jeopardy U.S. operations, military and intelligence personnel, and Americans at home."

America's Failure to Respond

Shockingly, U.S. officials still have done almost nothing to correct the ineptness and poor leadership that have brought us two decades of spy scandals. President George W. Bush has recognized the need for better and more active counterintelligence. The problem is that the government—and especially the entrenched intelligence bureaucracy—has not executed much-needed reforms.

In March 2005, President Bush approved a new National Counterintelligence Strategy, drafted primarily by Van Cleave and deGraffenreid, who had served as national security officials in the Reagan administration. The strategy followed closely the recommendations of several bipartisan congressional reviews from the past decade that recognized the urgent need for reform.

The adoption of the strategy seemed to represent a step forward, as it marked the first time the U.S. government formulated a comprehensive counterspy program that was aggressive rather than merely reactive. Van Cleave said in an interview, "In the past, our default posture was to sustain loss and then take swift action once that loss was detected—sometimes after nine, seventeen, or twenty-two years of successful espionage against us. Banking on acceptable loss was always a questionable approach to countering hostile intelligence activities. It is now intolerable given the changing foreign intelligence threat."

Van Cleave noted that major espionage cases in recent years— such as those of Ames, Hanssen, and Ana Montes, a Cuban mole in the DIA—have been utter disasters. "If you look at the devastating consequences of these successes against us, of the secrets stolen, of the lives lost, of the investments in major [intelligence and weapons] programs lost, of the compromises to U.S. national security, it is clear that we're being harmed terribly," she said.

So under the new counterintelligence strategy, the goal with foreign intelligence services, just as with terrorists, was to go on the offensive and engage them before they could do us harm. The Leandro Aragoncillo case provided a graphic reminder that simply installing more internal security measures won't prevent enemies from stealing our secrets. Van Cleave told me, "You can pile on so much security that you can't move and still there will be a purposeful adversary looking for ways to get at what it wants."

Therefore the new counterintelligence strategy called for "specific counterintelligence policies for attacking foreign intelligence services systematically via strategic counterintelligence operations." It required the FBI, the CIA, and other intelligence agencies to "identify, assess, neutralize, and exploit foreign intelligence activities before they can do harm to the United States." The strategy introduced for the first time "the concept of counterintelligence as a tool of national security policy," according to Van Cleave. She and deGraffenreid, and many others across the executive and legislative branches of government, had great hopes that with the president's imprimatur and a newly empowered counterintelligence office, they could finally push for tougher counterspying.

Both counterintelligence officials were gone within months. And with them went the immediate hope for an offensive counterintelligence program run by the NCIX.

The NCIX grew out of the damaging intelligence losses of the Cold War and, in particular, the devastating Ames and Hanssen cases. The office was created by President Bill Clinton's last presidential order in January 2001, known as Presidential Decision Directive 75. But it grew into a strategic or national-level office after the Republican Congress passed legislation in 2002. One of its major promoters was Porter Goss, then chairman of the House Permanent Select Committee on Intelligence, who later became CIA director. "The purpose was to provide strategic direction to U.S. counterintelligence," Van Cleave said. "An essential responsibility of the NCIX is to marshal the collective insights, talent, and resources of the several U.S. counterintelligence agencies to develop a strategy for the president to drive all U.S. counterintelligence."

Van Cleave recognized the urgent need to better understand foreign intelligence threats. "Foreign intelligence organizations aren't targeting an FBI field office, or a CIA station, or a military unit," she said. "They're going after America's national security secrets, plans, intentions, and capabilities to gain an advantage. It means looking at the problem across the board. In fact, the extensive foreign intelligence activities against us present opportunities we can exploit, provided we are organized for integrated, strategically directed CI [counterintelligence] operations, and seize the initiative."

As part of a planned upgrading of counterintelligence, Van Cleave reviewed the U.S. government's many damage assessments of Cold War spy cases. "I thought coming into the position that I had a fairly good understanding of how serious those losses had been," said Van Cleave, who worked in the Reagan White House's Office of Science and Technology Policy. "But when you look at it in the aggregate, it was truly staggering to see how much the United States lost and to know that if we had ever been in a shooting war with the former Soviet Union that some of the secrets that were compromised through espionage could have threatened our nation's survival."

Effective counterintelligence is needed more urgently than ever in the current war against terrorism. Every terrorist attack is preceded by an intelligence operation. "So you can't just stand back and hope for the best; you have to get at the threats," Van Cleave said. "That requires prioritized collection and analysis of these very difficult targets, to understand their 'order of battle.' It also requires creative operational planning to be able to degrade foreign intelligence capabilities as the president and his national security leadership may direct."

While Islamic extremists pose the most immediate danger, there are broader foreign intelligence and national security threats. "The sheer numbers of foreign collectors, the diversity and clandestine nature of the foreign 'presence' in the United States, and new attack modes enabled by technology exceed the reach of our CI resources as presently configured," Van Cleave said. In fact, she said, "we have every reason to think that creative adversaries are taking advantage of the fact that we are so properly consumed with the war on terrorism that we may have less time and attention to devote to what they're doing. So there is a window of opportunity right now that our adversaries are exploiting."

That is why the National Counterintelligence Strategy called for a new approach. "If we're not coherent in dealing with these very long-term, very grave threats to our security and our interests worldwide," Van Cleave said, "then we're going to suffer the consequences in the years to come."

Despite the pressing need for aggressive counterintelligence and the president's pledge to beef up counterspying operations, the functions and powers of the NCIX were limited once it was subsumed into the newly created Office of the Director of National Intelligence (ODNI). The intelligence and national security bureaucracy fought the kinds of changes that Van Cleave, deGraffenreid, and other reformers advocated, and bureaucratic turf battles stalled the new offensive counterintelligence strategy the president had just approved. "The CI community found itself answering to all of these new offices, and the coherence that was supposed to be behind the NCIX was lost in the effort to build a robust DNI structure," Van Cleave said.

The problem is not with the rank-and-file counterintelligence officials, who, as Van Cleave put it, are "dedicated and talented professionals" who support needed reforms. The problem is one of leadership. The intelligence and national security bureaucracy has long viewed counterintelligence not as a strategic offensive function but merely as a support or "gatekeeper" function. The CIA, for instance, has viewed counterintelligence as a means to support its intelligence-gathering operations, while the military has regarded it as a means of protecting its forces. Sure enough, under the new intelligence bureaucracy, "counterintelligence was seen by some of the leadership within the [ODNI] as being principally a support activity to collection, or a subordinate topic for analysis, or one of the many program areas the intelligence budget director would have control over," according to Van Cleave.

Van Cleave noted that "key CI insights and operations" need to be "integrated and directed to a common purpose" under a strategically directed counterintelligence program. But one of the first reorganizations under Director of National Intelligence John Negroponte, a career diplomat, involved setting up a new National Clandestine Service in which counterintelligence would be relegated to a support function for the intelligence gatherers. Van Cleave saw her position as the nation's top counterintelligence official undermined, as she was not even included in setting up the counterintelligence component of the new clandestine service.

Then the Office of the DNI concluded a budget deal with other intelligence agencies that took 75 percent of all centrally directed counterintelligence funds and gave it back to the Justice Department and the Pentagon. The budget deal effectively gutted the ability of the DNI or the NCIX to build a national program for counterintelligence.

Notably, the DNI's October 2005 National Intelligence Strategy omitted all references to the strategic counterintelligence mission or to the counterintelligence strategy the president had approved just seven months earlier. John Negroponte and his subordinates, many of whom have little intelligence experience, have essentially ignored the call for an aggressive and comprehensive counterintelligence strategy.

The leadership problem is not confined to the ODNI. Many different government agencies charged with dealing with foreign intelligence are resisting changes and insist that what they are doing now meets the new objectives outlined in the national strategy. "Strategic vision is not readily translated into effective action without leadership and insistence on accountability that must go behind its implementation," Van Cleave said.

Why does the intelligence establishment so strongly resist tougher and more aggressive counterintelligence? The issue is largely cultural. Middle and senior managers throughout the intelligence community are reluctant to have their work checked by someone outside their immediate agency. The head of FBI counterintelligence will take orders from the FBI director but no one else. Officials listen to strategic directives but then go about their business as they choose.

Another factor is the stigma attached to offensive counterintelligence. The 1970s witnessed a backlash against the aggressive operations devised by master counterspy James Jesus Angleton. Angleton headed the CIA's independent counterintelligence staff from 1954 to 1973. His main job was to find enemy penetration agents within the CIA, especially Soviet agents.

According to the conventional view within the intelligence bureaucracy, counterintelligence distracted the CIA from its true mission, to gather information on foreign entities. The National Commission on Terrorist Attacks Upon the United States, better known as the 9/11 Commission, promoted this view when it wrote that in the 1970s the CIA "developed a concern, bordering on paranoia, about penetration by the Soviet KGB." According to the report, Angleton was "obsessed" with the idea that Moscow had planted "one or more" penetration agents inside the CIA.

But the conventional view misses how inextricably linked counterintelligence is to effective intelligence operations. Good counterintelligence does not simply involve investigating suspected spies within the United States; it requires actively targeting and ultimately infiltrating foreign intelligence services and international terrorist groups.

As Angleton once told me, penetrating a foreign target's communications and using them—without the enemy knowing about it—is the essence of all intelligence work. And the best way to stop the enemy is to get inside the enemy's intelligence system and discover its plans before they are carried out. In essence, as veteran intelligence official Richard Haver put it, the goal is "to attack the adversary intelligence service before they attack you."

Intelligence operations depend on good counterintelligence. If a nation can't detect enemy spies, it can't fully trust the intelligence it collects, it can't protect its clandestine sources or recruit new sources, and it can't exploit the valuable weapon of turning foreign agents. As Angelo Codevilla told me, "It is almost better to have no intelligence service at all than to have one that is penetrated."

James Angleton, despite his faults, understood the value of targeting and defeating the intelligence services of America's enemies—what he called "strategic counterintelligence." He was forced out of the CIA in 1974 after a dispute with CIA Director William Colby involving an unprecedented leak of CIA programs that was designed to discredit Angleton. Angleton told me several months before his death that had he survived the confrontation with Colby, he would have reoriented the entire CIA toward strategic counterintelligence. Instead, the CIA turned its back on aggressive counterintelligence. After he left, any agency official who tried to probe into possible foreign spy penetration, a task that invariably required questioning the loyalty of employees, was ridiculed as "paranoid" and engaging in Angletonian "sickthink."

The demise of Angleton and his counterintelligence staff damaged the CIA beyond easy repair. It left the United States extremely vulnerable to foreign spying and opened the way to the numerous spy cases made public in recent years.

There was no more graphic demonstration of the damage done than the case of CIA turncoat Aldrich Ames, who was arrested in 1994 for spying for Russia. Ames devastated U.S. intelligence operations by secretly selling the names of almost every American source within Russia. The 9/11 Commission blamed the failure to discover Ames's betrayal on the CIA's obsessive concern for security, which the report characterized as a legacy of Angleton's. The commission said that security restrictions designed to prevent massive compromises from penetration agents had prevented the CIA from sharing intelligence information adequately. But in fact, had the CIA adopted the aggressive stance Angleton advocated, it would have been in a much better position to detect and halt foreign spy operations like the one Russia ran through Ames. The very risk aversion that the 9/11 Commission cited as a key failing of the U.S. intelligence community resulted not because of Angleton but in reaction to the proactive counterintelligence he championed.

The 9/11 Commission called for "transforming the clandestine service by building its human intelligence capabilities"—that is, reemphasizing the need to plant spies in foreign countries and within terrorist organizations. The reasons for such reform have become obvious in recent years—first with the failure to detect the 9/11 attacks and later with the pre–Iraq War intelligence failures. One top-secret intelligence report I obtained captured the CIA's inability to penetrate al Qaeda. The July 1996 report, regarding the Khobar Towers bombing in Saudi Arabia, admitted that the CIA "can neither confirm nor deny" most reports from a Middle East intelligence service, because "we have no unilateral sources close to bin Laden, nor any reliable way of intercepting his communications." U.S. intelligence was, in essence, helpless. As for Iraq, the presidential panel that investigated the weapons of mass destruction issue concluded that the intelligence community blew its assessment because it "had precious little human intelligence, and virtually no useful signals intelligence" on Saddam Hussein's Iraq. And the problem persists.

The failure to place spies in al Qaeda and Iraq reflected the CIA's cultural aversion to both human spying and aggressive counterintelligence. James Pavitt, the CIA's deputy direction of operations from 1999 to 2004, told the 9/11 Commission that when the White House had pushed the agency to conduct covert action against terrorist groups, it had "gotten the Clandestine Service into trouble." Pavitt said that he "had no desire to see this happen again." According to the report, he acted on the assumption that "a truly serious counter-terrorism campaign against an enemy of this magnitude would be business primarily for the military, not the Clandestine Service."

Pavitt wasn't alone. Intelligence officials took it as a given that the CIA couldn't place an agent inside a terrorist organization. Duane R. "Dewey" Clarridge, a flamboyant CIA operations officer who headed the agency's Counterterrorism Center before retiring in 1987, made this case explicitly. Clarridge said that it was impossible to place spies inside the Islamist terrorist groups operating in the Middle East be-cause the groups were close-knit, tied by family, and, basically, im-penetrable using spycraft. "We tried everything and it didn't work," he said.

Since the risk-averse CIA considered it too hard to spy on terrorists, intelligence officials approached terrorism as a law-enforcement issue. Clarridge formed "counterterrorism action teams"—commandos trained to capture suspected terrorists and bring them to the United States for prosecution. That move set the tone for U.S. counterterror-ism intelligence activities for years. Thus in the years leading up to 9/11, the U.S. government subverted the real goal of intelligence: to steal secrets. Passively analyzing reports and connecting the dots will never produce a penetration agent inside a terrorist organization, which is the ultimate objective of good intelligence and counterintelligence—and good counterterrorism.

Unfortunately, the problems haven't gone away, even five years after the 9/11 attacks.

The New Fight

In late 2004, President Bush instructed the new CIA director, Porter Goss, to clean house and reform the agency's stilted bureaucratic culture. A year later, in September 2005, Goss gave a progress report to agency employees in the classified auditorium known as "the Bubble."

"Improving our global capabilities is our main job," Goss told the several hundred assembled CIA employees. "After all, how can you disrupt terrorist actions without first knowing their plans and intentions?" The director claimed that the CIA was already having "great success recruiting agents on all the target sets" in the War on Terror.

But other senior intelligence officials have told me that Goss's progress report was misleading. Even today the CIA remains blind and deaf when it comes to finding out about al Qaeda's next major attacks, or about the North Korean and Iranian nuclear arms programs, or about China's massive arms buildup. As one agency official put it, "The CIA's problem can be summed up in two words: No spies." Indeed, by 2005, the CIA's Directorate of Operations had fewer than a thousand case officers, as its spy handlers and recruiters are called, deployed overseas, where they could do their jobs. Of those, several hundred were deployed to Baghdad to build the new Iraqi intelligence service.

Goss had acknowledged the problem during his Senate nomination hearing in September 2004. When asked whether it would take five years to develop a good system of spies around the world, Goss replied, "In terms of years, I don't believe five is enough. . . . The great bulk of what we need is more than five years out there, in terms of global eyes and ears coverage on the core mission, which is close-in access to the plans and intentions of the enemy, the mischief-makers, and other things we need to know in this country for our national security."

Even then, Goss underestimated the difficulty of reforming the CIA—and especially of overcoming the agency's cultural resistance to expanded human intelligence and active counterintelligence.

Sure enough, Goss lasted only eighteen months as head of the CIA; he was forced out in May 2006. The intelligence bureaucracy will not change without a fight.

But if a fight is necessary, America's leaders must take it on.

Rogue states and terrorist groups keep sending spies into our intelligence agencies, our weapons laboratories, and the most sensitive parts of the U.S. government, from the Pentagon to the White House. The United States has no choice but to act immediately to fix its counterintelligence failings. As Michelle Van Cleave put it, "Today we are far from where we need to be."

Refusing to plug the gaping holes in America's defenses will lead to still more devastating losses and even greater dangers in the future. If our leaders fail to take action now, it will be nothing less than dereliction of duty.

Chapter 1

PARLOR MAiD

She's been a Communist since the day she was born. Her bona fides are impeccable. I gradually converted her—she's now a rock-ribbed Republican.

—*FBI agent James J. Smith, introducing Chinese triple agent Katrina Leung to FBI China hands in 1993*

O n July 5, 2000, a brand-new, $120 million Boeing 767 jetliner flew from the Boeing corporation's airfield in Everett, Washington, to San Antonio International Airport. The Chinese military had purchased the jetliner for the leader of Communist China, Jiang Zemin. China Aviation Supplies Import and Export Corporation, which is run by the Chinese Communist state, purchased the aircraft for China United Airlines, which has been identified in declassified U.S. intelligence reports as a commercial entity operated by the People's Liberation Army. Once in San Antonio, the aircraft underwent a $15 million customization to outfit the plane with all the luxuries of a Middle Eastern sheik, including a special vibrating bed to help Jiang sleep.

On August 10, 2000, the modification work complete, the Boeing took off for Beijing's military airfield. Within weeks, Chinese security officials had found some twenty-seven sophisticated electronic eavesdropping devices in the aircraft.

How had the bugs gotten there, when the entire customization had been under the strictest, twenty-four-hour supervision by some twenty-five Chinese military intelligence officials? It turned out that clandestine operatives from the CIA and the National Security Agency (NSA) had covertly placed the devices in the plane in hopes of gathering intelligence from Jiang prior to a future summit meeting. (To this day, the details of the bugging remain secret.)

For the United States, there was a more pressing question: How had the Chinese uncovered the bugs so quickly? U.S. counterintelligence launched an investigation to find out. That probe led ultimately to the Los Angeles–based FBI counterspy James J. "J. J." Smith and his prized agent, Los Angeles businesswoman Katrina Leung—code name "Parlor Maid." A former FBI official, William Cleveland, would come under scrutiny as well.

The investigation turned up a revelation that would prove highly embarrassing to the FBI: Both of these officials, two of the Bureau's most senior counterintelligence officers, had had illicit, long-term sexual relationships with Leung. Contrary to the bed-hopping image of spies popularized in James Bond films, having intimate relations with a paid FBI informant violates one of the cardinal principles of the spy business, not to mention Bureau rules.

But to focus only on the soap opera element of the Katrina Leung story is to characterize the episode as something only vaguely resembling a spy case. And a spy case it is, without a doubt—a terribly damaging one at that.

The real story of Parlor Maid has never been told. The main reason the full account has not emerged is that the FBI and federal prosecutors mishandled the investigation from the beginning.

A small group of FBI officials did their best to keep the inside story from coming out. Rather than rage against the flagrant counterintelligence failures demonstrated in the Leung case, these officials focused on protecting the FBI's already-battered reputation from further damage. Later, prosecutors made poor tactical decisions that undermined the court case against Leung almost before it could begin.

Ultimately, prosecutors had to settle for a plea deal with Leung.

The deal, reached on December 16, 2005, spared Leung from serving jail time or having to admit anything about passing illegally copied classified information to Communist China.

After the plea deal was finalized, Leung's lawyers—having safely escaped a trial that would have aired the overwhelming evidence of Leung's espionage—issued a statement professing that their client wasn't a spy and suggesting that she would have been glad to tell her story in court. A spokesman for the U.S. Attorney's Office in Los Angeles, Thom Mrozek, responded, "It's fair to say the government, by virtue of how this case moved along, was never able to tell its side of the story either."

Mrozek's statement was accurate, but it only obliquely hinted at the reasons the case "moved along" as it did and at the powerful evidence that Katrina Leung was indeed a spy for Communist China.

The real story of Parlor Maid will be told here for the first time. The Leung affair, like many cases from the dark world of intelligence and counterintelligence, is rife with lies and betrayals, half-truths and truths, myth and reality converging and diverging. But this account, based on court papers and on interviews with numerous intelligence and law-enforcement officials who knew the case firsthand, reveals the inside story of what really happened with Katrina Leung, Communist China, and the FBI.

Parlor Maid is the story of a Chinese spy who got away. And not just any spy. U.S intelligence officials close to the case insist that regardless of the outcome of the prosecution, the Katrina Leung case represents one of the worst spy cases in American history—and one of the worst U.S intelligence failures, as well. The evidence buried as a result of the FBI's mismanagement and the prosecution's failures bears this conclusion out.

Further confirmation came in May 2006, when Department of Justice Inspector General Glenn A. Fine issued his report on the Leung case. Fine's highly critical report identified scores of FBI failures. The first among them was the fact that the FBI ignored intelligence from an informant who said a senior FBI agent was being "run" by Chinese intelligence in Los Angeles. The spy running the agent was Katrina Leung, and the agent was J. J. Smith. "The FBI's failure to fully investigate Leung early on," the report stated, "was a lost opportunity to obtain information concerning the PRC's attempts to acquire technology and her contacts with persons of investigative interest to the FBI." The inspector general also made it clear that Leung was in fact a spy for China, not the FBI. The report stated clearly that Leung "provided classified U.S. government information to the PRC without FBI authorization." It revealed that at every step of the way in Leung's career as an FBI informant, for which she was paid $1.7 million, there were glaring signs that she was not who she claimed to be.

The extensive record makes it clear that the People's Republic of China—an emerging world power that poses a direct threat to the United States—penetrated the FBI. For more than two decades Communist China ran a spy, Katrina Leung, who stole valuable secrets from the U.S. government and intelligence community. More than that, this penetration agent, who had more than 2,100 contacts with Chinese officials over the course of twenty years, helped the Beijing regime exert enormous influence in the United States.

As revealed by the inspector general's report, by many declassified intelligence reports, by FBI documents, and by other documents submitted in court, Leung compromised all the FBI's foreign counterintelligence investigations on China. The FBI already struggled at aggressive counterintelligence, the vital technique that represents the best way to discover our adversaries' true intentions and, if necessary, to thwart dangerous plans before they are executed. The Chinese agent did incalculable harm by ruining the few successful counterintelligence operations that the United States had in place.

Adding to the damage, Leung's frequent reports on China apparently contained strategic disinformation about Beijing's plans and intentions. For many years these reports, intelligence officials told me, reached the highest levels of the U.S. government—including the Oval Office. The Chinese government could tailor its deceptive information to conform with U.S. beliefs and expectations because it had access to the deepest secrets from within the U.S. government and intelligence community. One legal document in the court case quotes U.S. government officials as stating that given the magnitude of the compromises, the FBI "must now re-assess all of its actions and intelligence analyses based on [Leung's] reporting."

Parlor Maid is a textbook case of how Communist China uses its intelligence services and agents not simply to gather intelligence but also to run aggressive counterintelligence operations, to manage its adversaries' perceptions of the emerging Chinese superpower, and to conduct disinformation operations against the United States. The Katrina Leung case provides a harrowing reminder that Communist China has made the United States its number-one target. But largely because of the effectiveness of China's penetration and disinformation campaigns, we have reached the point where top U.S. government officials dismiss a nuclear-armed Communist dictatorship in Beijing as "not a threat" to the United States.

And at the end of the day, Parlor Maid is a story of criminal negligence and cover-up on the part of the FBI. The truth must be revealed.

The Intercept

On November 26, 1990, a decade before China discovered the electronic bugs on Jiang Zemin's Boeing 767, the telephone rang at the Chinese Ministry of State Security (MSS) in Beijing. MSS is the Chinese Communist equivalent of the FBI and CIA combined, with the political police aspects of Moscow's KGB added. The caller, a woman, spoke Mandarin and identified herself as Luo Zhongshan. She asked to speak to Mao Guohua, the head of the MSS Foreign Affairs Bureau, one of the units that runs China's intelligence-gathering operations in the United States. The conversation was intercepted and recorded by the NSA, the supersecret electronic spying and code-breaking agency.

MAO: Who's this?
LUO: Uh, greetings. Hey.
MAO: I recognize you now.

LUO: There are two situations right now. I don't want to disclose it over the telephone.

MAO: Uh.

LUO: The matter which I told you I was going to do.

MAO: Uh.

LUO: [It's] too late.

MAO: Oh.

LUO: He/she has arrived already.

Luo asked whether Wang Jingqiang, one of the MSS's couriers, had returned to China from the United States and given Mao something on his return. Mao replied that Wang had not returned yet. Luo told the intelligence official to call Wang, since one person had already arrived and was staying at the Traders Hotel in Beijing for a week. The person referred to was a visiting FBI official.

Within days, the intercept was translated and a copy provided to the FBI's San Francisco field office. It landed on the desk of Bill Cleveland, a supervisory special agent who ran counterintelligence for the FBI on the West Coast. Cleveland had spent more than two decades chasing Chinese spies and was widely considered the Bureau's premier Chinese counterspy.

When Cleveland saw the transcript, he recognized what the MSS was being told: that Cleveland himself and another FBI agent, I. C. Smith, were going to be in China and staying at the Traders Hotel. Cleveland immediately went to a secure room to listen to a recording of the intercepted phone call. He quickly identified the voice as that of Parlor Maid, the code name for Katrina Leung.

"That's her," he said.

The intercept was a shock. Leung was the Bureau's prize agent, one of the few people who, the FBI believed, had access to the inner circle of the Chinese Communist leadership and could get inside the secretive world of the Chinese intelligence bureaucracy. Her reports on China went to the CIA and the National Security Council in Washington, and even on to the president. But the Luo-Mao intercept revealed why counterintelligence has been called a wilderness of mirrors, where agents can trade loyalties as easily as they change clothes. The fact that Leung had a clandestine name for contacts with Chinese intelligence meant only one thing: She was working for the Chinese while pretending to be a paid FBI informant.

The intercept was an intelligence officer's worst nightmare, because it revealed that Leung was using a code name that was unknown to the FBI for what she believed was a clandestine conversation with her MSS handler.

Cleveland would have known immediately that the intercept meant trouble. The reason was simple: Since the late 1980s he had been conducting a secret extramarital affair with Leung. He would meet Leung, a Chinese-born naturalized American, in hotels in Los Angeles and San Francisco, debrief her about his visits to China, and then have sex with her. As Cleveland well knew, such illicit relations with a paid informant were taboo in the FBI.

There was another wrinkle: Cleveland wasn't the only FBI agent sleeping with Leung. According to counterintelligence officials, Cleveland suspected—accurately, as it turned out—that Leung was also carrying on an illicit affair with her immediate handler, James J. Smith, the agent who had recruited her in the early 1980s. As soon as FBI headquarters launched an investigation into the intercept, Cleveland's and Smith's secrets would be revealed.

The Confrontation

The intercept of one of the Luo-Mao phone calls prompted a meeting at FBI headquarters in Washington. On May 14, 1991, FBI officials gathered to discuss Leung's evident lying and betrayal. The fact that she had met with Mao in Beijing a month after the initial intercept raised further questions. But indicative of the hands-off approach FBI headquarters took to field operations, the officials agreed to let James J. Smith, her handler, deal with the situation. The FBI thus missed a key chance: either to end its relationship with Leung altogether, or to use the information to try to "turn" her back as a spy for the United

States against China—the ultimate counterintelligence challenge. As the inspector general's report put it, had the Bureau followed up properly at the time, it might have discovered the "fundamental flaws" in Smith's handling of Leung "10 years before the FBI actually began such an investigation." But, "incredibly," the FBI didn't think to ask "how it was that Leung had obtained the information she supplied to the PRC" in the first place. As Smith later admitted, the information all came from him.

Whatever doubts officials may have had about Leung, neither Cleveland nor Smith—known as J. J.—shut down Leung's penetration operation. Instead, J. J., Leung's handler and secret lover, confronted Katrina about the intercept.

The confrontation took place on May 31, 1991, which Leung later called the "worst day of my life." J. J. showed up alone at Leung's home in San Marino, California. Angry about the intercepts, he began questioning her about her conversations with Mao. Sitting at the kitchen table, Smith told her that the conversation they were having was the most important one they would ever have. The FBI knew she had a cover name, he told her, and that she was passing information to Chinese intelligence without FBI approval. He said specifically that the Bureau was aware she had notified the MSS of Cleveland's travel to China and his plans to stay at the Traders Hotel. In an earlier conversation she had told J. J. she did not know how Mao knew Cleveland had gone to China. Now J. J. called her on it. "I know what you have been doing and you have not been truthful," he told her.

"J. J., whatever you do, don't yell at me," she said. "We can have this conversation, just don't yell at me."

She then admitted to giving information to Chinese intelligence. Katrina Leung, it turned out, was what counterspies call a "triple agent"—she pretended to be a double agent controlled by and loyal to the FBI, but she had been trained by Chinese intelligence and secretly she remained loyal to Beijing.

The date the switch occurred is not clear, but court papers later indicated that the Chinese had turned her from an FBI asset to an MSS asset during the late 1980s, and certainly before the Luo-Mao intercepts were first identified.

Leung told J. J. that Chinese intelligence had turned her during one of her trips to China, when she met people from every branch of the Chinese secret services. On that particular trip, the MSS searched her luggage in her hotel room while she was out and discovered her FBI tasking list, outlining FBI objectives for her visit. The list revealed that she was supposed to find out what the Chinese knew about a Chinese intelligence officer who had defected. When she returned, an angry Mao, the Chinese intelligence official, was waiting with the FBI tasking list in his hand. Caught working for the United States, she made a full confession about her intelligence-gathering on China for the FBI, she told J. J.

In China, spying brings a sentence of between seven years and life. But instead of arresting her, Mao had offered Leung a deal. He directed her to open a post office box in Fullerton, California, for secret communications. And one of the worst spy cases in American history was off and running.

Mole Hunt

So as of 1991, the FBI had a confession from Katrina Leung that she had spied for Communist China. She had never revealed her work for China until her FBI handler, J. J. Smith, confronted her. Stunningly, the FBI still kept Leung active as an agent.

Why?

According to the 23-page unclassified summary of the inspector general's report, J. J. Smith told investigators after his arrest that he had "believed Leung was too important to be discontinued as an FBI asset." Her information would be of great value not only to the U.S. government but also to advancing his career, he felt. He believed, he said, that he could "obtain or reobtain" Leung's loyalty to the U.S. government. J. J. also admitted that he feared that exposing her treachery would have revealed his sexual relationship, ending both the case and his career. In other words, Smith had been caught up in a classic case of sexual entrapment. Cleveland's role in keeping Leung on the payroll is not known, and he could not be reached for an interview. But it is most likely that FBI headquarters could not allow J. J. to continue handling Parlor Maid without the support of Cleveland, who was a senior FBI counterspy involved with China operations.

Smith would simply be more careful about how Leung traveled and how her reporting was evaluated. But he did not exercise sufficient caution. Not only did he keep her working as an FBI agent, he also continued his sexual relationship with her. (After his arrest he would tell investigators that he was confident that Leung would keep the affair secret and not try to blackmail him, because "she had just as much to lose as he did.") At a 1993 gathering at the Bureau's training center in Quantico, Virginia, Smith introduced Leung to a group of FBI agents who specialized in chasing Chinese intelligence officers. He identified Leung by the cover name "Michelle" and boasted that she was "doing some great things for the Bureau." He also explained that Leung had "been a Communist since the day she was born" and that "she literally grew up in the student movement, the anti-Taiwan, the pro-PRC student movement." But, he bragged, "I gradually converted her—she's now a rock-ribbed Republican . . . and a terrific lady"—one whose credentials as an informant were "impeccable."

Years later it became clear to some U.S. intelligence and counterintelligence officials that Leung did not have impeccable bona fides. U.S. technical spying operations against China began drying up at an alarming rate. At least nine electronic spying operations went silent. The losses could not be explained by the expertise of Chinese counterintelligence. Some senior U.S. intelligence officials believed there was a mole selling the United States out.

The NSA was the most vocal in arguing within the secret councils of government that something was rotten inside the intelligence system. The NSA's extensive communications-intercept operations had begun going bad, and the agency couldn't explain why. The NSA spied on Communist China from U.S. diplomatic facilities in China by using military reconnaissance flights to intercept communications, and from listening posts in Australia, Japan, Pakistan, and Thailand. The sophisticated electronic ears used in the reconnaissance flights reached hundreds of miles inland from China's coast.

The biggest blow to U.S. intelligence efforts in China came in the late summer of 2000, when the electronic eavesdropping of Jiang Zemin's aircraft was compromised. The United States first suspected that the compromise had occurred in mid-October 2000, after several Chinese officials failed to show for business meetings. U.S. intelligence then learned that a team of counterspies from Chinese signals intelligence had discovered the American listening devices. Soon after the discovery, the Chinese regime had arrested about twenty Chinese air force officers and two officials from China Aviation Supplies Import and Export Corporation for negligence and corruption. Additionally, Beijing placed a senior air force officer under house arrest and investigated a senior officer of the Bodyguards Bureau of the General Staff Department of the People's Liberation Army suspected of tolerating the lax security.

Clearly the discovery of the bugs had prompted a swift response at the highest levels of the Communist Chinese regime. In fact, in an interesting twist, a classified State Department report said that Jiang himself became focused on the bugging. Jiang, according to the report, believed that fellow Politburo member Li Peng had ordered it to learn what the paramount Communist leader was saying about charges of financial corruption against Li's wife and children. But U.S. officials later concluded that the intelligence report might have been a smoke screen by the Chinese—one meant to protect the agent who had provided them with information about the aircraft bugging. In China, reports circulated privately that Li had planted the bugs in order to listen in on the pillow talk between Jiang and his mistress, Song Zuying, a famous singer in a People's Liberation Army band.

Within a matter of several months, it became apparent that the compromise of the Boeing eavesdropping was not an isolated setback for U.S. intelligence. Indeed, the NSA lost the ability to conduct electronic eavesdropping from nine major intelligence programs in China.

These losses were alarming enough to finally trigger what counter-spies call a mole hunt—the search for a traitor who was revealing se-crets to the enemy.

A team of counterintelligence officials began reviewing the secu-rity of the Boeing operation and who had access to information about it. That review led investigators to J. J. Smith and Parlor Maid, who was the key U.S. agent for intelligence on Jiang Zemin.

Officials now believe that J. J. learned of the bugging operation and relayed the information, knowingly or unknowingly, to Katrina Leung, and that Leung compromised the operation. Court papers show that the United States placed Leung under electronic surveil-lance in December 2001, and officials confirmed that she was the sus-pect in the aircraft bugging leak. According to senior intelligence officials familiar with the case, Parlor Maid was so highly regarded as a source of intelligence that she was briefed or informed about all U.S. intelligence operations against China, not just those being run by the FBI.

U.S. officials now believe that Parlor Maid compromised numer-ous CIA operations and agents, as well as scores of NSA technical operations. Smith would have violated intelligence compartmenta-tion rules by disclosing details of the operations to Leung. Leung also could have learned details of the operations by lifting classified intel-ligence reports from J. J.'s briefcase during breaks in her long debrief-ing sessions with him. According to U.S intelligence officials close to the case, J. J.'s hard-sided Atlas briefcase became a gold mine for Chinese intelligence thanks to Leung's work. FBI investigators would eventually discover in Leung's home classified documents taken from Smith.

"Everything the United States did was given to J. J., who gave it to Leung," one senior intelligence official told me. This official called the Katrina Leung case "the worst espionage case the United States has ever had," because of the growing strategic threat posed by China and the urgent need to find out the innermost secrets of the Communist government.

Smith, because of his seniority in the FBI counterspy program, was part of the inner circle of U.S. intelligence officials on China. He was frequently asked to join an interagency group of intelligence officials from the CIA, the Defense Intelligence Agency, the State Department, and the NSA. In these meetings J. J. learned the most secret details of U.S. spying operations against China. He also would have known about CIA domestic operations to debrief visitors to or from China and to acquire information from them.

Leung, for her part, was positioned perfectly to advance China's influence operations in the United States. Communist China has achieved extraordinary success in deceiving and manipulating U.S. government policies, all thanks to having well-placed agents like Leung.

Infiltrating the FBI

Just who is Katrina Leung, and how did she position herself to do so much damage to U.S. national security?

Leung was born Chan Manying on May 1, 1954, in the southern coastal province of China now known as Guangdong. One of four children, Katrina was adopted as an infant and raised by the wife of her mother's brother. Katrina's birth parents allowed the adoption as a family gesture to the woman, whose only child had died shortly after birth. When Katrina was three, her adoptive family moved to Hong Kong, and by 1970 they had arrived in New York City.

Two years later Katrina earned an academic scholarship to Cornell University, where she majored in architecture and engineering. Leung excelled in college, just as she had in high school. She graduated with honors and became an accomplished pianist, singer, dancer, calligrapher, and linguist. According to a 1984 FBI report that formed part of Leung's "asset file" outlining her career as an informant, a driving force behind her success was "the fact that she was given away by her parents." The report stated that "she became very much of an overachiever to dispel doubts of her self worth precipitated by her parents' willingness to give her to someone else."

Leung also became a political activist while at Cornell, according to the FBI report. She joined the pro-China student movement known as the Defend the Diao Yu Tai Islands; those islands were the subject of dispute involving China, Taiwan, and Japan. The 1984 FBI report stated that Leung supported Communist China because "her real parents, especially her father, opted to remain in China where he was a highly regarded hydrologist. The letters he sent spoke in glowing terms of China's progress and the socialist paradise that was China."

The Communist Chinese government was quick to exploit this student movement. FBI Chinese counterintelligence specialist I. C. Smith, now retired, said that the movement proved particularly important to the Communist government in the early 1970s, before the United States established formal relations with Beijing. "When the Chinese first came to the U.S., the Diao Yu Tai folks were their main points of contact," Smith said. "After all, they had demonstrated their allegiance to China by agitating for control of the islands to pass to China, holding demonstrations before the UN, et cetera." By the time U.S.-China relations were normalized in 1972, the Diao Yu Tai group stood too far from the mainstream of American politics to hold any real sway in the U.S. political and social system, but it did have some influence over Chinese diplomats in the United States. (At least initially: By the early 1980s Chinese diplomats had realized that Diao Yu Tai was giving them bad political advice, such as by reporting that Jimmy Carter would be reelected president in 1980.)

It was through the Diao Yu Tai movement that Leung first came into contact with Chinese government officials. From the FBI report it is clear that she began cooperating—informally, at least—with the Chinese government and its intelligence services as early as 1972. For example, while at Cornell she organized showings of Chinese movies, and to get the films she contacted officials of Beijing's Liaison Office. Leung also told the FBI that while in college she "may have met" the Liaison Office's Lu Ping, whom the FBI had identified as one of Communist China's top MSS intelligence officials.

Such contacts—and the vagueness of her recollection about meeting a key Chinese intelligence official—should have been a red flag to the FBI from the very beginning. I. C. Smith told me that he was astounded to learn in 2005, through court papers made public in the case, of Leung's links to the Diao Yu Tai group and to Lu Ping. Had he known of those connections, he said, he never would have permitted Leung to act as an informant. The information in the court papers was "simply devastating," he said. "If Katrina was part of Diao Yu Tai, one cannot dismiss the possibility that when she was first contacted by the FBI, she would have been told to target the FBI itself, a very likely situation." Indeed, after Leung's 1990 phone calls to the MSS, it became clear that she probably had been working for the Chinese all along.

After graduating from Cornell in 1976, she moved to Chicago, where she worked toward a master's degree in business administration from the University of Chicago and took a job as a bank teller. Leung told the FBI that in 1976 she attended a meeting of pro-Chinese activists in Chicago to commemorate the death of Communist China's founder, Mao Zedong. At the meeting, Leung introduced herself, described her activities at Cornell, and offered "whatever help she could provide," the FBI report said. The group of activists soon put her in charge of parties and entertainment. The pro-China organization regarded her as an asset because she wrote and spoke English well and was not a foreign student, meaning that she could "tout unpopular causes" without fear of reprisal. She even helped set up the Chicago chapter of the National Association of Chinese-Americans (NACA), which the FBI regarded as one of the more influential NACA chapters in the United States.

Leung later told the FBI that Lu Ping came to Chicago along with other Liaison Office officials. The FBI report noted that Leung and Lu "became friendly" and Lu asked her to organize a Chinese student meeting at which he would speak. According to the report, Leung also honored Lu's requests by meeting with him at least twice at the Liaison Office in New York and by organizing a delegation to China under the auspices of the government-run All-China Sports Federation.

Leung told the FBI that she "could not recall any recruitment pitch by Lu Ping or his associates," the report said. The reason, she said, was that she and others had already "made themselves available to the PRC government." "I asked for nothing and did my best to please them," she told the FBI. Still, she claimed that her contacts with Lu showed her how Beijing officials "secure the cooperation of overseas Chinese."

In January 1980, Leung moved to Los Angeles to work for Sida International, a business, started by pro-China students, that wanted to conduct trade with Beijing. In California, Leung again sought out and met other pro-PRC students and professionals. The Department of Justice inspector general's report revealed that in 1982 the FBI investigated Sida for espionage related to illegal technology transfers to China. The report also noted that at the time the FBI dubbed Leung's apartment building a "nest of spies," because of several suspects who had links to Chinese intelligence.

It was in California that Leung met up with FBI counterspy J. J. Smith. According to the inspector general's report, J. J. contacted her in 1982 as part of an FBI investigation into Gwo-Bao Min, a nuclear weapons engineer at Lawrence Livermore National Laboratory accused of passing W-70 nuclear warhead technology to China. The agent overseeing the Min investigation was Bill Cleveland. The report disclosed that in 1981 Leung herself had become the target of an FBI counterintelligence investigation based on her contacts with Chinese agents. Yet the Bureau took "no immediate action" to investigate Leung's "relationship" to Min. The inspector general deemed it "incomprehensible" that the FBI did not investigate.

Leung quickly went from being a spy suspect to an FBI informant with little or no investigation of her background. She soon became J. J.'s prize agent. The inspector general reported that Smith had her flaunt her contacts with the FBI in the Chinese community in the United States to draw the attention of Beijing intelligence officials. In the FBI counterintelligence culture, as in the CIA, officers had strong incentive to recruit agents as a way to advance their careers. But that incentive also represented a vulnerability for the United States, since it opened up U.S. intelligence to penetration by enemy agents. And

China's MSS specialized in turning spies against those who sent them.

Less than a year after J. J. recruited Leung, in August 1983, he began his sexual relationship with the informant. The inspector general's report disclosed that an FBI supervisor asked Smith about the affair as early as 1984. J. J. denied it—as he would on several occasions over the next nineteen years. At one point Smith's FBI supervisor would surprise Smith by picking him up at the airport after a vacation to London, only to discover that J. J. had traveled with Leung. Still, the supervisor told no one about the incident, according to the inspector general's report. It was a major management failure.

The FBI report from 1984 states that Leung changed her pro-China views in a variety of ways in the late 1970s and early 1980s. Her biological parents left China in 1975 and came to the United States in 1979. That is when Leung learned that her father's glowing tales about life in China had been fabrications; Chinese intelligence, which monitored all mail sent abroad, had added the messages to her father's letters. Now Leung heard her father recount the horrors of China's Cultural Revolution (1966–1976), when Mao Zedong unleashed the radical zealots known as the Red Guards on the entire country. Hearing the stories, and visiting China herself in the 1980s, changed Leung's perspective on China "a great deal," according to the report. After leaving academia, she reportedly distanced herself from pro-China activists, and then she quit Sida to work for General Medical Centers selling HMOs to businesses.

Investigators now believe that the Chinese groomed Leung as a triple agent and sent her to work for the FBI. In retrospect, it seems obvious that when she appeared to be trying to attract the attention of Chinese intelligence, she had already been recruited by Beijing and was really fooling the FBI.

The FBI interviewed Leung in June 1982 and described her as "tentatively cooperative." Earlier that year one of her fellow cofounders of NACA's Chicago chapter, a Hong Kong–born lawyer named Hanson Huang, had disappeared in Beijing, having been secretly arrested by the Communist Chinese regime; the Chinese government would later admit that it had convicted him of espionage. According to the 1984 FBI report on Leung, she convinced the Bureau of her worthiness as a source by revealing two good contacts in Chinese intelligence. One was Jin Xiao Qi, a China Travel Service employee who handled visits to China by Sida employees, and whom U.S. officials had identified as a Chinese intelligence officer working under cover in the United States. The other was "the madam of a [Chinese intelligence]-sanctioned prostitution operation in Beijing." Leung also began traveling to China once she became an activist in the Committee for Hanson Huang.

Katrina Leung was now working for the FBI—or so the United States thought.

The Art of Counterintelligence

The key to understanding China's modern spying system can be found in the ancient writings of the Chinese strategist Sun Tzu. His book *The Art of War* is well known among military and intelligence officers worldwide for the maxim that the acme of skill is defeating your enemy without firing a shot. Since battle exacts such huge costs in terms of both people and money, spies are essential, Sun Tzu argued. "What enables the wise sovereign and the good general to strike and conquer, and achieve things beyond the reach of ordinary men, is foreknowledge," he declared. "Now this foreknowledge cannot be elicited from spirits; it cannot be obtained inductively from experience, nor by any deductive calculation. Knowledge of the enemy's dispositions can only be obtained from other men."

Today, this foreknowledge is the essence of counterintelligence—the art and science of identifying and thwarting enemy spies. Sun Tzu identified—and China's current intelligence system is built around—five different types of spies. Three of them involve counterintelligence. "Inward spies" are recruited officials of the enemy who can provide inside information; "converted spies" are enemy spies who are bribed or otherwise tempted to work for China's purposes; and "doomed spies" do things for purposes of deception ("carry false tidings to the enemy").

Katrina Leung fit all three types of Chinese counterintelligence spy. She was someone on the inside with access to FBI secrets, who was converted to spy for China, and who furthered Chinese strategic-deception and foreign-influence activities. She was most essential to the Chinese as a converted spy, for as Sun Tzu noted, "knowledge of the enemy . . . can only be derived, in the first instance, from the converted spy."

The Leung spy case thus provides clear examples of the MSS's priorities. The intelligence documents she stole from J. J. Smith, which FBI agents found in her safe when they questioned her in 2002, demonstrate that China's primary spying objective is to penetrate U.S. intelligence agencies, and specifically America's extensive electronic intelligence-gathering networks. The classified documents investigators discovered in Leung's safe included a list of FBI counterspies involved in another failed FBI case code-named Royal Tourist, a transcript and summary of Leung's secret intercepted conversations with MSS official Mao Guohua, and, perhaps most important, a secret communication from the FBI office in Hong Kong.

Beyond the stolen secrets and compromised operations, the Leung case shows how China's Communist government emphasizes the use of disinformation, political influence, and policy manipulation as part of China's grand strategy of defeating its main enemy, the United States. In John Le Carré's acclaimed Cold War spy novel *Tinker, Tailor, Soldier, Spy,* the master spy Karla explains to his apprentice why purchased information—though false or misleading—gains easy acceptance at top levels of government, while accurate information gathered openly through diligent research is often dismissed. "Ever bought a fake picture, Toby?" Karla says. "The more you pay for it, the less inclined you are to doubt its authenticity."

U.S. intelligence officials invested a lot in Katrina Leung's authenticity. Officials close to the case emphasize that U.S. intelligence agencies never doubted her because she told them what they wanted to hear. The information she supplied was tightly controlled by the MSS to fit fundamental themes being promoted by Chinese Communist leaders. For a regime that since 1949 has murdered up to 70 million people through political purges, organized famines, and repression in prison camps, disinformation campaigns are essential.

China's strategy for influencing the United States goes back to the late dictator Deng Xiaoping, whose ruthless pragmatism was captured in the slogan "It doesn't matter whether the cat is black or white, as long as it catches mice." In a top-secret party directive in the early 1990s, Deng offered a "24-character strategy" to enable China to build up comprehensive power. Deng advised, "Observe calmly; secure our position; cope with affairs calmly; hide our capacities and bide our time; be good at maintaining a low profile; and never claim leadership." As the Pentagon observed in the report "The Military Power of the People's Republic of China 2005," "Taken as a whole, the strategy suggests both a short-term desire to downplay China's ambitions and a long-term strategy to build up China's power to maximize options for the future."

The strategy of deploying disinformation and influence operations seems to have worked well in the United States. Consider that in 2005 a top U.S. military officer downplayed an explicit Chinese nuclear threat against America. On July 15, 2005, Chinese General Zhu Chenghu, head of China's National Defense University, told reporters in Beijing that China was "determined to respond" with nuclear weapons against "hundreds" of American cities if U.S. forces defended Taiwan from an armed mainland attack. Several days later, Marine Corps General Peter Pace, then vice chairman of the Joint Chiefs of Staff (he would later become chairman), said that "there's absolutely no reason for us to believe there's any intent on their part" to use nuclear weapons. Pace repeated the soft line in September, stating, "I do not believe China is the next most likely peer competitor. I do not believe it is inevitable that we will be enemies." These statements reflected the ongoing efforts of pro-China members of the Bush administration and the American academic community to downplay the threat from Beijing.

Also in 2005, pro-China officials toned down the Pentagon's annual report on China's military strength, fearing that highlighting China's growing military power would create a new Cold War enemy. The report noted that the United States was developing "cooperative and constructive" ties to China. This despite the fact that the Chinese military had imprisoned twenty-three U.S. troops in 2001 after their EP-3 surveillance aircraft made an emergency landing in China, and despite the fact that Beijing supports North Korea, sells arms and technology to state sponsors of terrorism, and undermines U.S. alliances around the world.

The 2005 report also stated, "The U.S. Intelligence Community estimates that China will require until the end of this decade or later for its military modernization program to produce a modern force, capable of defeating a moderate-size adversary." American policy and intelligence officials familiar with the China estimates told me that this conclusion is fundamentally wrong. It does not express the Pentagon's true outlook, a more cold-eyed assessment that is reflected in the description of Deng's 24-character strategy, which was included in the same report. According to these officials, left-leaning analysts within the new Office of the Director of National Intelligence forced it into the Pentagon report. The CIA included the same naïve conclusion in the secret National Intelligence Estimate, intelligence sources told me.

The CIA is not alone in preaching the pro-China view. The U.S. stance toward China has been held hostage to the legacy of Henry Kissinger's gambit in the 1970s to use Communist China as a strategic counterweight to the Soviet Union. While the policy may have worked, the United States did not reevaluate its pro-China perspective after the Soviet Union collapsed. Kissinger himself, who has lucrative business deals with the Communist government and its state-run conglomerates, continues to champion China. In 2005, the former secretary of state told the official Xinhua News Agency, "Fundamentally, China is making a contribution to international peace and prosperity. China poses no challenges to the United States militarily."

The pro-China view suits many U.S. business leaders—including General Motors, Boeing, Microsoft, and other corporations—who prefer dealing with the dictators in Beijing as a way to reach the world's largest market, a supposedly modernizing nation that by 2005 had some 1.3 billion people. This business-oriented strategy is failing, however, at least insofar as a means to foster democratic change in China. President Bush has made global democracy a priority for his administration—most notably in his second inaugural address, in which he declared, "All who live in tyranny and hopelessness can know: The United States will not ignore your oppression, or excuse your oppressors"—but he has said little about the repressive system in China or about the Chinese military buildup.

The contradictory U.S. policies continue. After the summit meeting between President Bush and Chinese President Hu Jintao in Washington in April 2006, the United States offered to cooperate with China's space program. Human rights advocates opposed the cooperation, as did national security officials, who worried about how China had used U.S. space technology to improve its missiles—which are aimed at U.S. cities. A month later, the Pentagon issued its 2006 annual report, which showed for the first time that China is developing antisatellite weapons that could be used to knock out U.S. communications and intelligence systems in a crisis.

Behind the image perpetuated by Beijing leaders' discussion of their peaceful intentions and economic modernization, Communist China maintains its system of mass repression. Anyone who speaks or writes even the most innocuous criticism of the Communist Party or its rulers is severely punished, by being sent to one of the massive prison labor camps or by summary execution. The expanding economy that some Americans see as the key to democratization only fuels Beijing's repressive, military-dominated political system. China remains a nuclear-armed Communist dictatorship that continues a massive military buildup. And it is aggressively targeting the United States.

This message was brought home by a Chinese defector in 2005. Chen Yonglin, a diplomat posted to the Chinese consulate in Sydney, revealed that Beijing unrelentingly pursues its goal of targeting the United States. "The United States is always considered by the Chinese Communist Party as the largest enemy, the major strategic rival," Chen said in an interview several months after defecting. "I was often told that every matter regarding the United States is important no matter how trivial it is. China's [strategy] is actually focusing on the United States." Chen noted that the Chinese regime stepped up efforts against the United States after the 1996 standoff in the Taiwan Strait, when Chinese missiles were test-fired into waters north and south of Taiwan and the Pentagon responded by dispatching two aircraft carrier battle groups to the region as a show of support for the island.

Obscuring these darker realities and acquiring influence in the United States remain essential to the Chinese regime.

Buying Influence

Often the Chinese rely on a direct way to gain influence in the United States—by buying it. Here again, Katrina Leung played an important role. In the mid-1990s a fundraising scandal erupted after U.S. intelligence intercepted communications between Beijing and the Chinese embassy in Washington. The intercepts indicated that the Communist government was using go-betweens such as Indonesian entrepreneur Ted Sioeng to funnel millions of dollars into the campaign coffers of American politicians. The main beneficiaries were the Democratic National Committee and Bill Clinton's 1996 reelection campaign. Leung publicly defended Sioeng, telling the Los Angeles Times in 1997 that it was "nonsense" to suggest he was working as a Chinese agent. His worst offense, she said, was "that he got himself in the limelight for so long that he attracted . . . rumors and speculation." The "rumors and speculation" wording is typical of Chinese government reaction to news it does not like.

Leung did more than speak out in behalf of Sioeng. Intelligence officials now believe that she played an instrumental role in thwarting federal and congressional investigations into China's influence peddling in the 1996 elections. According to officials involved in the campaign-finance probe, China may have been able to tip off key targets of the investigation based on details Leung learned from J. J. Smith. Many of the suspects disappeared before they could be subpoenaed.

Leung's secret loyalty to Beijing would have allowed her, through J. J., to compromise the entire campaign-finance investigation, which J. J. was directly involved in supporting. China's intelligence service knew that the information it supplied to Leung was reaching the highest levels of the U.S. government. Leung boasted close relations with Chinese leaders, including Jiang Zemin and other top officials like Premier Zhu Rongji (she was photographed with both leaders). Therefore her reports were accepted easily at the CIA. The agency included her information in its annual estimates about China and its reports on China's leadership. Officials told me that her reports were sent to the White House National Security Council staff, and a review of intelligence reports that included Leung's information showed that she was able to influence every president from Ronald Reagan to George W. Bush.

Beyond thwarting the campaign investigation, Leung also fed money directly from Communist China's government into American political campaigns, according to FBI records. Except this time, the money didn't go to Democrats. It went to Republicans.

China's leaders used Leung's connections to target the Republican Party in the 1992 campaign, according to a once-secret FBI report from Leung's asset file dated March 15, 1991. At the time, President George H. W. Bush was setting up his reelection committee. The report—which is based on information Leung relayed to J. J. Smith—notes that Leung's MSS handler, Mao Guohua, approached her about how to "actively participate in this election." Leung told Mao that she was not active in party politics but that a person could join the Republican Party "inner circle" by making a $10,000 donation. She was apparently referring to the Republican Eagle program, the elite group of top donors who meet frequently with senior officials, including the president. To be an Eagle one had to contribute $15,000 or more to the party.

Leung told J. J. Smith that she met with Chinese President Jiang Zemin and MSS Minister Jia Chunwang at the sprawling leadership compound in Beijing known as Zhongnanhai. "We do not expect you to go into politics," Jiang said to Leung, "but we take every opportunity to support people we like because we do not have an organized lobbying effort. It would be nice to have friends like you [pro-China] to be involved in U.S. politics. Every little thing adds up. You could be involved at various levels. If your involvement makes you a friend of the Republican Party at the local, state or congressional level, then we have one less enemy. I am sure we will give you the support you need."

Later, Mao told Leung he had won approval from his superiors to "make contributions to the Republican Party." He worried that $10,000 would not be enough to make her a "major member" of the GOP, to which she replied, "[Ten thousand dollars] will get me in, but I will need a lot of money to sustain the effort over a long period of time."

Mao said that $10,000 was "nothing to the Republican Party or to us," and that "we do not expect you to manipulate anyone with $10,000." He said he recognized that the first $10,000 would trigger a "never-ending series of donations" but that China would be willing to support the effort. "Give me a budget and I will work with it," he said.

MSS Minister Jia subsequently told Leung that "we will give you the money" to donate to the Republicans. "Don't worry, there is no special tasking from us," Jia said. "I think it would do a great deal of good to have a higher profile which gives you more protection. If anything good comes your way for China, so much the better." Leung told Smith in recounting the meeting that she believed Jia was talking about political influence and not "information"—the intelligence she was secretly supplying Beijing.

In 2003, after Leung was arrested and identified as a Chinese agent, Senator Joe Lieberman, Connecticut Democrat, wrote to the Justice Department and FBI asking for an investigation into whether Chinese funds were channeled to Republicans. Referring to the earlier congressional investigation into the Chinese fundraising scandal,

Lieberman stated, "The committee majority chose to focus its investigation almost exclusively on individuals who had raised or contributed money to the Democratic presidential campaign of 1996. . . . The FBI apparently believes that Ms. Leung acted as a spy for the Chinese government, including during the period PRC officials apparently were trying to influence American political campaigns."

Ruining the Investigation

Ultimately, the case against Katrina Leung was doomed from the start. As soon as she knew she had come under suspicion, Leung could take steps to undermine any prosecution.

James Lilley, a former CIA Asian operations officer and ambassador to China and South Korea, told me he believes the same thing happened in the case of Los Alamos National Laboratory scientist Wen Ho Lee, who was convicted of illegally removing top-secret computer simulations of nuclear tests. Lee probably learned of the probe from Leung, and traveled to Taiwan as a way to thwart the investigation. Making telephone calls from Taiwan to Los Alamos would make it appear that he may have been spying not for Beijing but for Taipei.

The bigger problem was that the FBI badly mishandled the case. Most notably, of course, two of the Bureau's senior counterspies, J. J. Smith and Bill Cleveland, were compromised because of their long term sexual relationships with Leung. They kept her working as an active agent even though as of 1991 she had privately confessed to spying for Communist China. Cleveland left the FBI in 1993 to become head of security for the top-secret Lawrence Livermore National Laboratory, one of the Energy Department's key nuclear research facilities, but he continued to have contacts and sexual liaisons with Leung at least until 1997, according to an FBI report of a debriefing with Cleveland. J. J. Smith continued his sexual relationship with Leung until their arrests in 2003.

The FBI's failure to monitor and manage Smith also allowed the Leung case to spiral out of control. One FBI agent, Rita Chiang, told investigators into the Leung case that Smith's supervisor in Los

Angeles, Agent Dorothy Kelly, was a "relatively weak leader" who thought Smith "could do no wrong." Chiang reported that "Kelly relied very heavily upon Smith and promoted his asset Katrina Leung, code name Parlor Maid, to the detriment of other assets." She noted that Kelly and Smith would "minimize or suppress valuable information from other assets if the information would somehow take the limelight from Parlor Maid." Counterintelligence officials said that this was another damaging aspect to the case, namely that Leung's primacy as an FBI informant led to the denigration of other valuable intelligence sources. Leung's shiny reputation within the FBI made her the ideal disinformation agent for Beijing.

I. C. Smith, the veteran FBI counterspy, believes that the FBI should have noticed problems with Leung much earlier. As noted, Smith considers Leung's early connections to the pro-China group Defend the Diao Yu Tai and to Chinese intelligence officer Lu Ping to be astounding, believing that they should have disqualified her from serving as an FBI source. "Of course," Smith told me, "J. J. Smith and Cleveland were suckered, hook, line, and sinker."

I. C. Smith remembered that he had doubts about Leung's reliability as a source as early as 1991. The real problem was the quality of the reporting she did on Beijing. "I said, 'Where's the beef?'" Smith recalled. Leung's reports have contained some details of Chinese leadership meetings and what particular Chinese leaders were saying in private, but they did not provide intelligence truly valuable to the FBI, such as the identity of agents or methods of operation. "I saw a lot of gossip but no hard intelligence," he said.

Other officials share Smith's concerns. One intelligence official told me, "I think that the intelligence she was providing us on the Chinese will turn out to be a much bigger issue than the counterintelligence damage that she did to the FBI. Most people so far have looked at this case as a spy-versus-spy matter, but that is missing the point. She was considered one of the FBI's top sources on China, and her information was going to the president." Bill Cleveland and J. J. Smith were invested in the idea that Leung was providing a trove of information about the internal workings of the Chinese leadership and about its intelligence efforts. That became the standard view within the intelligence community. As if to validate the intelligence, CIA Director George Tenet gave J. J. Smith the National Intelligence Medal of Achievement in 2000.

The FBI's mishandling of the case became more shocking after the mole operation was finally detected. Bureau counterintelligence officials did their best to cover up the sordid saga, especially the sexual affairs, which would be an embarrassment to the FBI. The working-level FBI official put in charge of the investigation into the Leung case was thirty-year counterintelligence veteran David Szady.

Never mind that Szady was friends with Bill Cleveland, one of the subjects of the investigation. In the mid-1980s Szady had been posted to the FBI's San Francisco office, where he first met Cleveland. He became the special agent in charge in San Francisco in 1995, when Cleveland was still secretly sleeping with triple agent Leung. FBI agents also told me that they saw Szady staying at Cleveland's house in Monterey, California, when Szady worked in the area. When I interviewed Szady, he admitted knowing Cleveland "very well."

As revealed by court papers and the testimony of current and former intelligence officials like I. C. Smith, Katrina Leung enabled Beijing to obtain the crown jewels of U.S. intelligence operations against Communist China. Put bluntly, J. J. Smith and Bill Cleveland were taken to the cleaners by the MSS. But the Szady-led damage assessment did not reach those conclusions. In fact, Smith and Cleveland were allowed to escape with a slap on the wrist or less.

The small group of FBI agents who had come to control counterintelligence issues at the Bureau demonstrated no concern for addressing the severe counterintelligence failures in the Leung case. Their main interest, it seemed, was in keeping the FBI from having to air its dirty laundry—the fact that two of its most senior counterintelligence officials had illicit sexual relations with Leung.

Cleveland escaped any penalty whatsoever. Internally, the FBI's damage assessment concluded that the case was mainly about sex. Szady himself said that the problem with Cleveland had to do with his relationship with Leung. In an interview, he mainly defended his friend. Szady said, "To give Cleveland his due, there was no issue with him about giving away classified information." He did not impugn Cleveland for keeping Leung active as an FBI operative for years after she had been caught working for Chinese intelligence. Though Szady acknowledged "a lapse in management and discipline" at the FBI that allowed Leung to operate so long, he said that the negligence was spread evenly among headquarters managers, special agents in charge, assistant special agents in charge, and agents in the field. Szady admitted that Cleveland had failed to tell Lawrence Livermore security officials about his sexual relationship with a spy, but the FBI official dismissed the idea that Cleveland should have been prosecuted for the security breach. "I hope not or we'd all be in jail," he said.

Prosecutors initially planned to turn Cleveland against J. J. Smith and use him as a key prosecution witness. But eventually they abandoned the plan to make J. J. the fall guy, and allowed him to cut a deal by which he avoided jail time. An e-mail Smith sent to friends on May 21, 2004, suggested one reason prosecutors agreed to the deal: J. J. wrote that his lawyers had used the technique known as graymail, in which defendants request classified information that would be difficult for the government to release without compromising intelligence methods. The idea was to discourage the government from continuing prosecution. "We wanted more classified information declassified to demonstrate that I had ample reason to trust Katrina," he wrote. The ploy worked. To avoid losing wiretap rulings before a liberal judge, the Justice Department offered Smith a plea bargain. The resulting sentence: probation and no jail time.

I. C. Smith told me he was astonished that the government chose not to prosecute J. J. Among other points on which J. J. could have been prosecuted, he had been caught lying about Leung's refusal to take a polygraph test. According to J. J.'s indictment, in 1991 he asked Leung to take a polygraph test to help answer questions about the contacts with China. Leung refused. But J. J. refused to tell headquarters about the refusal and instead said she had passed the test. The omission was one of the key issues that led to the arrests.

Another reason prosecutors cut the deal with J. J. was that they hoped he would help in the case against Leung. But intelligence officials told me that Smith did not cooperate. On key dates and events, officials revealed, he suffered repeated memory lapses and could not recall what happened in his handling of Parlor Maid. Smith himself, in his May 21 e-mail, suggested that he had been uncooperative. He arrogantly complained about the prosecutors and spoke about how much he had supposedly suffered. "Since I was arrested a year ago," he wrote, "I was in a major sweat about losing my government benefits, including retirement and medical [valued at over $80,000 per year]." The good news, he said, was that he had gotten off, but he remarked, "I cannot own a gun, vote, hold public office or serve on a jury." He then gave what he called the bad news: "I am near broke, my relationships are shattered, I have to 'cooperate' with the same people who not so gently arrested me on April 9." It is telling that he used quotation marks to describe his legal obligation to cooperate with the U.S. government as part of the plea agreement.

Asked if Smith and Cleveland got off easy, Szady told me, "Well, it's a complex case. It depends on what you mean by 'got off easy.'" He said that if they did, it was the fault of the prosecutors in the U.S. Attorney's Office in Los Angeles or at the Department of Justice in Washington.

In any case, the prosecution's decision to reach a deal with J. J. Smith ultimately ruined the case against Leung. A provision in J. J.'s plea deal prohibited him from talking to Leung. This led District Judge Florence-Marie Cooper to dismiss the case on the grounds of prosecutorial misconduct. The judge ruled that the government had purposely denied Leung access to J. J., one of the case's most important witnesses, for information regarding her case.

Prosecutors did appeal, trying not to let a legal technicality submarine the government's entire case against one of the most damaging spies in American history. But the appeals court hearing the case, the Ninth Circuit Court of Appeals in San Francisco, was one of the most liberal courts in the United States. Consequently, prosecutors agreed to a plea deal with Leung on December 16, 2005.

Black Mark

The plea deal was Katrina Leung's get-out-of-jail-free card. Under the agreement, Leung admitted to lying to the FBI about traveling to Hong Kong and London with J. J. Smith, and to filing a false 2001 income tax return that omitted $35,000 she had been paid by the FBI. These were much less serious charges than the ones the government had initially pursued: illegally copying classified information and also tax fraud, evidence for which was uncovered during electronic surveillance of Leung and her husband. She did not have to go to prison, as she was sentenced to three years' probation and fined $10,000. Leung agreed to undergo debriefing sessions with the FBI and to take polygraph tests to determine the veracity of her testimony. But even if the debriefings revealed that Leung had spied for the Chinese, the government would not have been able to prosecute her. The plea deal stated that prosecutors had agreed "not to use in any way against Leung in any criminal proceeding any statements made by her during the debriefing sessions." Details of the debriefings remain secret, and officials familiar with them declined to discuss the details. Leung, through her lawyer, declined to be interviewed.

The U.S. Attorney in Los Angeles, Debra Wong Yang, hailed this agreement as a victory for the U.S. government. Yang trumpeted the specific debriefing arrangement, which, she said, "we hope will assist in ensuring that any damage caused by her activities can be remedied." But what this behind-closed-doors arrangement ensured was that the FBI's incompetence and corruption would remain covered up—exactly what officials had wanted from the beginning.

Meanwhile, Leung and her lawyers publicly proclaimed her innocence, now that the sweetheart deal ensured that most of the evidence against her would be locked away. Her attorneys, Janet I. Levine and John D. Vandevelde, said in a statement that Leung had been cleared of the spying charges: "More than two and one-half years ago, when some people assumed Katrina Leung was a Chinese Mata Hari who must have compromised U.S. intelligence efforts, we confidently told anyone who asked that Katrina Leung is and has always been a loyal American citizen, that this case was much ado about nothing, and that when the whole story was told she would be vindicated. Today the case against her is over and she has been vindicated." The lawyers said that Leung's only "mistake" was that "she tried to protect her handler," J. J. Smith, and prevent their secret relationship from being discovered.

Leung herself had a simple statement on the day of the plea deal: "I love America and I love American values." She argued in and out of court that the charges against her were ridiculous and trumped-up, claiming that she had been authorized to make contact with the MSS. She declined my request to interview her.

Again, though, the inside story is quite different from what Leung and her attorneys have led the public to believe. Leung's lawyers claimed that the only reason she aroused suspicion was that she had tried to protect J. J. But records in the case reveal that she made other incriminating statements to U.S. investigators. Most notably, she told investigators during one interrogation session prior to her arrest, "My approach is . . . it's like I felt badly [about] what I did, but for whatever reason I chose also to work with them [the MSS]. Because it's like you give a little, give a little."

During another interview, with FBI agent Peter Duerst on December 12, 2002, Leung offered to flee. "You know," she told Duerst, "I think the perfect way to end all this, if I just disappear, not disappear, oh well, wouldn't that be nice, I mean if I don't exist. If I do not exist anymore?"

A startled Duerst replied, laughing, "Uh, I don't know how we can do that."

"So nobody could, would be bothered by it, you know, you don't have to work so hard," Leung said.

"Well that's my job. I have to work hard at this," Duerst said.

Investigators dug up other evidence of her spying. Some evidence related to money. Chasing the money she received has proved difficult, but court papers show that she received at least $100,000 from the Chinese government. The figure could well have been much higher. Investigators discovered that Leung and her husband had sixteen different bank accounts in Hong Kong and China. The FBI believes the accounts were set up as the MSS's way of paying her covertly. The plea agreement also indicated that authorities in Australia had seized property belonging to the Leungs, probably more bank accounts. Any money she received from Communist China would have been in addition to what the U.S. government paid her: $1,197,449 for "expense reimbursement" and about $521,440 for "services" as an FBI agent.

All told, the Parlor Maid case is a frightening story of a relentless, two-decades-long Chinese espionage operation against the United States and of unforgivable U.S. counterintelligence failures. Of course, top FBI officials won't publicly admit the extent of the harm done. David Szady said "we're not sure at this point" of how much damage had been inflicted. "I don't think it's at the extreme as some people think, and [it's] probably not as minimal as others may think."

In contrast to Szady's low-key assessment, many other officials I spoke with told me they consider the Katrina Leung case in many ways more damaging than the more famous cases involving CIA turncoat Aldrich Ames and FBI mole Robert Hanssen, both of whom spied for Russia. While many U.S. government officials have gone to great lengths to ignore or minimize the danger posed by Communist China, the fact remains that China views the United States as its main enemy. Beijing represents a greater danger today because of its success in penetrating the FBI with Katrina Leung.

That penetration never needed to happen. Department of Justice Inspector General Glenn Fine, in his report on the Leung case, identified numerous counterintelligence failures that enabled Parlor Maid to keep operating as an agent for Beijing. Among the many missed opportunities the inspector general revealed:

- In late 1987, in a conversation with a Chinese consulate official in San Francisco, Leung requested that the official call her at a pay phone, an obvious sign that she had a clandestine relationship with China outside of FBI control. The FBI investigated the incident but closed the case when the investigator learned that Leung was an FBI informant.

- The first of two "red flag" warnings that Leung was a Chinese spy surfaced in June 1990, when the FBI learned that Leung had disclosed to Chinese officials the existence and location of an active sensitive technical intelligence-gathering operation and "aspects of a highly-classified FBI counterintelligence program." The FBI failed to respond. The failure was a "significant mistake." If it had been pursued, the compromise would have exposed the lack of control over the information Smith was giving Leung.

- The second red flag appeared in April 1991, when the FBI learned that Leung was using an alias unknown to the FBI in communicating with a Chinese intelligence official. In the discussions, Leung improperly disclosed "ongoing FBI operations and investigations."

- Several incidents in the 1990s showed that Leung was providing classified information to China without FBI authorization, and these should have raised serious questions about her loyalty to the United States. But "the FBI failed to document the incidents in Leung's file and relied on Smith to resolve the concerns about Leung, and then failed to follow up further to ensure that he had done so."

- In 1992 a "credible" report from an informant revealed that China had an agent "working in the FBI" named "Katrina" who was a double agent working for Beijing. An FBI agent, however, omitted Leung's name from a report on the matter to FBI headquarters. Headquarters ordered Smith to debrief the source, "unaware that the source had implicated Leung" in spying. J. J. reported that the source had identified Leung as a spy but dismissed the information because, he said, the source was a liar who disliked women. Though Smith frequently attended Chinese consulate functions with Leung, the FBI did not probe deeply into the nature of their relationship.

- In the late 1990s, after a series of compromises to U.S. intelligence operations, including detentions and arrests of agents in China, a U.S. government task force was formed to investigate and address the counterintelligence issues. Leung's file was slated for review, but the task force never pursued whether Leung was a spy.
- In the spring of 2000, FBI headquarters learned from a source that Leung "was an agent of the PRC intelligence service and had an internal source in the FBI." "Incredibly," the inspector general said, the FBI supervisor in Los Angeles informed Smith about the report, thus compromising any investigation of him and her. In mid-2000 another report from the same source stated that Leung was "in bed with" the Los Angeles division of the FBI. The fact that Smith was also informed about that report tainted any plan for an internal FBI investigation.
- In August 2000 the FBI's assistant director for counterintelligence dismissed the allegations against Leung and Smith as "sources pointing fingers at each other," a remarkable failure that contributed to the cover-up of negligence and incompetence.
- In November 2000, Smith retired from the FBI. He was not required to take a polygraph, even though FBI headquarters knew that Smith had been told about the allegations that Leung was a spy running an FBI agent in Los Angeles. Smith told investigators that he had assumed he would be investigated after retiring, but it would be fourteen months before the probe was launched.

After documenting the FBI's gross mishandling of Katrina Leung and J. J. Smith, the inspector general recommended that the FBI improve handling procedures for agents, create a system for placing red flags about informants in their files, conduct more background checks of informants and alternate case agents for informants, improve controls on documents provided to informants, limit the time an agent can handle an asset, and prohibit blanket exemptions to rules in handling informants. Even David Szady, when I interviewed him, admitted that the Leung case highlighted the FBI's need to better control its informants, to check the information they provide, and to make sure there are not handling compromises like the affairs Leung carried out with Smith and Cleveland. He also admitted that the FBI missed signals that should have alerted them to Leung's spying.

For the FBI, the Leung counterintelligence failures are another black mark on the reputation of a once-great law-enforcement and intelligence service. The FBI in its heyday ran one of the most successful spy operations of the Cold War: the penetration of the Kremlin through the number-two official in the Communist Party USA, Morris Childs. Childs worked as a clandestine agent for the FBI from 1954 until 1981, providing extremely valuable intelligence on America's main adversary. Those days are long gone.

Since the 1970s, the FBI has been hamstrung by lawsuits and self-imposed political correctness. During the Clinton administration, the FBI systematically eliminated its domestic intelligence capabilities, which were considered contrary to the Bureau's law-enforcement mission. The shortsighted decision to destroy the FBI's intelligence capabilities contributed directly to the Bureau's major intelligence failures leading up to the September 11 attacks. At one point prior to 9/11, FBI agents in Arizona and Minnesota reported a potential threat from men receiving pilot training at flight schools. An FBI field agent recommended conducting investigations of Middle Easterners who were undergoing such training, but FBI headquarters cabled back that to do so might amount to ethnic profiling—a practice forbidden by the politically correct leaders at the FBI.

The 9/11 attacks, and the intelligence failures they exposed, prompted loud calls for reform within the U.S. intelligence community. Cases like Parlor Maid reveal that those calls have largely gone unheeded. The critical area of counterintelligence has been the most neglected. As a result, the United States remains vulnerable to foreign spies like Katrina Leung.

In fact, there have been many other counterintelligence failures like the ones seen in the Parlor Maid case.

Chapter 2

RED FLOWER

Observe calmly; secure our position; cope with affairs calmly;
hide our capacities and bide our time.

—*Communist Chinese leader Deng Xiaoping on China's
military strategy*

Tai Wang Mak dialed the phone number in Guangzhou, China.
The man who answered the phone, Pu Pei-liang, worked as a researcher at the Chinese Center for Asia Pacific Studies at Zhongshan University, known to U.S. intelligence officials as CAPS.

"I'm with Red Flower of North America," said Tai, who was
working as an engineer in Los Angeles for the Hong Kong–based
Phoenix Television. He said he would be coming to China in nine
days. Pu told him to call from the airport in Guangzhou using a calling card so he could be picked up.

The telephone call, made October 19, 2005, was intercepted by
the long electronic ears of the U.S. National Security Agency. The reference to Red Flower of North America brought a breakthrough in a
yearlong investigation. Chinese spies used that code word to authenticate who they were when making contact with Communist China's
intelligence bureaus. Other often-used Chinese code words included
"Winter Chrysanthemum" and "Autumn Orchid."

U.S. intelligence knew that CAPS received funding from the

People's Liberation Army and conducted operational research for the powerful Chinese military. This phone call revealed that CAPS was working one of its most valuable spies inside the U.S. defense industrial system. In fact, Tai and Pu were military intelligence officers working undercover for the Second Department of the People's Liberation Army, the spy service well known to U.S. counterspies as 2 PLA.

It was Tai's brother Chi Mak who headed the Chinese spy ring. Chi was an electrical engineer with a major American defense contractor who had been supplying extremely sensitive U.S. Navy weapons secrets for more than twenty years.

From this NSA intercept, U.S. intelligence would roll up one of the most damaging losses of defense technology in American history. The fact that the spy ring went undetected for some two decades was a major counterintelligence failure in itself. Worse, the U.S. government would bungle the case once investigators discovered the espionage.

Botched Job

Chinese mole Katrina Leung compromised every single U.S. intelligence and counterintelligence operation aimed at China. The emerging Communist global power learned about all the operations and turned them to its purposes, either to protect its secrets or to deceive the United States about its intentions and policies.

So after the Leung case had been wrapped up, U.S. intelligence needed to find all new sources who would not be immediately revealed to China's Ministry of State Security intelligence service. It was this vigorous recruiting that produced a break in the Red Flower case.

Former CIA director R. James Woolsey has said that the U.S. Constitution is one of the best intelligence recruiting tools. His point is that those living under oppressive, dictatorial regimes—of which Communist China is surely one—will sometimes take incredible risks to step forward and secretly help in the battle for freedom and democracy. In the fall of 2004, the CIA recruited just such a source from China, a person who worked within the Chinese military and security establishment.

One of the first questions the CIA poses to these sources is "Who is 'picking our pockets'?" in the jargon of the intelligence business. The Chinese source identified a Chinese military intelligence spy ring in Los Angeles headed by Chi Mak. Through this network, the source reported, China's PLA was gaining sensitive technology and information on U.S. Navy warships. The source also revealed that China was buying ostensibly commercial goods but diverting them to the military.

The Los Angeles case offered a chance for the U.S. government, and the FBI in particular, to reverse the damage caused by the Leung counterintelligence failure. The Leung case had exposed corruption in the FBI's management of special agents and informants, as well as poor management within the counterintelligence section. Under pressure to adopt a counterintelligence culture instead of a "cop" mentality, the Bureau hoped to play the Los Angeles spy ring and see where it led. Counterintelligence is part art, part science, and an intelligence discipline aimed at identifying and exploiting or stopping foreign spies. Law enforcement is easier: You identify the bad guys and arrest them.

But the U.S. government mishandled the case. One problem was that the FBI and the CIA had conflicting goals. The CIA was afraid to lose its prized source, the Chinese recruit, so it did not want the FBI to immediately arrest those involved in the L.A. spy ring, since that swift action would alert the Chinese to a mole within its ranks. The investigation continued for about a year, until the NSA intercepted Tai Mak's "Red Flower" phone call in October 2005.

Days after the intercept, the FBI arrested Tai and his wife, Fuk Heung Li, at Los Angeles International Airport as they prepared to travel to China. When he was arrested, Tai was carrying disks on which were hidden encrypted files that contained sensitive data on U.S. Navy technology plans. Many of the documents were labeled "proprietary" and "restricted"—meaning they could not be exported. As we will see, even this arrest was mishandled.

The FBI also arrested Tai's brother Chi Mak and Chi's wife, Rebecca Laiwah Chiu. According to investigators, Tai served as handler and courier for a Chinese spy ring that Chi ran. The FBI affidavit accompanying the arrests laid out an extensive case against the four people. And the charges leveled in the affidavit represented the maximum that could be applied, including conspiracy to steal U.S. military information on restricted U.S. Navy warship technology, smuggling information to China in violation of export laws, and theft of government property.

The FBI produced the affidavit to secure arrest warrants for Chi, Tai, Rebecca, and Fuk, as well as search warrants for the individuals' homes, workplaces, and vehicles. Having spent a year conducting extensive electronic surveillance of Chi, Tai, and their wives, investigators believed that the searches would uncover classified data and other information that would lead to more serious espionage charges. After the arrests, judges underscored the seriousness of the charges by denying bail for Chi and Tai, with one judge telling Chi's lawyer, "You're talking about billions of dollars of technology that puts our country at serious risk."

But by the time a formal indictment was issued a couple of weeks later, on November 15, the most serious charges had been dropped, and one person, Fuk Heung Li, was excluded altogether. (She was charged separately with running an illegal marriage-fraud network that helped immigrants gain entry into the United States.) The three remaining people were indicted for the relatively minor offense of failing to register as foreign agents. While the initial charges could have resulted in prison terms of up to twenty-five years for each person, the failing-to-register charges carried maximum sentences of ten years. Chi, his wife, and Tai all pleaded not guilty to the reduced charges.

So what changed? According to sources within the U.S. government, petty squabbling between the prosecutors and the investigators jeopardized the case from the start. The most serious charges were dropped at that point because the FBI counterintelligence team that had conducted the investigation got into a dispute with the U.S attorneys in Los Angeles in charge of the prosecution. The FBI had fully expected that search warrants would unearth classified data, so

prosecutors balked when it was revealed that much of the data found
was not officially classified as secret. In fact, one of the first things
that Chi Mak told investigators after his arrest was "Nothing I
passed [to China] was classified." He was right. According to U.S. investigators, the lack of classified documents revealed that the spies
had done their homework.

The Chinese intelligence-gathering services thought they had
learned how to get what they needed without violating U.S. laws on
classified information. Their agents exploited the fact that Navy
weapons officials underclassified some of the most sensitive information about their systems in order to make it easier for private defense
contractors to use the information. In short, even though the information compromised was not officially secret, revealing it to Communist China proved quite damaging.

David Szady, the head of FBI counterintelligence until 2006, explained how the loss of sensitive yet unclassified information can do
real harm to U.S. national security. He said that the technology data
in the Mak case was proprietary corporate trade secrets or export-
controlled but did not carry the "secret" or "top-secret" label. This
case "probably murdered the Navy" because of the loss of military
technology, Szady said. The loss of contract documents to Beijing
will allow the Chinese to build their own version of the Navy's developmental DD(X) destroyer warship and then possibly "sell it in com-
petition to us," he noted. Chi Mak was a specialist in electrical
power, and he had access to the Groton, Connecticut–based submarine manufacturer Electric Boat "as if he was one of their own," according to Szady. The Chinese, he said, are very good at positioning
people who can obtain advanced technology in the developmental
stage, before it is classified as a military technology. "The [spy] business is getting more complex, more subtle," Szady remarked. "It's
smarter business than the old cloak-and-dagger."

Still, a federal judge in the case seized on the lack of classified data
to criticize prosecutors for overselling the case. "From what I'm getting now," U.S. Magistrate Judge Marc Goldman said to Assistant
U.S. Attorney Gregory Staples, "while the documents [seized from

Chi Mak and Tai Mak] have security implications, they're not the classified documents you said. I'm more concerned about the representations you made to me about the seriousness of these charges."

Behind the scenes, investigators were frustrated by the difficulties of proving the damage in the Mak case. "There is no question that this case has caused serious damage to U.S. national security," one official told me. The problem was that U.S. espionage laws are so difficult to apply that prosecutors almost need a confession to be able to make their case. The current U.S. espionage statute, passed in 1917, says that for espionage charges to stick, prosecutors need to prove that the information involved in the spying was used "with intent or reason to believe that the information is to be used to the injury of the United States, or to the advantage of any foreign nation." This standard is extremely difficult to meet in court, and it often requires the release of intelligence or defense information to prove that U.S. national security was harmed.

"It's kind of sad you have to wait until you have a landslide of information on a guy in order to be confident your charges can't be denied no matter how many liberals you go up against," one intelligence official said. "The Leung and [Wen Ho] Lee case failures, even though they were both guilty as sin, on top of worries over press perception of profiling, make it a hostile atmosphere to prosecute these cases. An average American knowing all the details would lock up this whole family and throw away the key."

Claims of anti-Asian racism also appear to have influenced the decisions of judges and prosecutors. The aftermath of the Wen Ho Lee and Katrina Leung cases still lingered in legal circles, especially in areas like Los Angeles, where there are large populations of Asian-Americans. Both Lee and Leung claimed they were investigated and charged because they were Asian and were ultimately victims of racism.

David Szady said that when he visited academic institutions and U.S. Energy Department research laboratories, he usually got asked have-you-stopped-beating-your-wife questions about why the FBI targets Asian-Americans. Szady emphasized that it's the Chinese who do the racial profiling, not the FBI. Chinese Communist officials "use ethnicity," he said. "They don't consider there's anything such as American-Chinese," he said, noting that Beijing considers ethnic Chinese in America simply "overseas Chinese." Szady added, "It's a dilemma for us, because I talk at the nuclear labs and the Chinese-American scientists will always ask why we're profiling them. Our answer is: We're not profiling you. The Chinese are. And they're very good at doing that."

The Mak case offers a good example of how China uses ethnic scientists and engineers. Tai and Chi were born in Guangzhou, China.

Although the U.S. government mishandled the Mak case in many ways, federal officials, and the FBI in particular, did not want to let another espionage case go down the drain. Investigators' frustration over the Mak case led to a debate within the Justice Department, the FBI, and the Naval Criminal Investigative Service about what to do.

A decision was made in May 2006 to upgrade the charges in a new indictment that would go beyond the one issued in November 2005. The new charges were to include conspiracy to export defense articles and unlawful export of defense articles. But the big difference would be to indict Chi Mak on the new counts of unlawful export of defense articles and gathering defense information, an espionage charge, according to officials close to the case. Also, Tai was said to face the added charges of aiding and abetting and possession of property to aid a foreign government. The case was still pending as of the summer of 2006.

The plan for the new charges was disclosed to me but was not announced publicly, and at the time of this writing had not been added. In June 2006, however, federal prosecutors indicted two members of the spy ring—Tai's wife and son, Fuk Heung Li and Billy Yui Mak—for failing to register as foreign agents and lying to the FBI. Fuk had discussions with prosecutors shortly after her indictment that led some to believe she was ready to cooperate, a move that would have sealed the entire case for the government. But no deal took place. FBI officials were hoping the Mak case would be successful and restore the FBI's tarnished reputation after the disastrous cases of Katrina Leung and Wen Ho Lee.

Picking Our Pockets

The revamped and upgraded indictment offered a clear signal of just how much damage the Los Angeles spy ring did to U.S. defenses. U.S intelligence conducted an in-depth investigation that revealed the extent of the damage.

Chi Mak exploited his position as an electrical engineer at the defense contractor Power Paragon—a subsidiary of the Fortune 500 company L-3/SPD Technologies/Power Systems Group, known as L-3. Ranked ninth among aerospace companies in 2005, with revenues of $6.9 billion, L-3 "serves the Department of Defense, select U.S. government intelligence agencies, aerospace and defense prime contractors and commercial telecommunication and cellular customers," according to the company website. The site adds, "Power technology systems from L-3 Power Systems Group"—the division where Chi worked—"are virtually the 'service standard' for the United States Navy and many international navies." Chi received a secret-level security clearance in 1996.

It appears Chi began operating the Chinese spy ring in the early 1980s, well before he received his security clearance. The earliest dated document that investigators discovered in Chi's residence comes from 1980. Meanwhile, the FBI affidavit revealed that Chi told investigators two days after he was arrested that he had been sending sensitive but unclassified documents on Navy weapons research to China since 1983. Investigators later discovered a private notebook Chi used in Hong Kong during the 1960s that indicated he was working for Chinese intelligence back then. Entries in the notebook, which appear to date from around 1968, indicated that Chi gathered intelligence on U.S. Navy warships that stopped in Hong Kong on the way to Vietnam. "He was doing HUMINT [human intelligence gathering] for the Chinese," one investigator told me.

Under questioning, Chi told investigators that when he began passing data to the Chinese in the 1980s, he would travel to Hong Kong and give it to his brother Tai Mak, who then supplied it to the Chinese government. In 1985, Tai and his wife moved to Los Angeles and became permanent residents, at which point Tai became a courier for the ring. "Chi Mak admitted that much of the information he provided to his brother was designated NOFORN, meaning that it could not be given to foreign nationals, and that other portions were export-controlled, protected by the International Trade in Arms Regulations, and should not be passed to a foreign nation," the FBI affidavit stated. "Chi Mak said that he knew that Mr. Pu [Peiliang] was providing the information to members of the Chinese government's science and technology community."

Chi said he was motivated to provide information to China because he knew it would help Beijing's science and technology community develop similar technology, officials familiar with his interrogation told me.

According to the affidavit, Chi admitted sending to the Chinese data on the following:

- Direct-current-to-direct-current converters for U.S. Navy submarines.
- A 5,000-amp direct-current hybrid circuit breaker for Navy submarines.
- Electronics known as an autobus transfer system for Navy submarines.
- The Electromagnetic Aircraft Launch System (EMALS), the Navy's latest technology for launching aircraft off carriers, using electromagnetic technology in place of the steam catapults that are currently standard.
- The power distribution system for the Aegis battle management system, the most modern combat system in use by the Navy.
- A study called the "Survivability of Battleships Paper," which reveals the methods used by U.S. warship personnel to continue operating after being attacked.

- Modifications and Additions to Reactor Facility (MARF), a nuclear reactor located at the Navy's Knolls Atomic Power Laboratory that is used for testing prototype nuclear reactors; investigators found a detailed, hand-drawn map of that facility in Chi Mak's house.

The thousands of documents investigators found at Chi's home support what he admitted to interrogators. The document trail led investigators to conclude, for example, that Chi passed information to the Chinese that will allow Beijing to track the Pentagon's new Virginia-class attack submarine, which uses L-3 technology. The compromise also will allow the Chinese to develop countermeasures against the submarine and to copy the submarine's unique electronic systems.

In addition, investigators believe Chi gave China schematics and design information on the latest generation of the Aegis weapons systems, which L-3 helped develop. The Aegis—meaning shield—is currently being upgraded to become America's most advanced and mobile antimissile system, used on guided-missile cruisers, guided-missile destroyers, Sea Wolf–class submarines, and aircraft carriers. Aegis-equipped ships will use the radar and tracking system to provide data to ground-based missile defenses and to ship-based Standard Block-3 missiles.

During the period Chi was supplying data to the Chinese, he worked on four classified Navy contracts related to Aegis. Investigators believe that the Los Angeles spy ring was the main supplier of Aegis technology to China, which is the most visible compromise. A U.S. defense official told me that the Chinese quickly incorporated the Aegis technology into their Luyang II guided-missile destroyer. The official said that the Luyang II is clearly based on U.S. technology and weapons and thus is "distinctly different" from the Luyang I, which is based on Russian radar and weapons. "This is one of the technologies handed over by this ring and we've been scratching our heads on it for years."

Moreover, Chi provided the Chinese with the frequency of the electrical systems on all these warships and submarines, according to investigators. By knowing that frequency, China will now be able to set up sensors near key points in the ocean that will allow them to track U.S. submarines near Chinese shores and around the world. The compromise makes ships and submarines floating noisemakers; the vessels will be sitting ducks for China's antisubmarine weapons, including torpedoes and missiles.

The information about EMALS that Chi gave the Chinese will teach China's military not only how to build its own high-technology aircraft launch system for an aircraft carrier. It will also show the Chinese military how to produce a "rail gun"—a high-tech weapon that uses EMALS technology to fire projectiles at seven times the speed of sound and at a range of up to 300 miles. The United States is considering this high-tech gun for the next-generation destroyer known as the DD(X). Chi had access to information on the DD(X) and is believed to have passed it on to China's military.

One of the most important military projects Chi is believed to have compromised was a U.S. Navy silent propulsion system for warships known as Quiet Electric Drive (QED). The Office of Naval Research contracted out the project to Power Paragon. The QED is part of the Advanced Capability Electric Systems (ACES), which the Navy calls "the backbone" of future warships. The FBI affidavit stated that QED is "an extremely sensitive project." If China obtained QED, it would be a major setback for future Navy warfighting.

It is probably not a coincidence that many of the compromises relate to systems that directly threaten China in any conflict with the United States over Taiwan: destroyers, submarines, aircraft carriers, and related weapons and systems. "If you want to know the damage, think destroyers," an investigator involved in the case told me. The technology compromises occur at a time when there is the looming danger of a military confrontation with China over Taiwan.

"Certainly Against the Law"

It was the "extremely sensitive" QED that provided the immediate trigger for the breaking up of the Los Angeles spy ring.

In October 2005, FBI surveillance at Power Paragon's Anaheim office detected Chi Mak as he e-mailed documents to his home; intercepts of the e-mails revealed that he had sent reports on the QED program and photographs of the system. The surveillance also showed Chi placing computer disks and other items at his desk into his briefcase. Video and audio surveillance of his home showed that Chi transferred the data to CDs and then delivered the disks to Tai Mak's house. There, Tai and his son used encryption software to convert the data into codes that could be read only using special software.

Electronic intercepts of conversations between Tai Mak and his wife, Fuk, on October 18 revealed that she had booked two tickets to Hong Kong on Cathay Pacific Airlines flight 883, scheduled to depart on October 28 at 10:22 P.M. The FBI soon discovered that Tai and Fuk were also heading to mainland China. During a telephone conversation on October 21, Tai told Chi that during his planned trip to Hong Kong, he would "swing by" mainland China. "Good," Chi replied, adding that it would "be beneficial" for the two of them to meet before Tai's trip. Four days later, on October 25, the FBI searched Tai's trash and discovered a travel document confirming that Tai and Fuk's ultimate destination was Guangzhou, in southern China.

On Thursday, October 20, U.S. intelligence intercepted a conversation at Tai's home that indicated a handover of data was about to take place. Tai confided to his wife that he would need to carry the disks because Chi was nervous about the plan to carry them. Fuk asked, "Doesn't he [Chi] know how to do it?"

"He has to give it to me to do it," Tai replied. "It's on my notebook [computer]; he definitely has to give it to me; he can't do it." Later in the conversation, Tai again noted that his brother and Chi's wife, Rebecca, were "very nervous" about passing the QED encrypted disks to the Chinese government.

Two days later, on Saturday, the FBI recorded a conversation at Chi and Rebecca's home that indicated why the couple felt so anxious about the QED documents. Chi was working with the most recent QED research information that he had obtained from Power Paragon. When Chi said that he would take the disks to his brother,

Rebecca reminded Chi that the "things" he had asked Tai to take to China were "certainly against the law."

On Sunday, October 23, Chi was videotaped downloading information from several compact disks onto the hard drive of his laptop computer at home. As he copied the downloaded data onto new disks, Rebecca asked him what would be on the disks. "These CDs are all about programs," Chi told her, referring to the Defense Department programs he was working on for Power Paragon.

It was at this point that Chi appears to have handed off the material to his brother. Late that morning, Chi and Rebecca drove to Tai's house. After twenty-six minutes inside, the two families left Tai's house together. The next day, the FBI overheard Tai telling someone in his house to buy three or four rewritable computer disks. "I need to do something when I get home tonight," he said. During a phone conversation that day, Chi asked Tai if everything was ready to go and Tai replied, "Not quite."

On Tuesday, October 25, FBI surveillance detected Tai's son Billy helping his father to encrypt the information on Chi's disks. Billy asked his father where he could find the "small disk"—a reference to a so-called smart card, which is used to unlock or to encrypt data. Later in the day, Tai called his son, who was out of the house, and said, "I saw that your computer up there kept on spinning." Tai was referring to the IBM notebook computer on the second floor of the house, which was the only computer that could be used to encrypt disks. Billy explained to his father that the computer was spinning because he was burning a disk for Tai.

With Tai Mak and his wife scheduled to leave the country in just a few days, investigators from the FBI, the CIA, and the Naval Criminal Investigative Service (NCIS) met in Washington to discuss whether the couple should be allowed to depart with the valuable QED technology. CIA officials argued that Tai Mak should be permitted to go; the agency wanted to protect its source. But the Navy admiral overseeing the investigation concluded that the QED technology could not fall into the hands of the Chinese military, so he said the disks should not be allowed to leave the United States under any circumstance.

At around 10 P.M. on October 28, FBI agents swooped down on Tai Mak and his wife as they waited on the security line at Los Angeles International Airport. As they moved in, agents noticed that an Asian man had begun to videotape the arrest. The FBI arrested this man, too. Later, intelligence officials determined that the man videotaping the incident was an intelligence officer for the Chinese Ministry of State Security. It showed that China's intelligence service was protecting its prized agent as he was preparing to deliver U.S. Navy high technology.

Where the United States Went Wrong

Though U.S. authorities now had Tai Mak and Chi Mak in custody, they had mishandled the case, as indicated by the subsequent difficulties with the initial indictment.

Counterintelligence specialists told me that the FBI botched the case, first of all, by arresting Tai at the airport. The public arrest gave Chinese intelligence important information that its prized agent had been arrested and that its spy ring had been discovered.

The public arrest of Tai (who was charged in June 2006) also meant that the United States had wasted an opportunity. U.S. counterspies could have exploited the knowledge of the Maks' spy ring in order to run operations against the Chinese and feed Beijing false information on U.S. weapons systems.

To that end, counterintelligence experts say, the government should have arrested Tai's son Billy as part of the spy ring. By implicating the son as an accessory or as a conspirator, counterintelligence officials would have had great leverage over Tai and possibly Chi. The FBI would have been in a position to tell Tai that he had a choice: either become a double agent for the United States or see his wife, his son, and himself go to jail for a very long time.

Instead, the FBI's hope for making a high-profile arrest and the Navy's fears of losing the QED technology won out. Certainly the Navy's concerns about losing the QED technology were legitimate, but a properly run counterintelligence operation could have addressed this issue. Specifically, counterintelligence could have designed special technology or material that would have led the Chinese to build weapons that contained trapdoors or vulnerabilities. U.S. weapons designers and military planners could exploit those vulnerabilities in any future confrontations.

Investigators gathered plenty of incriminating evidence before and after the arrests. Tai Mak refused to cooperate in any way when he was questioned by agents on October 28. He denied he even had a brother and said that the disks he was carrying contained only music files. Still, officials had evidence to demolish those claims. On the statement about the music files, for instance, Tai failed to realize that the FBI had obtained from his home the electronic smart card used to read the coded files.

Chi Mak told interrogators more than his brother did. For starters, he acknowledged that he and Tai were brothers. He also said his brother voluntarily joined the PLA, the Chinese military. Chi said that Tai was in charge of organizing propaganda gatherings and running audiovisual equipment for the PLA, and was involved in military television projects through his experience at Phoenix Television.

More significantly, Chi admitted supplying weapons information to China. After initially saying that he had given the disks to Tai only to help his brother decide which electrical engineering books to buy in Hong Kong, Chi eventually admitted to investigators that the disks were for Pu, the PLA intelligence handler.

Other evidence that investigators discovered indicated Chi's links to Beijing. Found in Chi's residence were business cards from such Chinese officials as a senior engineer with the government-run Shanghai Mechanical and Electrical Industries Administration; a senior engineer working for the Ministry of Aviation, Civil Aircraft Bureau; and a deputy director of the Department of Facilities and Financial Support of the Commission of Science, Technology, and Industry for National Defense (COSTIND), a major collector of weapons technology abroad.

Chi told interrogators—truthfully—that he had "never crossed the threshold" of passing classified information to China. The information he supplied on the Aegis and on submarine and aircraft carrier technology was unclassified. The case highlights the U.S. Navy's failure to recognize that its sensitive weapons technology should have been classified.

Chi admitted that his wife traveled with him when they delivered documents, proposals, and technical manuals to Tai Mak. He also admitted that she helped him send the information to the Chinese government and that she "knew it was illegal," the FBI affidavit reported.

Furthermore, Chi said that he and his wife kept their original Hong Kong government residency cards for the purpose of traveling to China without having their U.S. passports stamped by the government. The residency cards allow holders to travel to mainland China without a passport. Chi would not say during the interrogations why he wanted to travel to China without passports, but the FBI affidavit said that "a person spying for a foreign government would avoid evidence associating them with travel to that country."

Hong Kong residency, the FBI knew, also helped Chi and his wife protect their money. On September 18, 2005, electronic surveillance had recorded a conversation between Chi and Rebecca in which they talked about using their status as U.S. citizens to open a bank account in Hong Kong, at the Hong Kong & Shanghai Banking Corp. (HSBC). In discussing the return to China, Chi told his wife, "We have to get to Hong Kong. Even if we reside in Guangzhou and Shanghai, we still need to keep a household registration in Hong Kong." Most of Chi's money is in the form of cash deposits, and cash in checking and saving accounts.

It all was strong evidence that the Maks had indeed operated the spy ring and done serious harm to the United States.

Assassin's Mace

The military technology the Los Angeles spy ring targeted indicates that Communist China's intelligence penetration operations have very specific objectives. "What we're finding," the FBI's David Szady told me, "is that [the Chinese spying is] much more focused in certain areas than we ever thought, such as command and control and things of that sort. In the military area, the rapid development of their 'blue-water' navy—like the Aegis weapons systems—in no small part is probably due to some of the research and development they were able to get from the United States."

Similarly, a second FBI affidavit in the Red Flower case, dated November 19, 2005, noted that "the government of the PRC is vitally interested in acquiring technology regarding U.S. Navy research projects as part of its efforts to build a deep water navy" and that Beijing "does not allow research or development of military programs to occur without the instigation and control of the government." It certainly appeared that Beijing was calling the shots with the L.A. spy ring. According to the first FBI affidavit, Chi Mak admitted receiving, through his brother Tai, tasking lists from the Chinese government—in this case, lists of specific U.S. military technologies to pursue.

U.S. investigators actually discovered copies of such tasking lists, which provided the first solid proof of the direction of China's massive military buildup.

On February 7, 2005, FBI agents searching the trash outside Chi's house found documents that had been torn into small pieces. The FBI put the documents together and translated them from Chinese to English. One document instructed Chi to join more specialized associations like the American Society of Naval Engineers. A second, hand-printed in Chinese characters, listed specific military technologies the Chinese government sought, including:

1. Water-jet propulsion, which is used to increase warship maneuverability.
2. Propulsion technology that allows nonnuclear submarines to stay submerged longer.
3. Power-system configuration technology, weapons standardization, modularization.
4. Early-warning technologies, command-and-control systems technology, defense-against-nuclear-attack technology.

5. A permanent electromagnetic motor as a solution for shipboard power systems.
6. Shipboard internal and external communications systems.
7. High-frequency, self-linking satellite communications.
8. High-frequency transient launch technology, which uses extremely strong magnets to create kinetic energy used to launch aircraft or projectiles. This is believed to be related to electromagnetic-pulse (EMP) weapons technology.
9. DD(X) advanced destroyer technology.

That list of targeted technologies fit in perfectly with Communist China's strategy of seeking "Assassin's Mace" weapons—select weaponry and technology to enable a smaller, weaker military power to defeat a larger, stronger one. Michael Pillsbury, a Pentagon consultant who served as a Defense Department policy official during the Reagan administration, was the first to identify China's Assassin's Mace plan. Writing in a report on Chinese technology development, Pillsbury stated that this strategy relies on "correct and detailed assessments of the opponent's weakest points and the best means to surprise and to shock into paralysis the powerful opponent." He noted that the assessments are like "acupuncture points" for military planners to target.

The Los Angeles spy ring provided the Chinese with exactly the kind of detailed knowledge of American vulnerabilities that Beijing needs to execute the Assassin's Mace strategy. According to intelligence officials, one of the most damaging documents discovered in Chi Mak's house was a listing of the electronic vulnerabilities of U.S. warships. Also, Chi supplied China with the details on the extent of electronic "hardening" of U.S. weapons systems against attack. Knowing the level of hardening, China will be able to develop its electromagnetic-pulse weapons so that they are effective against U.S. systems. From a military standpoint, that kind of intelligence is absolutely devastating for an adversary like China to obtain.

Chinese military officials have themselves written about the value of the kinds of technologies the L.A. spy ring targeted. In a 1995 report on twenty-first-century naval warfare, PLA Captain Shen Zhongchang wrote that "certain cutting-edge technologies are likely to first be applied to naval warfare." Shen noted, for example, that in a military conflict, "the side with electromagnetic combat superiority will make full use of that Assassin's Mace weapon to win naval victory." Similarly, in March 2000 the *Chinese Military Digest* stated that in future wars, electromagnetic-pulse warheads will be essential to targeting enemy command centers and knocking out enemy electronics.

Of course, electromagnetic weapons are just part of a long list of technologies that China's military theorists have written about as Assassin's Mace weapons that can be used to defeat the United States. The Los Angeles spy ring allowed the Chinese to make extraordinary strides in their massive military buildup, which is aimed at making Communist China a global power that can challenge the United States. But the damage to U.S. national security would not be nearly so bad were it not for America's counterintelligence failures—first the failure to detect the spy ring for more than twenty years, then the repeated mishandlings of the case. Investigators only hope that prosecutors will be able to salvage the case after so much government bungling.

In the case of Communist China—a regime that follows Deng Xiaoping's dictate to "hide our capacities and bide our time"—the true extent of the damage done may not be apparent for some time, and perhaps only after it is too late.

Chapter 3

THE SPIES WHO GOT AWAY

If the Americans draw their missiles and position-guided ammunition onto the target zone on China's territory, I think we will
have to respond with nuclear weapons.

—*Chinese Major General Zhu Chenghu, July 2005*

In 1999, a small group of U.S. counterintelligence officials asked
for a meeting with CIA Director George Tenet. The officials were
part of a special task force that was set up in utmost secrecy to
look into how China had compromised just about all the useful U.S.
electronic eavesdropping operations and other technical spying in the
Communist nation. They told Tenet they needed more than two
hours of his time because of the explosive nature of the information
they had uncovered.

The officials met in Tenet's seventh-floor office at the CIA's Langley headquarters, with a view of the woods in the northern Virginia
suburbs. What they told him was shocking: At least three CIA officers
from the storied Directorate of Operations, the agency's espionage
branch, had betrayed the United States and had worked as spies for
Beijing. One of the officers was paid $600,000 for U.S. secrets.

The CIA traitors had been tracked and identified with the help of
a Chinese intelligence defector who had revealed for the first time
that there was a special section within China's military intelligence

organization, the Second Department of the People's Liberation Army, known by the name 2 PLA. The special section was known as the First Department, and its sole mission was to recruit spies from within the U.S. government, and from within the fifteen-agency U.S. intelligence community in particular.

Tenet, stunned that China had been able to penetrate his agency, ordered the group to pursue the officers, who had already retired from the CIA. But the investigation went nowhere and ended without any action against the Chinese spies. It was typical of the U.S. intelligence community's "see-no-evil" approach to Communist China and Chinese intelligence operations.

The spies could still be operating, officials said. The First Department remains mostly a mystery to U.S. counterintelligence officials. The one thing known for sure is that it has had many great successes in penetrating the U.S. government. Along with the Parlor Maid and Red Flower cases, the First Department reveals that Communist China's intelligence operations aggressively target a wide range of U.S. government agencies for a vast array of sensitive information. Katrina Leung worked with the FBI and stole mainly intelligence secrets; the Chi Mak spy ring targeted some of America's most important and sensitive military secrets; the First Department spies discovered in 1999 were embedded within the CIA itself.

As indicated by the CIA's dead-end investigation of the First Department penetration, the Parlor Maid and Red Flower cases mark merely two of a number of intelligence and counterintelligence failures related to Communist China. Beijing's massive intelligence-and-influence operation in the United States has been active for some thirty years, and the FBI, the CIA, and other U.S. agencies have been negligent in addressing the China threat.

U.S. counterintelligence officials who have begun reviewing the intelligence community's assessments of China since 1982 said that the review has turned up a number of current and old cases of Chinese government penetration of the U.S. government. Some of the spies were identified and allowed to retire quietly. Other cases were botched by public disclosures or ineptitude on the part of the FBI.

The list of mishandled Chinese spying cases does more than call into question the competence of U.S. counterintelligence. It also raises the prospect that China has penetrated the U.S. government to such a degree that it can run its intelligence operations against the United States with impunity. Having a free hand to run espionage operations means that Beijing can not only steal America's most important intelligence and defense secrets but also influence U.S. policy toward China in ways that threaten the future security of the United States.

Despite these significant dangers, many U.S. officials and so-called China experts still insist that Communist China does not represent a serious threat to the United States. Former FBI official I. C. Smith, who understands the full scope of Chinese spying and influence operations as well as anyone in the U.S. government, said that for decades it has been fashionable in U.S. academic and government circles to dismiss the threat from China because of China's ostensibly "agrarian character." Smith remarked, "In essence, the inference by many of the China-is-no-threat group is that an agrarian country could not pose an intelligence threat to such a technological marvel as the United States. In fact, an FBI internal study that was controversial in itself made that argument, an argument that was made throughout the intelligence and diplomatic communities."

Larry Wortzel, a former U.S. military intelligence officer who tracked Chinese intelligence activity for thirty-five years, agrees that the Chinese spy threat is pervasive. "I know of no more pervasive and active threat to America's national security than that posed by the People's Republic of China," Wortzel said in congressional testimony. "The manpower available to the Chinese government and its corporations to devote to gathering information in the United States is nearly limitless."

Given the growing threat from Communist China, the U.S. government must conduct a major review of all counterintelligence activities directed at China. If the United States does not reform its counterintelligence system quickly, we will fall victim to many more spy operations like Katrina Leung's, Chi Mak's, or any of the numerous cases that follow.

Stealing America's Nuclear Secrets

Notra Trulock, the former security official at Los Alamos National Laboratory who first investigated the loss of U.S. nuclear secrets to China, believes that the Katrina Leung case answers many questions about the inability of U.S. counterspies to succeed against China. Regarding the earlier case of Los Alamos nuclear weapons specialist Wen Ho Lee, Trulock told me years after the debacle that "the Chinese seemed always to be one step ahead of us."

Lee, like Katrina Leung, appears to have immunized himself from FBI scrutiny in the 1980s by becoming an informant to the FBI and supplying supposedly good information on Chinese nuclear scientists. Volunteering information reduced suspicions and provided better cover for spying.

When, in early 1999, the FBI informed Lee that he was a suspect in the loss of the most sensitive U.S. nuclear weapons secrets to China, the Bureau undermined its investigation of Lee, much as it would that of Katrina Leung. Lee was charged with removing magnetic computer tapes from Los Alamos's X Division, where nuclear weapons are designed. According to court papers in the case, the missing tapes, which were never recovered from Lee, contained blueprints of the entire U.S. nuclear warhead arsenal, including the exact shapes and dimensions and the materials used in design and construction. They included the crown jewels of America's nuclear arsenal, such as computer codes and databases from forty years of research and more than a thousand nuclear tests. With the tapes, China could simulate the performance of the warheads without having to conduct actual nuclear tests.

The FBI and the Clinton administration abandoned the Lee case, settling for a deal in which he pleaded guilty to the lesser charge of mishandling classified information. Inexperienced FBI agents were to blame for torpedoing the Lee probe. David Szady, the FBI's former chief of counterintelligence, said that FBI agents working in New Mexico at the time of the Lee case did not even know about the presence of the Los Alamos National Laboratory and other nuclear facilities, or the military base there, or private-sector defense contractors or universities involved in sensitive research. More important, they were unaware of the espionage and intelligence-collection targets the facilities presented to foreign intelligence. "We sent agents out to help and we put them on the Indian reservation," Szady said—FBI agents focused on crimes on a reservation while secrets related to the W-88 nuclear warhead were compromised at Los Alamos. "It was our mistake, our errors."

Lee sued the Energy Department, the Justice Department, and the FBI over his case, claiming that his privacy rights were violated by disclosures to the press that he was a spy for China. He also claimed that he was a "scapegoat" in the loss of nuclear secrets and a victim of anti-Asian racism. Several news reporters were held in contempt of court for refusing to identify sources who provided information about the case. Lee settled the civil suit in June 2006, winning $1.6 million from the government and five news organizations. The Associated Press, the *New York Times,* the *Los Angeles Times,* the *Washington Post,* and ABC Television made the unprecedented payment to avoid court fines and to keep their reporters from going to jail for refusing to disclose their sources. The government did not admit it had violated Lee's privacy rights and stipulated that the money could be used by Lee only to pay legal fees and taxes. The news organizations said in a statement that the accuracy of their reporting on Lee was not challenged.

The accusation of racism has made it extremely difficult for U.S. counterintelligence to aggressively pursue Chinese spying at a time when Beijing's activities are increasing. Federal prosecutor Randy Bellows concluded in a report in 2001 that Lee was not a target of investigation because of his ethnicity.

The FBI still claims that it is investigating the loss of U.S. nuclear secrets, but not a single person has ever been identified as a source of the most damaging leak of nuclear secrets since the time of Julius and Ethel Rosenberg. Los Alamos has conducted a detailed classified study on the Wen Ho Lee case that, according to officials familiar with the study, concludes that Lee was the source of the loss of nuclear warhead secrets to China. The study has never been made public. Officials fear that even talking about it will lead to lawsuits.

The FBI doesn't have even a single person who comes to work each day to pursue the supposedly ongoing nuclear-secrets investigation. The Bureau didn't learn about the loss of nuclear secrets until Notra Trulock drew attention to the matter, and even then the FBI never did a serious counterintelligence operation to find out what had happened. Worse, the FBI then persecuted Trulock, who had made the FBI look bad. Intelligence officials say it is clear that espionage allowed China to steal nuclear warhead design secrets from Los Alamos's X Division. The information was known only to a handful of scientists and in fact went beyond what even Wen Ho Lee knew. Therefore there may still be other spies who were never discovered.

Tiger Trap

Before the Wen Ho Lee case there was another nuclear spy case, that of Gwo-Bao Min, code-named Tiger Trap. Min was the scientist working at the Lawrence Livermore National Laboratory in California who provided China with secret warhead information that allowed the Chinese military to build and actually test a neutron bomb, noted for its capability to kill people while leaving buildings and other structures relatively undamaged. Under a secret U.S. government project that began in the 1980s and lasted ten years, U.S. nuclear weapons scientists were allowed to conduct exchanges with their Chinese counterparts. The result was a massive illicit transfer of nuclear information to China. The damage allowed a Communist dictatorship to arm itself with nuclear missiles that currently are aimed at U.S. cities.

According to U.S. officials close to the program, security officials at the Energy labs opposed the exchanges for just such reasons. But they were overruled by the Defense Intelligence Agency and U.S. Air Force intelligence, which were desperate to find out any details they could about China's nuclear arms programs. The program was the brainchild of Los Alamos scientist Daniel Stillman and his deputy

Terry Hawkins. Stillman was head of Los Alamos's intelligence unit, which investigated foreign nuclear arms programs. He was pro-China and had a naïve belief that formal exchanges would produce intelligence. They did—but not for the United States. Unfortunately, they helped Chinese intelligence to identify and recruit the top scientists in the U.S. nuclear weapons program and ultimately to access a trove of secrets.

Stillman's visits to China as part of the program and his connections to Chinese scientists led the FBI to investigate him on suspicion of leaking nuclear secrets, according to U.S. officials. One security official told me that the FBI suspected that Stillman and others at Lawrence Livermore "had been a little too accommodating in their 'information exchanges' with Chinese counterparts," especially since U.S. intelligence had no way to monitor exactly what took place during the trips to China. "I have long believed that these guys passed stuff they shouldn't have," the official said. But nothing came of the investigation. I asked Stillman about the China exchange program, but he said in an e-mail that he did not want to discuss the program. He dismissed claims that the exchanges helped China's nuclear weapons efforts as "ridiculous accusations." Stillman said he was "certainly unaware of any FBI investigation of me" regarding leaks of nuclear information to China.

Gwo Bao Min traveled to China in 1979 on one of the program's exchanges. U.S. intelligence officials believe that Min disclosed to Chinese nuclear officials extremely sensitive information on how to manufacture a small warhead. He was forced to resign from Livermore in 1981, but not before a clumsy FBI attempt to turn him into a double agent. The effort failed, and the prospect of prosecuting a Chinese nuclear spy was lost. The lead investigator on the case was FBI Special Agent Bill Cleveland, who would later become a key player in the Katrina Leung case. Cleveland had interviewed Min in the early 1980s, years before he became a squad supervisor, and claimed to associates that he almost succeeded in getting Min to confess to spying. But at the last moment, Min backed off.

Tiger Trap was an outgrowth of the case of Larry Wu-Tai Chin, a

Chinese mole who had burrowed deep within the CIA for more than three decades. Chin was a translator for the CIA's Foreign Broadcast Information Service, which conducts language translations of foreign press reports and broadcasts. Chin escaped justice by committing suicide in his cell. I. C. Smith told me the Chin case was the last case, and perhaps the only case, of consequence that the FBI worked successfully against Chinese intelligence.

Significantly, Min's case would set in motion both the Katrina Leung and Wen Ho Lee cases. The investigation of Min first brought Leung to the attention of the FBI. The Bureau questioned her about Min and tasked her to find out what she could on the case from the MSS. Min became more directly linked to Leung's spy case years later, when he appeared at the same hotel in Shenyang, China, where FBI agents Bill Cleveland and I. C. Smith were staying. This encounter occurred in 1990, just after Leung had been overheard telling her MSS handler that Cleveland and Smith would be traveling to China. So it appears that Leung's tip-off had prompted the MSS to send Min to Shenyang. Was the meeting an attempt to recruit Cleveland? Cleveland told the FBI that it was strange meeting someone who had been the target of an investigation he had led years earlier.

The Min case also first brought Wen Ho Lee to the attention of the FBI. After Min resigned from Los Alamos, the Bureau recorded a telephone call Lee placed to Min at his California home. Lee offered to help Min. The conversation showed that both men were sympathetic toward China.

The connections among these various China spy cases indicate that Beijing was carefully coordinating and directing the intelligence operations.

Royal Tourist

The Chinese nuclear spy case that ended in near failure was the case of Peter Lee, code-named Royal Tourist. Like Tiger Trap, Royal Tourist involved a nuclear scientist working at the Lawrence Livermore National Laboratory. The Chinese government saw weak security at the weapons laboratories and even weaker FBI counterintelligence. U.S. intelligence learned that China had targeted the U.S. Stockpile Stewardship Program, which sought to test the reliability of nuclear arms without underground tests.

According to a classified U.S. intelligence report, Lee traveled to China in 1985 with a group of scientists at the invitation of a Chinese visitor to Los Alamos. On the trip, he was visited late one night in his hotel room by two Chinese officials from the State Science and Technology Commission. The officials "pitched" him to work for China, and they secured his cooperation by appealing to his Chinese ancestry and cultural ties, according to the report.

Eventually Lee would become the focus of an FBI investigation, and he was arrested in 1997. He admitted to passing information on nuclear weapons and antisubmarine warfare technology.

Despite the admission, the Clinton administration soft-pedaled the case. Lee could have received a life term for leaking sensitive nuclear weapons secrets, but Justice Department officials limited the prosecutor and kept him from seeking tough charges. Lee was allowed to plea-bargain, and he received minimal punishment—a five-year suspended sentence, twelve months in a halfway house, and a $20,000 fine.

Why? The soft line on Lee reflected the pro-China policies of the Clinton administration, which had been caught taking cash donations during the 1996 elections from a number of people linked to the Beijing government. Also, congressional investigators learned that the Chinese government had threatened the administration by saying that a tough handling of the Peter Lee case would upset U.S.-China relations. The threat worked. And so another nuclear spy escaped serious punishment.

Intelligence Break or Chinese Disinformation?

A major intelligence break appeared to help the CIA learn about China's nuclear weapons program. In 1995, a Chinese scientist involved with the ultrasecret nuclear program walked into a U.S.

embassy overseas with a packet of Chinese-language documents that included secrets on China's military program—missiles, nuclear warheads, and even advanced weapons research on electromagnetic-pulse (EMP) weapons. The documents showed that China could now produce the most advanced warhead in the U.S. arsenal, the W-88, which is used on submarine-launched missiles and multiple warheads. The Chinese version had almost the identical dimensions as the W-88. The Chinese warhead was believed to be in mass production.

But then China put out word that the "defector-in-place" was actually a Beijing-controlled double agent. This information discredited the documents the scientist had passed to the United States. Were the Chinese telling the truth about a double agent, or were they practicing classic tradecraft and trying to make the CIA doubt its intelligence breakthrough? CIA Deputy Director of Operations Jack Downing, who was involved with the walk-in documents, said through a spokesman that while the matter was still subject to debate, the defector was probably controlled by Beijing, "at least at the later stages of events." Downing is a former CIA station chief in Beijing who back in the late 1970s promoted a program of U.S.-Chinese intelligence cooperation (a program that ended after the Tiananmen Square massacre). He recognizes that China spies on the United States, but he reflects the typical CIA mindset, which views China as a nonthreatening power.

U.S. counterintelligence officials recognized that the Chinese could easily have fed the United States still more disinformation. They began looking into whether Katrina Leung had alerted the MSS to the defector-in-place and whether the tip-off led to the passing of disinformation. Interrogators probably asked Leung about this possibility in her post–plea bargain debriefing sessions; those debriefings remain secret.

"Mother"

The full details of one Chinese case have never been made public. This case involved a 1987 sting operation against a Chinese intelligence officer.

Hou Desheng was a junior officer in the PLA's military intelligence unit who was posted to the Chinese embassy in Washington, D.C. The talkative officer complained to a reporter that he had a difficult time surviving on the $75 a month he was paid by the Chinese military. The information found its way to the FBI's Washington field office and the foreign counterintelligence section. The complaint about money was a tantalizing indicator that perhaps Hou could be lured to work secretly for the FBI.

To "pitch" him for recruitment, the U.S. government would need to set up a sting operation. If the government could catch Hou trying to take American secrets, U.S. officials could offer him a deal: either come work for the FBI in secret or be publicly exposed as a Chinese intelligence agent and have your diplomatic cover blown.

The sting operation lasted a year. It came to a head on December 21, 1987, when two U.S. government officials posing as employees of the NSA approached Hou and told him they had classified communications codes that would allow China to read secret U.S. communications around the world. They offered Hou the codes for $500. The group arranged to meet that night at the Mongolian Restaurant in the heart of Washington's Chinatown. There they exchanged the fake codes for the money. FBI agents moved in and arrested Hou and another Chinese intelligence officer, Zang Weichu, who was working undercover as a Chinese consular official posted in Chicago.

The government offered both the recruiting pitch. Hou and Zang turned it down. Both Hou and Zang had diplomatic immunity, so the United States could not arrest them. The Chinese intelligence officers were expelled from the United States and forced to return to China.

Months later U.S. intelligence officials learned why the two Chinese officers might not have accepted the U.S. recruiting pitch: because the MSS in Beijing already knew about the possibility of their getting caught and was worried about protecting the identity of an agent inside the U.S. government far more important than either Hou or Zang.

Sensitive intelligence revealed that shortly before Hou's meeting at the Mongolian Restaurant, the MSS dispatched a courier to the

Chinese embassy in Washington. The courier carried a message on edible paper—so that it could be eaten if he was caught—that said the Hou meeting should not go through.

"The message said that if the meeting takes place, 'Mother' may have a heart attack," one intelligence official said. U.S. officials interpreted the message as an indication that the meeting might disclose the identity of a senior Chinese agent working clandestinely inside the U.S. intelligence community or government.

Chinese ambassador Han Xu and the Chinese defense attaché in Washington argued over whether the meeting should go ahead as planned. The defense attaché objected strongly to the meeting, but in the end Han overruled him. Beijing would recall the attaché a short time later.

U.S. intelligence officials now believe that "Mother" may have been Katrina Leung, who in 1987 was a key asset in Los Angeles providing extremely valuable secrets to the MSS through her relationship with J. J. Smith. The other possibility is that "Mother" was another high-ranking Chinese agent in the government who was never found, and who may still be operating.

Agent of Influence

Another failed Chinese spying case involved an analyst for the Defense Intelligence Agency (DIA) named Ronald Montaperto, who would eventually be convicted for illegally having classified documents but who avoided harsher espionage charges.

Montaperto began work in 1981 in DIA's China military estimates branch. That year he was among six DIA analysts directed to have contacts with Chinese embassy military attachés, who were intelligence officers. But his contacts went far beyond his professional work and ended with him providing Top Secret and Secret classified information to Chinese intelligence. He had a particularly close relationship with Yu Zenghe of the People's Liberation Army, a military attaché at the Chinese embassy in Washington. Montaperto was so close with Yu—who would later become head of the PLA's ultrasecret spy section known as the First Department—that the Chinese military intelligence officer attended his wedding in 1990. Such close associations should have signaled the U.S. intelligence community that there was a serious problem. But beginning in the late 1980s the FBI's and the DIA's internal counterintelligence security service failed to notice Montaperto's unprofessional Chinese contacts. It would take a Chinese government defector to provide the first clues to his activities.

Montaperto had defenders in high places within the DIA, people who liked his conciliatory views of China. According to counterintelligence officials, that allowed Montaperto to operate both as an information source and as an agent of influence for Communist China. "He was valuable to Chinese intelligence for the secrets he passed and for his role in facilitating Chinese deception of U.S. intelligence by providing Beijing with a feedback mechanism," said a Pentagon official.

In the early 1990s, DIA officials began to suspect that China had penetrated the agency. For much of the 1980s the United States had cooperated with China on electronic intelligence operations aimed at the Soviet Union, but that was severely limited after the Tiananmen Square massacre in 1989. The few operations that continued were supposed to be closely monitored by the Defense Intelligence Officer (DIO), but it became apparent that the DIA was not properly supervising Chinese contacts. For example, the DIO's own Focal Group, also known as the "Small Group," was not required to file foreign contact reports. Those reports are normally standard procedure for all U.S. intelligence personnel, as they allow the United States to monitor contacts for counterintelligence purposes. Montaperto was part of the Small Group, so he did not report his contacts with Chinese military officials in Washington. As in the Aldrich Ames case, formal contacts with a target embassy would spiral out of control and lead to a damaging loss of secrets.

Montaperto aroused suspicion within the DIA, but according to one intelligence official who worked with Montaperto, the DIA resisted making a full investigation. "DIA, as an institution, did not want one of its senior people busted on spying charges," the official said. "I got that firsthand from one of the DIA security investigators after he resigned in disgust and joined a counterintelligence contractor."

When multiple intelligence sources, both electronic and human, showed that China was operating a spy in the United States code-named "Ma"—Chinese for "horse"—the FBI launched a search for a Chinese mole. On January 29, February 6, February 12, and February 20, 1991, the Bureau confronted Montaperto about his contacts with Yu Zenghe. Montaperto told investigators that he had "close relationships" with Yu Zenghe and another Chinese military intelligence officer working at the Washington embassy, Senior Colonel Yang Qiming. "Montaperto admitted to verbally providing these attachés a considerable amount of information that was useful to them, including classified information," a court statement said. But he denied being a spy. After he refused to take a polygraph test, he left the DIA.

Officially, that initial investigation of Montaperto faltered for lack of evidence, but court papers in the case indicate that the U.S. government at the time was uninterested in pursuing Chinese spies. The papers reveal that as early as 1989, Montaperto had informed security officials that he had maintained unusual contacts with Yu and others at the Chinese embassy.

Worse, after leaving DIA, Montaperto was allowed to keep his top-secret security clearance and moved to a new China analysis center at the National Defense University in Washington. "He had protectors in high places, at DIA, CIA, and in the academic community," the intelligence official told me. It would take more than a year after Montaperto moved from the DIA before the FBI began to reinterview witnesses from his previous investigations in the early 1990s. Around the same time, conservatives in Congress began pressing the National Defense University to remove Montaperto, since they did not believe he was the right person to conduct threat assessments on China. So Montaperto moved on to Hawaii, where he went to work as the academic dean at the U.S. Pacific Command's Asia-Pacific Center for Security Studies.

It didn't take long for him to come under suspicion there. In August 2001, the FBI and the Naval Criminal Investigative Service opened an investigation of Montaperto in Hawaii. As part of the probe, they arranged a sting operation, pretending to offer Montaperto a job as leader of a new DIA intelligence-sharing program with the People's Liberation Army. They told him that intelligence officials in Washington needed to know whether Chinese intelligence had enough confidence in him to head the new program. The sting worked: During questioning by agents in October and November 2003, Montaperto made the following admissions:

- He met with Chinese military attachés Yu Zenghe and Yang Qiming numerous times over a period of many years.
- He knew when he met the men that they were both trained intelligence officers.
- He often discussed classified issues with the attachés by talking "around" the information.
- He had verbally disclosed to Yu Zenghe information classified by the U.S. government at the Secret and Top Secret levels; he said he could not recall the specifics, except for two discussions in the late 1980s involving Top Secret information about Chinese military sales and missile transfers to the Middle East.

At one point during the questioning, one official told me, Montaperto realized he had been had and pretended to play the victim of Chinese intelligence recruitment.

A search of Montaperto's residence in Springfield, Virginia, on February 4, 2004, provided the final details of Montaperto's treachery. Numerous classified documents on U.S.-China military and intelligence relations were found, including one called "The Maturing US/PRC Military Relationship."

In early 2004, the Asia-Pacific Center ousted Montaperto for mishandling classified information. It would take another two years before the case would finally come to a close—and even then he would be let off on the most serious espionage charges.

On June 21, 2006, Montaperto pleaded guilty to one count of unlawful retention of classified documents. The plea agreement meant that he would undergo debriefings and that he was barred from meeting any foreign agents. He would serve jail time, but the sentence was relatively light considering his betrayal of secrets and his help in facilitating Chinese deception efforts.

I reached Montaperto's wife by telephone at their home in Morehead City, North Carolina, days before the plea deal, but she declined to comment. Montaperto's lawyer, Steve Anthony, also declined to comment.

Montaperto's friends swung into action, though. Lonnie Henley, a Montaperto protégé who had recently been appointed deputy national intelligence officer for East Asia, e-mailed several groups of U.S. and international China specialists to criticize the FBI for persecuting Montaperto. His e-mail triggered an internal investigation within the Office of the Director of National Intelligence (ODNI), since it could be viewed as an ODNI-sanctioned criticism of the FBI. Intelligence officials told me that Henley should not be investigated by the ODNI ombudsman, Nancy Tucker, since she at one time was romantically involved with Montaperto.

U.S. officials also said that Montaperto's friends spiked stories about the case by telling reporters that if they wrote about it, they would end up in court like the reporters in the Wen Ho Lee case. Perhaps that helps explain the remarkable fact that almost no major news organization besides the *Washington Times* saw fit to report that a former high-ranking DIA analyst had pleaded guilty to an espionage-related charge and had, according to court papers, passed both secret and top-secret information to Chinese intelligence.

Regardless of what Montaperto's friends said, U.S. counterintelligence officials told me that Montaperto was a spy for China—one of the many who got away. A senior counterintelligence official disclosed that Montaperto admitted passing secrets to the Chinese. "He told us, 'If I saw it, it was gone'" to the Chinese, the counterintelligence official said. FBI officials defended the less-than-stringent prosecution, saying that their information was based mostly on Montaperto's own admissions and that using classified information in court is always difficult.

Montaperto represents one of the more difficult challenges in the counterintelligence field. Catching a spy red-handed passing classified documents to foreign officials is a relatively cut-and-dry investigative and legal affair. The real counterintelligence challenge lies in identifying agents of influence. These are the people who subtly advance the interests of foreign entities or governments. When such agents work within the intelligence community, they distort the intelligence picture and can skew policy decisions and judgments. They can downplay emerging threats by ignoring important intelligence reports and by raising the standard of evidence so high that it is hard to reach the level of confirmation. Or they can simply issue a "nonconcur" with an analytic position that runs counter to what the agents' foreign tasking officers want to portray. By failing to agree, they effectively quash the opposing assessment. Assessments that differed from Montaperto's could not get published, or at least they were delayed until the publication was outside the decision-making time frame. This is where Montaperto did damage.

In July 2006, Congressman Dana Rohrabacher, chairman of the House International Relations oversight and investigations subcommittee, asked the Government Accountability Office to investigate policy documents Montaperto had "prepared and influenced" and, more broadly, whether Montaperto had influenced U.S. policy toward China. "I am deeply concerned about the damage that has been done by Ronald N. Montaperto to our country's formulation and implementation of foreign policy related to the People's Republic of China," Rohrabacher wrote.

Economic Espionage

The U.S. intelligence community is not the only place that China planted agents. Still another botched Chinese intelligence case involved a Chinese national who penetrated the Securities and Exchange Commission (SEC).

Mylene Chan was a Chinese national who worked as a computer and online-service analyst with the SEC. Ten months in to her time at the SEC, coworkers discovered that she had sent sensitive economic data on American computer companies to Shanghai. U.S. intelligence officials said that Shanghai is the headquarters of the MSS division that is responsible for targeting the United States. Chan was forced to resign. On July 1, 2002, security guards escorted her from the SEC building and sealed her office.

"She was clearly expropriating things from the commission that weren't hers—things that were not public information and that would cause competitive harm to the companies involved," one official close to the case said. The case showed how the Chinese conduct economic espionage in the United States.

The SEC never reported the matter to the FBI. Apparently to avoid the embarrassment of having hired a Chinese agent, the commission covered up the data leakage. The U.S. companies were never informed about the compromise of their corporate data until I broke the story in the *Washington Times* on November 11, 2002.

Chan denied being fired and told coworkers in an e-mail that she had resigned for personal reasons and would be returning to Hong Kong. In an e-mail to SEC coworkers, she said it was her responsibility to work with officials of the China and Hong Kong securities commissions to educate them on SEC functions. In the course of those contacts, Chan stated, "I provided a small number of SEC materials mistakenly, all of which were retrieved as soon as I learned of the mistake."

But SEC officials believe Chan supplied China with confidential-treatment requests, or CTRs, which are secret reports U.S. companies provide to the SEC. The CTRs contain proprietary and other sensitive information that companies do not want disclosed to the public or to competitors. Intelligence officials told me that the SEC leak to China constituted either economic espionage or state-sponsored espionage.

Documents from the SEC showed that Chan had access to sensitive information from more than fifteen high-tech companies, including several involved in cutting-edge software development. She had also processed numerous CTRs. Several of the companies who suffered information compromises in the case are involved in security-related work for U.S. defense and intelligence agencies. All the sensitive information Chan sent would be useful for China in assisting its state-run industries to compete with their U.S. counterparts.

Rare Breakthrough

In dealing with Communist China, U.S. counterintelligence has made very few breakthroughs. One counterintelligence break that came the government's way occurred in 1985. That year, a Chinese intelligence officer named Yu Qiangsheng defected to the United States.

Yu had realized that the Communist system he worked for was wrong and he agreed to work against it. From 1983 until he was safely resettled outside China, the former MSS official provided valuable leads to U.S. intelligence. Yu helped identify some fifty MSS agents working for China against the United States. Most notable among these agents was Larry Wu-Tai Chin, the CIA translator who was a Chinese mole for decades.

Unlike the operational security of the Soviet Union (later Russia) and its Cold War satellites, which produced scores of intelligence defectors and recruitments of agents "in place," China operational security is extremely good. In fact, since the 1980s there have been only six major intelligence defections from China; the defectors are known within the U.S. intelligence community as "The Big Six."

Yu remains under federal government protection and still fears for his life from Beijing agents.

The B.G.s

The Chinese have also managed to influence U.S. analysts, prompting them to issue favorable reports that ultimately soften U.S. policies toward China. Two members of the clique of pro-China analysts in the United States were sucked in as part of an intelligence coup for Beijing.

Bonnie Glaser and Banning Garrett—"the B.G.s"—were a husband-

and-wife team of contractors paid by the CIA to travel to China and meet with Chinese officials. There was only one problem: The couple, ostensibly part of the CIA's cadre of unclassified, open-source intelligence collectors, was influenced by a Communist Chinese campaign of deception. China's Ministry of State Security (MSS) created and funded a think tank, the China Institute of Contemporary International Relations—known as CICIR, or "kicker"—that supplied information to the B.G.s for years.

Glaser initially was employed by the System Planning Corporation in Arlington, Virginia, and Garrett worked for Palomar Consulting. They began operating as CIA consultants in 1980 and were backed by officials at the highest levels of the U.S. government. Those officials were the same people who read and were obviously influenced by the top-secret reports provided by Chinese intelligence agent Katrina Leung. Among the pro-China officials who supported Glaser and Garrett were several Asia directors for the White House National Security Council, including Douglas Paal, who served under President George H. W. Bush; Robert Suettinger and Kenneth Lieberthal, each of whom held the post during the Clinton administration; and Dennis Wilder, the Asia specialist under George W. Bush.

On a regular basis, Garrett and Glaser traveled to Beijing and stayed at the exclusive Shangri-La Hotel. The hotel was well known to U.S. intelligence as having a special MSS intelligence unit based there. The unit was in charge of recording all hotel-room conversations of visiting foreign guests. The Shangri-La was located conveniently close to the CICIR offices. They would meet Chinese officials and write up memoranda of their conversations, known as "memcons"— all unwittingly and carefully controlled by the strategic disinformation specialists at CICIR.

At the heart of the deception fed to Garrett and Glaser is a fundamental precept of Chinese strategic deception—namely, that China does not practice deception. What you see is what you get. If this is the case, then unlike all Communist governments in the past, Beijing must be accepted at its word, and any suspicions about its motives and objectives should be dismissed. If China did practice deception, it would be improper for the CIA to have conducted the long-running collection effort using Garrett and Glaser. The CIA paid the couple as much as $100,000 per year, plus expenses, to make two trips annually to China.

Around 2000, Garrett and Glaser got a divorce, at which point Glaser took over the unclassified CIA contract work. She had her own conflict of interest in that her father owned a factory in Guangdong, in southern China. She eventually was given a job as senior associate at the Center for Strategic and International Studies, a think tank in Washington, D.C. In October 2005, she hosted two CICIR "researchers," whom she described in an e-mail to me as "experts on Sino-U.S. relations and U.S. foreign policy."

Glaser and Garrett's work with the CIA, while unclassified, was deliberately "secretive." They were not clandestine CIA officers and they did not hold security clearances, but often they made it seem that way, according to U.S. intelligence officials. They signed their published articles "Consultants to the U.S. Government" and invoked the CIA in seeking background interviews with U.S. officials before going overseas. In that way, Glaser and Garrett got dozens of U.S. officials they talked to over some twenty years to reveal sensitive information that they would then use in discussions with their Chinese hosts during annual visits.

Glaser declined to discuss her contract work other than to say she did not have access to U.S. intelligence analyses. Garrett could not be reached for comment.

Bush administration officials said there is evidence that Garrett and Glaser have informed the Chinese of U.S. political policies that threatened the pro-China approach that still prevails. For example, one senior U.S. official told me that several years ago Garrett and Glaser alerted Chinese officials to the fact that Senator Jon Kyl, Arizona Republican, tried to include language in a bill to increase military contacts between the Pentagon and Taiwan's military. One of the key elements of China's disinformation campaign in the United States is that Beijing wants to peacefully resolve its dispute with Taiwan, which broke from the mainland in 1949 and has been home to Chinese

Nationalists since. In fact, China's military buildup is aimed directly at eventually using force against the island. A bill strengthening U.S. ties to Taiwan's military would complicate those plans. China was able to lobby against the language Kyl wanted to include; it was cut out in a House-Senate conference.

Panda Huggers

Garrett and Glaser are part of a small group of pro-China CIA private specialists and government analysts that has played a key role in shaping U.S. policy relating to China. These analysts are not the only government officials to take a soft line on China, by any means, but their reporting has given them inordinate influence within government. In conservative political circles the analysts have become known as "panda huggers"—a derisive term used to describe U.S. officials who aggressively promote pro-Beijing policies. They gained substantial influence during the Clinton administration, and their work exerts a hold on U.S. policy to this day.

In recent years one of the most influential of these CIA intelligence analysts has been Dennis Wilder. Wilder joined the CIA in the 1980s as a military analyst. Both he and his wife, Ursula, are left-leaning liberals, according to officials who know the couple. He got his start in the corridors of Washington power after he helped arrange the secret July 1989 visit to China by National Security Adviser Brent Scowcroft and Deputy Secretary of State Lawrence Eagleburger. The two officials visited Beijing as part of a shameless and immoral effort to assure Chinese leaders that their brutal military crackdown on unarmed protesters in Tiananmen Square a month earlier would not harm ties with the United States.

As the CIA's top China military analyst in the late 1990s, Wilder came under investigation by the agency's ombudsman, with his management of China analysis triggering more than a half-dozen formal complaints of politicization. Analysts accused him of skewing or suppressing their reports on China's worsening human rights situation, China's rapid military buildup, and its swift development of its scientific and technical base with help from American corporations. Wilder modified or killed the reports because he claimed that they exaggerated the threat posed by China. To deal with the analysts, he saw to it that they were moved out of the China analytical division to other posts. Wilder skillfully deflected the criticism of himself by arranging the transfer of those who made the accusations or by outright denials.

Wilder was also instrumental in blocking Chinese dissidents from meeting President George W. Bush in a period from 2003 to 2006, despite the president's declaration in his second inaugural address and the 2005 State of the Union message that his administration had launched a major effort to promote democracy and freedom. Instead of bringing Chinese dissidents to meet the president, Wilder arranged White House meetings for several Chinese Communist officials. For example, he set up a meeting between National Security Adviser Stephen J. Hadley and Chinese Communist Party official Zheng Bijian, who is often touted by pro-China officials in the Bush administration as a reformer.

Wilder provoked more controversy in 2005 when he had a hand in producing a highly classified report for the new director of national intelligence on U.S. spy agencies' failure to recognize key military developments in China over the previous decade. The June 2005 report used the term "intelligence surprise" more than a dozen times to describe the failures to anticipate or discover significant Chinese arms developments, including Beijing's development of a new long-range cruise missile, precision-guided munitions, surface-to-surface missiles for targeting U.S. aircraft carrier battle groups, and a new attack submarine. Thus the report placed the blame squarely on intelligence collectors. According to officials familiar with the report, this perspective reflected Wilder's work behind the scenes to try to exonerate himself and his fellow pro-China analysts, who had downplayed or dismissed intelligence on the military buildup.

"This report conceals the efforts of dissenting analysts [in the intelligence community] who argued that China was a threat," one official told me. The official added that covering up the failure of intelligence analysts on China would prevent a major reorganization of the system. Meanwhile, a former U.S. official told me that the report should help expose a "self-selected group" of specialists who fooled the U.S. government on China for ten years. "This group's desire to have good relations with China has prevented them from highlighting how little they know and suppressing occasional evidence that China views the United States as its main enemy," the former official remarked.

Similarly, an analyst told me that key officials like Wilder had contributed to the intelligence failures on China by "carrying out their own private foreign policy" aimed at minimizing China's military buildup.

The 95-page report received a limited distribution, but when intelligence analysts who had been excluded from taking part in the review challenged some of the report's findings, the distributed copies were recalled and destroyed, apparently to prevent congressional oversight panels from seeing them.

Wilder's handling of the secret China review angered conservatives in Congress and the executive branch who say that this kind of downplaying of threats had softened U.S. policy toward China. In many cases the skewed reporting involved cooperation between intelligence analysts like Wilder and political appointees. During the Clinton administration, as head of the China analytical division, Wilder spoke privately and regularly with the Asia specialist on the National Security Council staff, Kenneth Lieberthal. Most major media ignored such interaction, and the politicization questions it raised. Yet any similar interaction with CIA analysts by Vice President Dick Cheney and other Republican officials raised cries of politicization by liberal pundits. Politicization exists only, it seems, when a Republican administration is in power.

Disinformation

The persistence of naïve views on, and policies toward, Communist China reflects the astounding success of the Chinese government's "perception management" operation in the United States.

One of the key disinformation themes the Chinese emphasize is that China wants to adopt a democratic system like that of the United States. Chinese leaders and apologists outside China frequently point to the village-level democratic elections held in China as a sign that the nation is becoming democratic. But Chinese government reports make clear that China has no intention of abandoning its Communist system. Its idea of democracy is to have the ruling Communist Party vote among its million members for a collective dictatorship of about seven top rulers. This small collection of rulers holds the real power in the country. Any movement toward democratic reform ended suddenly with the Tiananmen Square massacre in 1989, when the regime cracked down on democracy advocates, killing hundreds of protesters and imprisoning and deporting many others.

One revealing Communist government white paper emerged in October 2005. The paper showed that Beijing had no plans for Western-style democracy. "China's democracy is a democracy guaranteed by the people's democratic dictatorship," the report said. Under that dictatorship, "democratic centralism" is used to rule collectively by party leaders. The report stated that the Communist Party regarded itself as a "vanguard of the working class" and that therefore the party had rejected copying the "Western bourgeois political system," which "would lead them nowhere."

China's deception operations also put out stories about alleged splits between "hawks" and "doves" inside the ruling Communist leadership. Portraying such a split allows China's perception managers to explain away hard-line policies as those of a faction. The message usually sent is that if political pressure is applied on the Chinese government—whether over human rights abuses, arms proliferation to terrorist states, or trade disputes—it will only strengthen the hand of the hard-liners and delay China's move toward democratic reform. In fact, China has no significant split within its leadership. Note that many China analysts hailed Jiang Zemin as a leader who would institute Western-style political reforms, when in fact he came to power after the bloody Tiananmen crackdown, and he proved not to be a reformer during his years in power. Today, so-called China experts make similar claims about the current Chinese president, Hu Jintao, another supposed reformer.

A third Chinese Communist disinformation theme is the deliberately spread notion about China's "collapse." The collapse theme has been used by Chinese propagandists and others outside China to argue for conciliatory policies toward Beijing. The program has been very successful in fooling U.S. and other Western leaders into not pressuring China toward developing democracy and has led to downplaying or ignoring China's widespread human rights abuses, lest pressure force a collapse.

In 2003, China demonstrated its influence on U.S. policy yet again when the State Department scuttled the Library of Congress's plan to buy from a Chinese national a treasure trove of classified Chinese Communist Party documents on the Cultural Revolution, the decade-long reign of terror carried out by Mao Zedong's Red Guards that ended in 1976. The State Department intervened just as the deal was about to be settled, prohibiting the documents from being transferred. It turns out that State had been tipped off to the sale by the pro-China official who had run the China collection at the Library of Congress for forty-eight years. After the document incident, Wang Chi, the Library of Congress China collection director, was quietly allowed to retire in 2004.

Underestimated

Why do so many U.S. officials deny that China poses a threat when so many intelligence operations have been detected in the United States?

A major reason, as former FBI counterspy I. C. Smith pointed out, is that analysts have simply underestimated China's intelligence and military capabilities. Another reason is that U.S. counterintelligence concluded that Chinese spies typically don't emphasize traditional espionage practice. For example, FBI China analyst Paul Moore, who was among those fooled for decades by Katrina Leung, is fond of telling audiences that "China does not spy as God intended." Instead of dead drops and secret communications, they use a much more benign form of intelligence collection, Moore and others maintain.

Smith summarized this view when he said the Chinese "aren't out there making dead drops, communicating via shortwave radio, paying cash concealed in hollow rocks, et cetera, as is the expected norm for the spy business." From this, Smith said, U.S. officials have mistakenly concluded that "China doesn't pose a threat." He added, "This view became dominant in the FBI and even, to a large extent, the intelligence community, and this resulted in the FBI essentially deemphasizing counterintelligence in general and in the China CI [counterintelligence] program in particular."

Even if the Chinese were indeed ignoring traditional espionage techniques, their targeting of nuclear secrets and other vital information should have been cause enough for concern. As it happens, though, U.S. intelligence might have underestimated China's traditional spying skills. It is known, for instance, that the Chinese use the tried-and-true technique of running "illegals"—deep-cover agents dispatched to the United States to help other spy networks—and operate schools and training centers for spies and intelligence officers. Also, the United States gained a wealth of knowledge about the inner workings of Chinese intelligence from a key defector. Senior Colonel Xu Junping, a close aide to the head of PLA intelligence, General Xiong Guangkai, defected in late December 2000. Xu's information contradicts Paul Moore's theory that China spies differently.

Other information challenging the Moore thesis comes from Ambassador James Lilley, the former CIA officer and envoy to Beijing. Lilley has revealed to friends how Chinese intelligence in Laos and Cambodia carried on traditional spying operations, including the use of dead drops and theft of classified documents.

The fact is that there are substantial gaps in our knowledge of China's intelligence services. Michelle Van Cleave, the former top U.S. counterintelligence official, expressed great concern over these gaps. "What's really unacceptable is how little we know about Chinese intelligence capabilities and how they operate," she said in an interview. "We should be able to say, with high confidence, how big the MSS is, how many people make up that service. But we can't. Why not? Because there hasn't been a focused collection and analysis effort on the foreign intelligence threat as it is engaged against U.S. national interests." The CIA might be interested in knowing what the MSS is doing in China to try to stop CIA activities there.

It is high time that the United States revise its misguided assessments of Communist China. The assessments are not just those of the intelligence community. I. C. Smith noted that Republican and Democratic presidents alike, including George H. W. Bush and Bill Clinton, have taken conciliatory views toward China. And in return, all they have encountered is a tougher posture from Beijing. When presidents are viewed as strong, Beijing backs off, he said.

"One must recall that the PRC's Communist government needs an adversary," he told me. "Having an adversary is key to Communism remaining in power, hence a justification for a violation of their very constitution that exalts freedom, et cetera, and the police apparatus that keeps them in power."

But one doesn't typically hear such frank assessments within the intelligence community or in other corridors of power. "To state such views is to be cast by the pro-PRC intellectuals in this country as a warmonger, of limited intellect, a gumshoe, and viewed with contempt," Smith said. "In effect, a hard-liner toward China was simply ostracized and banished to the fringes of policymaking in government and certainly within some individual agencies."

The soft line on Beijing has prevailed for years. The more information emerges on China—the *real* China—the more misguided that position appears.

Chapter 4

THE FBI'S WILD-GOOSE CHASE

The worst thing, the absolute worst thing, is that some of your
colleagues would call you a traitor to your country.

—*CIA counterintelligence officer Brian Kelley*

The FBI's mishandling of the Katrina Leung case and numerous
other Chinese intelligence cases reflects a much wider problem:
gross ineptness at counterintelligence work.

The Bureau demonstrated its inability to conduct real counterintelligence in the case of veteran CIA counterspy Brian Kelley, whom
the FBI hounded for years in an effort to prove that he was a Russian
mole selling secrets to Moscow. The Bureau turned Kelley's life into a
living nightmare. For more than three years, investigators put him
under blanket surveillance—twenty-four hours a day, seven days a
week. They also resorted to tactics that seemed more appropriate for
a political police force like the Soviet KGB than for an American law-
enforcement agency. Kelley's family members, including his octoge-
narian mother, received not-so-veiled threats. The investigation ruined
Kelley's career at the CIA, as the FBI continually told CIA bureaucrats that the case against Kelley was "100 percent" solid. Agency officials, including CIA Director George Tenet, refused to go to bat for
their counterspy. Tenet, just as he had falsely promised President
George W. Bush that Iraq's hidden weapons of mass destruction were

a "slam dunk" from the intelligence viewpoint, also believed that the FBI's case against Kelley was 100 percent proven. Thus no one challenged the FBI's assumptions and investigative findings.

There was only one problem with this relentless investigation: Kelley wasn't a Russian spy. In fact, the real mole was operating right under the FBI's noses the entire time. The Bureau was betrayed by one of its own—FBI Special Agent Robert Hanssen. The FBI never detected it, until an audiotape recording provided irrefutable evidence of Hanssen's guilt.

The Bureau, which is among the most secret agencies of government, was quick to claim credit for catching Hanssen. It released surveillance video of Hanssen's arrest in northern Virginia on a cold Sunday morning in February 2001. FBI Director Louis Freeh boasted, "The successful investigation is a direct result of a CI [counterintelligence] coup by the FBI. Their [the FBI's] actions represent CI at its very best. . . . Their success represents unparalleled expertise and dedication to principle and mission. . . . This investigation and arrest represent for me a brilliant CI and investigative success."

While trumpeting its achievement in ferreting out a Russian spy, the FBI had nothing to say about Brian Kelley and the more than thirty-six months spent on what turned out to be the single most expensive counterintelligence wild-goose chase in American history. "This was not an investigation to be proud of," said Kelley's lawyer, John Moustakas, in an interview. "It was an investigation to be ashamed of."

Worse, once the furor over the Hanssen case died down, the FBI essentially went back to business as usual. The counterspies involved in the Kelley affair and the failed Hanssen investigation were not held accountable for their failures. In fact, two of the agents were given awards and cash bonuses for their counterintelligence work. One of them, FBI Agent Rudy Guerin, stayed on as the FBI's top counterspy for China until he retired in 2006. Kelley's other main persecutor, Michael T. Rochford, retired from the FBI but ended up with a lucrative position as the director of security for the U.S. Energy Department's Oak Ridge National Laboratory. When I contacted him about the Kelley affair, Rochford was surprised that I had located him. He noted that he had put himself "on the equivalent of the retired agent's witness protection program," although he did not say why.

Brian Kelley shared with me some of his serious concerns about the fact that the same people who were in place for a series of FBI intelligence disasters are still there. "Not one person was held accountable," he said, "and I just want to make sure that what happened to me never happens again to anyone else." Kelley, a career counterintelligence officer, reluctantly agreed to discuss how the wrongful investigation destroyed his career and hurt his family. He had spoken earlier to CBS's *60 Minutes* and to the Discovery Channel. But he said he felt it was important to expose the FBI's "extraordinary incompetence" in conducting the three-year investigation of him. Some of the key details of his case are reported here for the first time.

How could the FBI have bungled the case so badly, and unceasingly pursued an innocent man? The story begins in the late 1980s.

Seeds of Trouble

On April 27, 1989, CIA counterspy Brian Kelley experienced a Eureka moment in his investigation of so-called illegal spies from the Soviet Union's KGB. Investigating illegals—those intelligence officers who operate under deepest cover by posing as anything but foreign government officials—is without doubt the most challenging job in counterintelligence work. Retired KGB general and master spy Yuri Drozdov—who directed KGB illegals for years in Germany, the United States, and China—told me in a 1992 interview that illegals spend years preparing to look, speak, and act like a national of the country they spy on. Drozdov also revealed that illegal spies are not run by the "residencies" that control official spies but rather they receive their taskings from special clandestine "centers," making the job of finding illegals almost impossible. But Kelley, who had spent twenty years as a U.S. Air Force counterintelligence case officer before moving to the CIA full-time in 1984, had developed a unique methodology for finding these elusive spies. And now, as he investigated a KGB illegal who had been using the identity of a dead Finn named Reino Gikman, he hit pay dirt.

Sitting at CIA headquarters in Langley, Virginia, Kelley learned of a telephone call Gikman had placed to longtime U.S. diplomat Felix Bloch at his home in Washington, D.C. Bloch two years earlier had been the deputy chief of mission at the U.S. embassy in Vienna, and had served previously as the chargé d'affaires in Vienna, the senior American diplomat in Austria. He was recalled to the United States in 1987 by Ronald Lauder, the U.S. ambassador to Austria and son of cosmetic magnate Estée Lauder. The CIA had already determined that Gikman was a spy through its surveillance of Russians working in Paris for UNESCO. But it still wasn't clear how the Soviet intelligence services documented, communicated with, and directed their illegals. Once Gikman called Bloch and asked for a meeting in Paris, Kelley knew: Gikman was running a penetration agent within the U.S. State Department. None other than Felix Bloch.

Kelley knew that it was essential to protect the new information about Bloch, since any leak could undermine the investigation and squander the opportunity to "turn" Bloch into a double agent working for the United States, one of the goals of counterintelligence operations. To protect the information about the Russian spy, Kelley briefed only five people within the CIA—Richard Stolz, the deputy director of operations; Gardner "Gus" Hathaway, the assistant deputy director of operations for counterintelligence; James Pavitt, who was Stolz's executive officer; Ted Price, the chief of the counterintelligence center; and a psychologist who was working as Price's executive assistant. Even the CIA director at the time, William Webster, was not notified at first.

Under government rules regarding information about Americans linked to spying, the CIA was required to notify the FBI immediately upon learning of the contact between Gikman and Bloch. Kelley did brief the case to the FBI, and this briefing would prove to be incredibly costly. Unlike the CIA, the FBI had almost no internal security (as is the case even today). Within a short period of time, Kelley would learn later, the FBI had notified more than a hundred people that Bloch had been identified as a spy. One of those who learned about the CIA's discovery was Robert Hanssen, who worked in FBI headquarters as a supervisory special agent in the intelligence division's Soviet affairs unit—the unit that would be directly involved in the case.

The FBI immediately opened its investigation of Bloch, and on May 14 it tracked him as he traveled to Paris for his meeting with Gikman. Bloch met Gikman for dinner at Paris's Meurice Hotel. French intelligence covertly filmed the entire meeting. At the beginning of the meal, Bloch placed his large duffel-type bag under the table, but he did not take it with him when he left. Gikman departed a few minutes after Bloch, with the bag in hand. The next day he left Paris with the bag. Bloch and Gikman would meet again in Brussels on May 28.

If the CIA was correct in its assessment, Bloch was a valued spy for the KGB and was handled by what officials characterized as one of Moscow's most important illegals. For those reasons many counterintelligence officials regard the Bloch case as the most damaging penetration of the State Department—even more damaging than the espionage done decades earlier by Soviet spy Alger Hiss.

The success of the Paris surveillance was reported within the FBI, and Hanssen found out about it, according to the FBI affidavit in the case. "Hanssen passed the reporting on to the KGB," Kelley said. Indeed, on May 22, 1989, Hanssen put a package for the KGB underneath a footbridge in Idylwood Park, a wooded area west of Falls Church, Virginia, near the intersection of Interstates 66 and 495. One of the items in Hanssen's package—which included some eighty pages of classified intelligence documents, as well as requests for cash and a Swiss bank account—was a note explaining that the CIA and FBI were tracking Bloch.

In early June, several weeks after the package reached KGB headquarters in Moscow, Gikman suddenly left Vienna for Moscow.

Then, on June 22, the FBI intercepted a telephone call to Felix Bloch's Washington apartment. A man who identified himself as

"Ferdinand Paul" told Bloch he was calling on behalf of "Pierre." Pierre Bart was the name Gikman had used in meeting Bloch. The caller said Pierre "cannot see you in the near future" because "he is sick" and "a contagious disease is suspected." Paul then told Bloch, "I am worried about you. You have to take care of yourself."

The FBI knew that its investigation of Bloch, opened only weeks earlier, was in trouble. The Bureau called him in for questioning on June 22 and 23. Bloch denied that he was a spy and declined to answer further questions. The FBI investigation came to a screeching halt.

On July 21, ABC News reporter John McWethy disclosed the Bloch investigation in a report on *ABC World News Tonight*. The publicity totally undermined the investigation and even garnered sympathy for Bloch from within the ranks of the State Department. The diplomat continued to maintain his innocence, and eventually the FBI abandoned its round-the-clock surveillance of Bloch. He left Washington and ended up driving a bus in North Carolina.

In 1990, Brian Kelley was given the CIA's Intelligence Collector of the Year award for developing a unique counterintelligence tool and using it to find Felix Bloch. CIA Director William Webster presided over that secret ceremony and another one the following year at which Kelley received a second prestigious CIA medal for his work in catching other spies. But the case that Kelley broke would come back to haunt him years later.

Target

Trouble for Brian Kelley emerged in the wake of the Aldrich Ames spy case. Ames, a CIA officer who was a KGB penetration agent, was arrested in February 1994. He was eventually convicted of espionage and is serving life in prison. Ames had compromised an extraordinary number of U.S. intelligence sources, causing American agents in Russia to be imprisoned and even executed. CIA and FBI counterintelligence officials launched a damage assessment and soon concluded that Ames could not have been responsible for all the intelligence losses. There were some agents and operations that Ames did not know about. That realization eventually triggered a search for a second mole.

The mole hunt ultimately focused on the Felix Bloch case, to which Ames had had no access. In fact, the Bloch case had raised concerns about a mole well before Ames was arrested. Back on July 28, 1989, I reported in the pages of the *Washington Times* that the public disclosure of the Bloch investigation "has raised questions among counterintelligence officials involved in the case about how the KGB learned of the investigation, which was a tightly held secret known only to a small group of officials." One official told me at the time that "the leak may have come from within the government—raising the possibility of a Soviet agent in the government—or possibly as a result of a mistake by FBI or CIA counterspies that somehow alerted the KGB to the secret probe of Mr. Bloch."

It would be almost a decade before the search for a second mole became a full-blown probe. As the mole hunt intensified, the FBI learned from CIA sources within Russian intelligence services—correctly, it would turn out—that the person who had compromised the Bloch case in June 1989 was also the person who compromised the entire U.S. counterintelligence program in the Soviet Union and later Russia. FBI officials reasoned that if they could identify the mole who had compromised Bloch, the rest of the pieces would fall into place.

The agents in charge of the investigation—Mike Rochford, Rudy Guerin, and Jim Milburn, the FBI's senior Russia analyst—reasoned that no one within the FBI would sell out the Bureau. As one FBI agent involved in the failed probe noted, "No one with a badge would ever do this [spy for Moscow]." So the investigators never even considered the more than one hundred FBI agents and administrative employees who had been notified about Bloch in 1989. They falsely concluded that the mole had to be in the CIA. From the beginning, then, the investigation was based on a bizarre assumption: that this one CIA officer would have intimate knowledge of scores of the FBI's most protected and highly classified operations, and would have sold this information to the KGB, compromising the FBI's entire counterintelligence program against the KGB at the height of the Cold War.

Suspicion soon centered on Kelley, since the FBI quickly dismissed the other CIA employees who had known about Bloch—Stolz, Hathaway, Price, and Pavitt. Rochford convinced himself that Kelley was the guilty party and set up the Washington field office investigatory unit to catch him.

In July 1998 Rochford and David Szady, the FBI counterintelligence official who oversaw the investigation, told Kelley they wanted him to join a compartmented program to work with a Soviet defector who had information on the person who had compromised the Bloch investigation. To be "read in" to the program, Kelley would need to take and pass a polygraph test, a routine step for the most sensitive intelligence investigations and programs. Kelley recalled that he eagerly accepted, because "I had spent so many years and no one, no one, wanted that name more than I did, because that person took away all the years of work I had done on [the Bloch case]."

The FBI intended it as a sting operation. During the polygraph exam, the FBI asked Kelley specific questions related to espionage, such as had he ever supplied classified information to a foreign power. The sting failed. Kelley took and passed the examination, administered by the FBI's most senior polygraph examiner. "There wasn't even a wiggle out of place," Kelley said, referring to how the tests measure heart rate, breathing, and skin response to questions. Still, the Bureau refused to believe that Kelley was innocent. He was in a no-win situation: If Kelley had failed the test, investigators would have taken it as proof that he was the mole. When he passed, they concluded that he was too clever and had outsmarted the counterspies again. Only the FBI could have produced such tortured thinking.

After two months of working on the special project, Kelley noticed that his telephones did not work and he heard strange sounds, all signs of electronic surveillance. The counterspy began to suspect that he was the one who was being hunted as a mole. At another point, Kelley found a screw on the floor of his house, a sign that someone had conducted a surreptitious entry. "Although I didn't want to believe someone was in my house," he said, "that was clear evidence that somebody was there and dropped a screw in the middle of the floor. Now if I was a spy, that would have worried me a great deal."

When neither the polygraph nor the surveillance worked, Rochford and Szady decided to employ the same technique that the KGB had used to warn Felix Bloch that he had been discovered. The FBI sent an agent who posed as a Russian to Kelley's house in Vienna, Virginia. "As I was getting ready to leave the house, the doorbell rang," Kelley said. "And [the person at the door] said, 'Someone who knows your situation may have told the authorities who you are. We have an escape plan for you. We want you to go tomorrow night to the Vienna Metro and you will meet someone who will provide you with a passport and an escape plan. Take this piece of paper, it will give you the instructions.' And he turned around and walked into the darkness."

Kelley was stunned by the crude approach. He made sure to protect the note, placing it in a plastic bag to preserve the fingerprints. Then he reported the incident to the FBI agents assigned to security at CIA headquarters. Szady immediately took the note out of the bag and handled it, ruining the fingerprints and tainting the note's evidentiary value. Kelley concluded later that the FBI was interested in his reaction to the approach, not in any fingerprints. Kelley subsequently learned that the FBI investigators became convinced that he was simply outsmarting them, that he always stayed "one step ahead." The mole squad apparently refused to believe anything other than that Kelley was a spy. The FBI concluded that Kelley was an "evil genius." This mindset caused Rochford to redouble his efforts to catch and prosecute the alleged spy.

John Moustakas, Kelley's attorney, told me, "Every test they used to try to snare Brian, to prove he was a spy, he passed with flying colors. And what is the government's explanation? He's the ice man. He's the perfect spy. He's one step ahead of us. It never dawned on these nincompoops that the guy isn't a spy—the reason he 'passed' every test was because he was absolutely innocent. And that most simple explanation eluded the government's crack investigators because they had become so biased and their investigation's trajectory had become so skewed that by the end they could hardly tell fact from fantasy."

Convinced that Kelley had fooled everyone but them, FBI investigators apparently dismissed information that could have cleared the CIA counterspy of wrongdoing. According to people close to the probe, several senior CIA officers who were intimately familiar with the investigation said that the FBI's Washington field office developed information indicating that Kelley could not have been a mole, but the Bureau never shared such evidence with the CIA. Kelly confirmed that he heard this and was told by several FBI sources that if the information developed did not fit Rochford's thesis that Kelley was the mole, it was not briefed to CIA, nor apparently to FBI headquarters.

Ineptitude

When the Kelley probe intensified, FBI bungling allowed the real mole, Robert Hanssen, to keep tabs on the mole hunt. According to a report produced in 2003 by Justice Department Inspector General Glenn A. Fine, FBI employees mistakenly uploaded numerous highly restricted reports on the investigation to the Automated Case System computer network (ACS). Here the FBI had embarked on what it considered one of the most important investigations in the Bureau's history, and yet it was making the tightly controlled information in this critical investigation available to a wide array of FBI employees, any of whom could have been Moscow agents. That is how Hanssen found out that the FBI's mole squad was focused on Brian Kelley.

"While searching the ACS system in the spring of 1999," Fine stated in his report, "Hanssen stumbled upon the FBI's most significant ongoing Russian espionage investigation. This case was a search for the KGB mole who turned out to be Hanssen. At the time, however, the FBI's investigation was focused on a CIA officer [Kelley]. Although the FBI did not intend for documents related to this highly sensitive investigation to be uploaded into the ACS system—because of widespread concerns about the system's security—many such documents were uploaded due to failures in training, simple human error, and insufficient concern about maintaining operational security."

Hanssen had broken off contact with the KGB in 1991 after learning that the U.S. intelligence community was on the lookout for a mole (who turned out to be Ames). At this point he went to the SVR, the KGB successor agency, and offered to spy again. It was his third period of espionage since he had first started passing secrets to Moscow in 1985. The Fine report stated, "Over the next two years [1999 to 2001], Hanssen provided the Russians with information concerning some of the FBI's most significant KGB sources and most sensitive espionage investigations. Hanssen had obtained most of this information from improper searches of the FBI's ACS computer system."

Why did Hanssen swing into action at this point, after being inactive for years? According to the inspector general's report, Hanssen craved the "excitement" and "stimulation" of espionage, and he also badly needed money. But there was another reason. If the FBI was focusing its entire investigation on another spy, Hanssen felt he would be safe reentering the espionage game, at least for the time being. "Hanssen was watching my case," Kelley said. "He was watching it very carefully. So that he could continue to do what he did, because the whole focus of the FBI investigation was on me and not against anybody else."

According to counterintelligence officials, Hanssen believed Kelley was a real spy, because, like other FBI investigators, he accepted the FBI reporting about the case. He never thought through the consequences of his restarting his work for the Russians. He could have sat back and watched as the FBI followed the wrong man. Hanssen's decision to jump back into spying for the Russians baffled investigators. "It makes no sense to anybody," one official said. "Hanssen just was not thinking."

The old KGB hands running the new SVR were delighted at the FBI's ineptitude. They knew, from Aldrich Ames, that Kelley was the counterintelligence officer who for decades was responsible for tracking down and neutralizing some of Moscow's most secret and important deep-cover agents. Now that the FBI had targeted Kelley, one of the U.S. government's premier counterspies would be unable to take part in the search for Mole 2.

Intimidation and Harassment

On August 18, 1999, the FBI decided to confront Kelley. He recalled that FBI Agents Doug Gregory and Rudy Guerin met him at CIA headquarters and told him bluntly, "We know who you are. You're a spy." The agents accused Kelley of having alerted the KGB that the FBI was investigating Felix Bloch. This idea was absurd, given that it was Kelley who had discovered the link between Gikman and Bloch. But the FBI concluded that Kelley must have been partnering with the Soviets, who would have deliberately sacrificed a soon-to-be-terminated agent in order to catapult Kelley to the top of the CIA's counterintelligence bureaucracy. This utter nonsense was the key to the "evil genius" theory that FBI investigators spun to superiors.

Gregory and Guerin conducted a grueling four-hour interrogation, trying to force Kelley to admit he was a spy. Kelley told the agents, "Your facts are wrong. Your conclusions are wrong. Your underlying hypothesis is wrong." Clearly the agents were not in any mood to listen, Kelley said; they wanted to prosecute him. Almost as shocking to Kelley as being falsely labeled a traitor to his country was how incredibly inept the two agents showed themselves to be during the interrogation.

Faced with an accused traitor in its midst, the CIA put Kelley on administrative leave that day. The agency confiscated his "blue badge" pass for CIA headquarters—the equivalent of a white collar for the priesthood of CIA officers—and escorted him out of the building.

The FBI shifted its investigation of Kelley into high gear, convinced that he was set to flee to Russia. The Bureau intensified the already-tight electronic and physical surveillance, which required the services of more than fifty FBI agents and "technicians," as its surveillance personnel are called. From this point on, watchers stood outside his house twenty-four hours a day, mobile trackers followed his every move, and pervasive electronic surveillance captured all his telephone conversations and other communications. This relentless surveillance would last for another fifteen months, until officials identified Hanssen as the mole. U.S. intelligence officials told me it was the most expensive surveillance operation aimed at one person in American history, costing U.S. taxpayers millions of dollars. And it was all a waste of time.

From 1999 to 2000, while the FBI focused its entire investigation on trying to prove a case that had no basis in reality, Hanssen passed several packages of extremely sensitive documents to the SVR.

Blanket surveillance on Kelley may have been understandable, but according to Kelley, the FBI resorted to disturbing tactics to try to force him to admit he was a spy. Especially troubling was the harassment of Kelley's family. Kelley's daughter, who was especially close with him, had followed her father into the CIA. Kelley said that FBI agents confronted her at CIA headquarters the same day that Gregory and Guerin interrogated Kelley: "They said to her, Your father is a spy. Not only is he a spy, but he's the worst spy in American history. People died because of him." Kelley's daughter did not believe the FBI agents, but the experience was agonizing, and she eventually left the CIA after fifteen years of loyal service to the agency.

Later that evening, two FBI teams descended on the homes of Kelley's two sisters in Connecticut. The FBI teams told them that their brother had a secret life and was a traitor to his country. The agents explained that the issue at that point in their investigation was not whether Kelley had committed espionage—they were 100 percent certain he had, they said—but why he had. One sister, Marylou Raider, said that the agents said the FBI considered her brother's espionage "as big a case as the Julius and Ethel Rosenberg case."

The FBI agents even threatened to interrogate Kelley's eighty-four-year-old mother, who was in a nursing home. According to the sisters, the two sets of agents interviewing them simultaneously said, "If you don't tell us what we want, then we will go to the assisted-living facility where your mother is and get that information from her."

When the sisters hysterically begged the FBI teams not to interview their mother, one agent replied, "Well, if we find out the information we're looking for, we don't need to."

The next day, the FBI detained one of Kelley's sons, Barry, while he was on a business trip to New York City. The agents told him that his father's arrest was "imminent"; they warned him, "Brace yourself for the publicity." The next morning, the FBI interrogated Kelley's other son, Brian T. Kelley, who was living in the Cincinnati area. Kelley had told the FBI not to question the son because he and his wife had just had their first child. The Bureau ignored him. Brian T. Kelley, the son, said, "They came in the office and the first thing that hit my mind was that this was one of those Candygram things and they're going to say Surprise, congratulations for your daughter. They started saying We're with the FBI. Quickly I knew they weren't joking. Talk about being on top of the world to the bottom in a short time! It was pretty tough."

It was a terrible burden for all three children to be told that their father, with whom they were very close, was about to be the target of national front-page stories identifying him as a spy. They had to deal with this possibility every day for more than a year and a half, until the arrest of Hanssen cleared away the doubts about their father's innocence.

Kelley remains bitter about the threat against his late mother and the treatment of his family by bumbling FBI counterspies. "It's one thing to beat me up, to come down hostile on me," he said. "My family was another matter. What the FBI did to my family—the threats, the outright lies, and the intimidation—was inexcusable." As for his mother, the FBI threat to question her was serious. "It would have killed her," he said.

The intimidation was not limited to family. The FBI went after a CIA case officer who had worked for Kelley. Kathleen Hunt had carried out a deception operation initiated by Kelley and designed to keep Soviet intelligence from discovering how the United States had caught Felix Bloch. Hunt had actually worked for two CIA officers who were truly guilty of espionage, Aldrich Ames and James Nicholson, and she understood the personalities that drove them to betray their country. With Kelley, she saw no possibility that he was a spy. "That's what made the accusations against Brian all the more upsetting, disconcerting to me," she said in a Discovery Channel documentary. "But I also know that the FBI does not accuse people of espionage, which carries the death penalty, without solid evidence. And I certainly didn't think they'd accuse a CIA officer without having incontrovertible evidence of his guilt."

Hunt felt that she had also come under suspicion. "Even though Brian was the focus of the investigation," she said in the documentary, "I felt that I too could be caught up in it. And that perhaps one day there could be a knock at my door." The pressure against Hunt finally took its toll, and she resigned from the CIA after nineteen years of service, just a year short of getting her pension. The FBI, to its lasting discredit, never apologized to her.

Kelley endured the months of the investigation with the stoicism of a professional intelligence officer. He was required to call in to the CIA security office every day to say he was still at home. He said that the months under suspicion were "a psychological Chinese drip water torture." Once when he was told to come in to the office, he thought his arrest was imminent. He brought a bag of toilet articles and a Bible, since "those are the things I would take to jail with me." Another time, he saw a man in a windbreaker run by his window as he worked on his home computer. He thought this was it, that he was to be arrested by the FBI. It turned out the man was a lawnkeeper.

The FBI was so far off that it also believed that Kelley had created a "family" spy ring, like that of U.S. Navy radioman John A. Walker Jr., who recruited his son, his brother, and a Navy coworker into his Soviet spy ring in the 1980s. Kelley's sister Pamela Baim recalled that the FBI told her Kelley was using her husband as a cutout or surrogate in dropping off packages for Russian intelligence. As a result, she and her family were under investigation and surveillance. "I assumed we were always being watched," she said.

The Breakthrough

The campaign against Kelley did not let up, regardless of the fact that the FBI's case against him was flimsy. Incompetent FBI counterspies adopted a theory and stuck to the theory despite large amounts of evidence to the contrary.

For example, the FBI's most senior and experienced financial analyst examined Kelley's financial records in detail and concluded that Kelley was not a spy. The analyst, who will not allow his name to be used, told both Szady and Rochford repeatedly that they were on the wrong track, but they ignored him, according to the agent and others at the CIA. Though this analyst was considered the best in the business, Szady and Rochford pressed on with the bogus investigation. Kelley recalled that when he was interrogated by the FBI, "I was told that I was so clever that I knew that if I were to come under suspicion that they would be looking at my finances so I took the payment in diamonds." The agents even insisted that his KGB code name was "Karat," as in diamonds.

The FBI relied on a couple of tiny clues to make their weak case against Kelley. The main one was that a Russian intelligence officer had once been spotted in Nottoway Park, which was very close to Kelley's home. The FBI believed the spy had been there to "service," or communicate with, Kelley, Kelley said. When the Bureau interrogated Kelley about this issue, he reminded the agents that if he really were a spy, he would never be so careless as to conduct operational activities so close to his house. Nottoway Park would be "the last place" he would go, he told the FBI. "Every foreign intelligence operations officer, whether he works for the KGB or the CIA, is trained never, ever to do operational activities in an area close to your home," Kelley said. "The clueless counterspies never knew this fact."

At that point in the interrogation, an FBI agent pulled out a piece of paper that the Bureau had taken from Kelley's house during one of many covert searches. The paper was a small hand-drawn map of Nottoway Park that Kelley used for jogging. Kelley asked the agents why they classified the note as "secret." He was told that it was "an operational site map" and that he couldn't deny it.

"And I corrected him and said, no, it was a photocopy of a small Post-it that I had made up approximately ten years before," Kelley recalled. He had used the paper to record his lap times on an eight-mile jogging route. "They were stunned at that revelation. That was the only piece of evidence that they put forward to me." A senior FBI official later confirmed to Kelley's lawyer, John Moustakas, that the FBI never had any real evidence against Kelley. It was all based on an assumption, and a false one at that.

Curiously, while Kelley's proximity to Nottoway Park fueled the FBI's zeal to nail him, the Bureau didn't even consider that the mole might be the other intelligence official who lived near the park: Robert Hanssen. The bridge at Nottoway Park was fifteen yards away and in a direct line of sight from Hanssen's home, which was less than one-tenth of a mile from Kelley's. As it turned out, the Russian spy who had been spotted in the park was there to pick up a package left by Hanssen. According to an FBI affidavit, Hanssen and the Russians used the same site on seventeen occasions—showing a stunningly careless disregard for conventional tradecraft. It was equally dangerous for Hanssen to defy intelligence training and conduct operational matters so near his home.

Nor did the FBI ever notice the red flags in Hanssen's financial situation. He had large amounts of cash in his house and was living way beyond his means, with six children in expensive private schools. He had also paid $100,000 in cash for an addition to his house—proceeds from his illicit activities for Russian intelligence.

It took a KGB defector to finally open the Bureau's eyes to the stupidity of the Kelley investigation. After the demise of the Soviet Union in 1991, scores of KGB officers turned against the collapsed Communist empire. In early 2000, one of them offered to sell the CIA and FBI, as part of a joint operation, a tape recording and other evidence that he said would allow U.S. intelligence to identify the mole once and for all. But it would cost them. The defector wanted

$7 million for the KGB material. The United States agreed. It was the largest sum ever paid to a defector. The FBI expected the material to provide the firm evidence needed to arrest Brian Kelley after years of fruitless investigation.

In late 2000, the transaction complete, the FBI held a meeting at its headquarters to go over the defector's materials. The assembled officials expected to hear Brian Kelley's voice on the audiotape. But as soon as the tape started playing, one FBI counterspy realized the stunning truth. "That's Bob Hanssen," the agent said.

The FBI was listening to a recorded phone conversation in which Robert Hanssen spoke with his Russian handler. They discussed how there had been a botched package drop in Nottoway Park, in which Hanssen's Russian contact had left the package under the wrong end of the Nottoway Park bridge.

Hanssen was a good spy, but even the best spies make mistakes. In Hanssen's case, he had attempted to keep his identity secret from his KGB/SVR masters in order to prevent any defectors from identifying him down the road. But when he was unable to communicate with his Russian handlers through dead drops, he made a fatal mistake. Taking a chance, he set up a telephone exchange with the Russian embassy; he would call from a pay telephone and leave a telephone number for a Russian intelligence officer to call him back. The particular phone call the FBI was now listening to had been recorded by Russian intelligence. It had found its way into the Russian archives, where the defector accessed it and eventually sold it to the United States.

For Mike Rochford, Rudy Guerin, and Jim Milburn, the revelation was devastating. According to a source present when Kelley's innocence was confirmed, Rochford said to Milburn, "Our careers are ruined." It is telling that the FBI agents first thought of their careers rather than what they had done to an innocent American intelligence officer over more than three years, and to all the U.S. agents whose lives had been lost because of Hanssen's treachery. Of course, they needn't have worried: They would eventually be rewarded with promotions and cash bonuses. (Milburn was given a manager's position but was later demoted.)

After Hanssen was identified on the tape, the FBI obtained two of his partial fingerprints from a plastic bag he had used to wrap classified documents he sent to the KGB. This time, the FBI made sure that it kept secret its probe, to prevent tipping off Hanssen.

On February 18, 2001, Hanssen was arrested after dropping off a package of documents in Nottoway Park. The second mole had been captured.

Apology Denied

Even after Hanssen was in custody, the troubles did not end for Brian Kelley. The day before Hanssen's arrest was made public, an FBI agent called in Kelley and asked him to review a transcript of an interview the FBI had conducted with him on August 18, 1999. According to Kelley, the agents who conducted the interview had misstated or altered the transcript as a way to cover the FBI's tracks from the failed thirty-six-month investigation. "They had misstated significant parts of the interview log," Kelley said. "They claimed I said things that I never said."

At six o'clock on the morning the Hanssen arrest was announced, Kelley received a call from his son Barry. Barry told him that he had heard on the radio that the FBI had arrested a spy for Moscow. The son was thus relieved that his father was home to answer the phone, and not under arrest.

The FBI refused to clear Kelley and still harbored suspicions that he was a spy weeks and even months after Hanssen was arrested. It would take a liberal Democratic senator to finally force the FBI to clear Kelley's name. When Robert Mueller came before the Senate Judiciary Committee on July 30, 2001, for his confirmation hearing to become FBI director, Senator Patrick Leahy, Vermont Democrat, asked him about reports of a CIA officer who had been initially suspected of espionage before Hanssen was uncovered. "This officer was forced to go on leave from his job at the CIA, caused great stress for himself and his family," Leahy said. "Among other things, members of the family kept constantly being told, 'This is a capital offense.'

Now he's been cleared of all wrongdoing. He's been allowed to return to his work in the CIA. He has back pay, full security clearance restored. The FBI totally regrets this happened, but they did not notify him or his family that he's no longer suspected of any wrongdoing. Can you take a look into some of these matters?" Leahy, it turned out, had been a classmate of Kelley's at St. Michael's College in Vermont.

Mueller told Leahy, the committee's ranking Democrat, "I certainly would, Mr. Chairman. It's critically important to do investigations quickly, and if the allegations prove not to be true, to make certain that those who were under scrutiny are told of that immediately, and to the extent possible, any appropriate response given to that individual who has been exculpated from the allegations."

On August 16, 2001, the FBI dispatched Jim Lyle, the FBI agent who headed the CIA's Counterintelligence Center, with a message for Kelley. Lyle drove to the CIA's training center near Williamsburg, Virginia, known as The Farm, to give Kelley a letter of apology from FBI Acting Director Thomas Pickard. The letter cleared Kelley of wrongdoing and stated, "It was not the intent of the FBI to either discredit you or to cause you or your family any embarrassment. If this has occurred, I'm sorry." The letter was disgraceful, telling Kelley, in effect, that if he had been harmed during the course of the Bureau's mole investigation, the FBI didn't mean it.

Kelley said that he would have appreciated the letter more if it had been sent in February or even March, weeks after Hanssen's arrest, instead of five months later. There was no question in Kelley's mind that he received the apology only as a result of Senator Leahy's intervention. Kelley's lawyer, Moustakas, had sent a letter to FBI Director Louis Freeh a hundred days after Hanssen's arrest, asking the director to send Kelley an official letter of exoneration. Freeh had promised CIA Director George Tenet that this would be done in the weeks after Hanssen's arrest. But Freeh never answered the letter before he retired. It appeared that the letter was expedited so Mueller could tell Senator Leahy that he had exonerated Kelley.

The CIA did the right thing and welcomed Kelley back into his old job, but the experience weighed heavily on him. "I wanted to go back just to make sure there was never any cloud hanging over my head," Kelley said. "If I got back in the building with my security clearances fully reinstated, that meant that I was fully and completely cleared by the system. I had to clear my name and my reputation." Family and colleagues threw him a surprise exoneration party in January 2002. It was an emotional affair, as fellow officers from the CIA, the Department of Defense, and the FBI apologized for doubting Kelley and said they were ashamed of the way the FBI and the CIA had treated him.

Kelley continued to work for the CIA until 2006. His last assignment was with the Office of the National Counterintelligence Executive, a counterintelligence unit that is part of the newly formed Office of the Director of National Intelligence. He did his part to shore up a counterintelligence system badly in need of repair.

The Need for Wholesale Change

The FBI clearly mishandled the mole investigation to a staggering degree. Still, the Bureau denied that it had done anything wrong in hounding Kelley for years. David Szady, who had overseen the investigation and had repeatedly assured CIA Director Tenet and others at the CIA that the case against Kelley was rock-solid—told *60 Minutes* that the focus on Kelley was valid and necessary. "We haven't pinpointed Brian Kelley for any other reason except he fits into the facts as we know them, the information as we have it," Szady said.

Szady also defended the mistake of not investigating any FBI employees. "What you have to understand is when the investigation was moving forward, the type of information that we're receiving clearly focused on the CIA and led us in that direction." Never mind what Inspector General Glenn Fine had pointed out in his 2003 report, that "the FBI had access to information suggesting that the mole might be an FBI employee, and believed that the mole had compromised certain FBI assets and operations." In the *60 Minutes* interview, Szady said it was "an insult to the FBI," and a "personal insult" to him, to suggest that the Bureau refused to investigate its own people. But in fact, as the inspector general's report revealed, the FBI "never opened even a preliminary inquiry on any FBI employee in connection with the search for the mole ultimately identified as Hanssen."

Responding to the suggestion that a simple financial analysis of Robert Hanssen would have pointed the finger at the FBI agent, Szady insisted, "We can't go and do a total financial analysis on every employee of the FBI because we think there may be a mole within the FBI."

What about the fact that Hanssen had been caught improperly accessing FBI computer data? "You have to put this in perspective," Szady said. "Let's say we knew nothing about a mole, and all we have is the fact that Robert Hanssen hacked into a computer or Robert Hanssen paid $75,000 for a home improvement. Do we have a spy on our hands?"

Many within the FBI were horrified by Szady's *60 Minutes* performance, believing that he had made a fool of himself and by extension the Bureau. The only exceptions were officials like Mike Rochford, Rudy Guerin, Jim Milburn, and Bill Cleveland—close associates of Szady's who were known collectively as "the posse." All these men owed their careers to Szady. They remained loyal, telling him they were proud of him for falling on his sword and not owning up to FBI incompetence. Many of these Szady associates were involved in the FBI's counterintelligence debacles going back to Wen Ho Lee and would later emerge in the Katrina Leung case.

Rudy Guerin himself offered another example of how FBI agents who were marginal at best were not held accountable for numerous failures. Guerin would reappear throughout several FBI counterintelligence failures, and yet he would continue to be supported by senior FBI managers and rewarded. It was Guerin who misled a House Permanent Select Committee on Intelligence subcommittee about the damage in the Katrina Leung case. At one point in a closed session, Guerin told a member of Congress that the U.S. intelligence community got very little good intelligence from the electronic spying operations that Leung had compromised. In fact, the loss of technical spying operations in China did serious damage to U.S. national security. Guerin's testimony was part of an effort to downplay one of the FBI's worst failures. Said one senior U.S. intelligence official who is critical of the FBI, "People who protect the Bureau get promoted, and in the Bureau, self-promotion is often above what is good for the national security of the country."

The inspector general's report, which came out in August 2003, provided the most damning indictment of the FBI. The IG revealed that despite the weakness of the case against Kelley, the FBI produced a 70-page investigative report for the Justice Department to try to get Kelley prosecuted for espionage. The Bureau's report "was written as if the FBI had no doubt that the CIA suspect was a KGB mole who was the most damaging spy since Ames," despite the fact that some "several senior FBI managers had serious doubts that the CIA suspect was the correct target." Fine chastised the Bureau for presenting a misleading case. One FBI insider told me that the investigative report was the work of an inexperienced "first office agent" with no counterintelligence background. The report was anything but honest, the insider told me, and reflected Mike Rochford's desperate effort to get the arrest. After all, capturing this mole would be bigger than the Ames arrest. It would have allowed Rochford to finish his career and retire in a blaze of personal glory.

The inspector general said that the FBI's failure to find Hanssen reflected "long-standing systemic problems" in its counterintelligence program. Aside from the FBI's demonstrated reluctance to look within the Bureau itself, there was the problem of "ineffective oversight" of the Hanssen investigation. According to the IG report, FBI supervisors too often deferred to Rochford and his team of investigators, "even when the managers harbored serious doubts about the progress of the investigation—resulting in a tacit endorsement of erroneous analysis and conclusions." Also, congressional oversight has been almost nonexistent as far as the FBI is concerned, although Congress has at least four committees that are required to keep tabs on FBI activities.

The IG report said that the FBI had failed to detect Hanssen's spying even though he was reckless in his espionage tradecraft. In August 1990, FBI Agent Mark Wauck, who was Hanssen's brother-in-law, learned that Hanssen's wife had discovered $5,000 in cash in a dresser drawer in their home. Wauck reported the cash and significant related suspicious incidents to his FBI supervisor at the Chicago field office, Jim Lyle. But according to the IG report, Lyle ignored the information, never asking for a written report and never communicating the information to FBI headquarters. It is simply astonishing that an FBI supervisor would never follow up on a report from an FBI counterintelligence agent (one with a law degree on top of it) suggesting that the agent's own brother-in-law could be a spy. Lyle thus missed the chance to catch one of the worst spies in American history. In typical FBI fashion, he was later promoted to head the Counterintelligence Center at the CIA.

The failure to investigate the discovery of Hanssen's unexplained cash reflected the weakness of the FBI's internal security. Clearly the Bureau needed to set up a system in which derogatory information on agents could be pooled and investigated. And there were many other problems, all of which made the FBI an easy target for spies like Hanssen. The Fine report stated that "the absence of adequate security controls at the FBI made espionage too easy for Hanssen to commit. Because of inadequate document security, he felt comfortable removing thousands of pages of classified documents from FBI offices. Because of lax controls over even the most sensitive information and violations of the 'need to know' principle, he knew that he could compromise the FBI's most important Soviet/Russian assets and operations with little risk that the loss of these cases would be traced to him." Fine noted that the security problems represented years of neglect. The FBI had failed to comply with Executive Orders, Justice Department regulations, and intelligence-community procedures for internal security.

After the Hanssen arrest, the FBI took some steps to shore up internal security. For example, because Hanssen was never made to take a polygraph test, it required agents to take polygraphs more often. The Bureau also developed financial-disclosure requirements and created a Security Division. But the inspector general noted that serious problems remained. The lingering weaknesses "expose the FBI to the risk of future serious compromises by another mole," the IG report said, months before Katrina Leung and J. J. Smith were uncovered.

Even today, the FBI's security problems are pervasive, from personnel security, to computer security, to document security, to security training and compliance. For example, the core computer system, the Automated Case System, is vulnerable, as was shown by the case of FBI analyst Leandro Aragoncillo, who pleaded guilty to espionage in May 2006 for passing secrets to officials in the Philippines. This case shows that the FBI never learned the horrible lessons from its many mistakes in the Hanssen case and still had no computer audit capabilities in place to detect other spies.

The larger problem is cultural: The FBI has continually resisted efforts to change, even in the aftermath of the Hanssen case and the September 11 attacks. The need for change applies at all levels, from high-level officials to agents in the field. Since the government hasn't held FBI officials accountable for significant intelligence failures, directors and senior managers on whose watch these failures occurred remain in key security-related positions in government. Almost as problematic, according to the inspector general's report, is the fact that FBI agents in the field have failed to "reconsider initial conclusions and judgments in the face of investigative failures," as most vividly demonstrated in the Kelley investigation. The IG report concluded that "what is needed at the FBI is a wholesale change in mindset and approach to internal security. The FBI must recognize and take steps to account for the fact that FBI employees have committed espionage in the past and will likely do so in the future."

These problems are not going away, and they certainly won't be fixed by the relatively minor reforms that have been instituted. The FBI has failed to protect its people, its secrets, and U.S. national security. Until the government takes the bold steps needed to shore up our intelligence apparatus—especially the neglected field of counterintelligence—we will be extending an open invitation to our enemies to come through the gaping holes in our defenses.

Chapter 5

KGB REDUX: RUSSIA'S AGGRESSIVE ESPIONAGE

The only thing worse than having a spy in the DO is having a spy uncovered in the DO.

—*Unidentified CIA Directorate of Operations (DO) officer at an internal meeting following the 1994 arrest of Aldrich Ames*

n March 2006, the U.S. Joint Forces Command in Norfolk, Virginia, released a report on how Saddam Hussein's regime prepared for and responded to Operation Iraqi Freedom in 2003. The 210-page study, based on captured Iraqi documents, contained two startling revelations about Russia. Back in 2003, Americans knew that Moscow tried at every turn to block military action in Iraq. But the extent of Russia's betrayal became clear only with the release of the "Iraqi Perspectives Project" report in 2006.

The report, citing a "secret and urgent" Iraqi document dated March 25, 2003, revealed that just days into the war, the Russian ambassador in Baghdad provided Saddam's regime with details of the U.S. military's top-secret warfighting plans. And how did the Russians obtain this vital information? They had planted a spy in the heart of the U.S. Central Command's warfighting headquarters in Doha, Qatar.

The Russian government publicly denied the treachery. Despite the fact that the United States had documents in hand indicating the leak, the U.S. Central Command said it did not even plan to investigate the matter. The loss of secret warfighting information did not seem to concern military commanders. And as usual, counterintelligence was not a priority.

It should become a priority, and quickly. The United States cannot make the mistake of thinking that the end of the Cold War marked the end of Russian spying against the United States. It is no coincidence that the two most devastating spy cases in recent American history—those of Robert Hanssen and Aldrich Ames—involved Russia, and were exposed after the collapse of the Soviet Union.

The problem of Russian spying has reached a critical point. Amazingly, there are as many Russian spies in the United States today as there were during the Cold War.

FBI counterintelligence chief David Szady told me, "The Russians are up to Cold War levels in both intelligence presence and activity." According to FBI officials, Moscow is running more than one hundred spies who operate under official cover out of the Russian embassy in Washington and consulates in other major U.S. cities. These "legal" spies are supplemented by an unknown number of "illegals"— deep-cover agents dispatched to spy here while posing as businessmen, academics, journalists, students, and other visitors. The growth in spying reflects the fact that KGB veterans now run the Russian government. President Vladimir Putin is himself a former KGB officer once posted to East Germany.

The head of Russia's GRU military intelligence service, General Valentin Korabelnikov, told an interviewer in 2003 that his agency spies throughout the world to support Moscow's military and defense industry needs. That statement highlights why Russia represents a particularly dangerous intelligence threat to the United States: because Moscow has targeted our defense secrets. A major intelligence target for Moscow is the network of sensors, radar, communications, and interceptors that make up U.S. missile defense. Russia views missile defense as a threat, even though the Pentagon insists its limited long-range missile defense system, which includes just ten anti-missile interceptors deployed in Alaska and California, cannot stop

Russian strategic missiles. U.S. plans for a third missile defense interceptor site in Britain, Poland, or Romania have rattled Moscow,
which responded by building a new nuclear warhead that can change
altitudes to defeat the defenses. Beyond stealing U.S. defense secrets,
the Russians also want to learn inside details of U.S. policymaking
plans for former Soviet republics and Eastern bloc states, as well as
for China and the Middle East.

The United States remains highly vulnerable to this aggressive espionage, because the government has done little to fix our severe
counterintelligence problems. Those problems were glaringly exposed
in the Hanssen and Ames cases. The Hanssen spy ring revealed the
FBI's utter incompetence in countering Russian intelligence activities.
Even today, the FBI seems to be failing at one of its core missions: to
stop our enemies from spying on us. Meanwhile, the Ames case
showed how the CIA's lack of counterintelligence against Russia destroyed the agency as an intelligence service.

The CIA is still crippled by the damage done in the early 1990s.
The damage is acute. From Cold War levels of nearly 10,000 case
officers—spies in the field—the CIA's once-proud Directorate of Operations has been decimated by retirements and low morale. By 2005,
the agency had fewer than 1,000 case officers in the field. Many CIA
stations had been reduced to single CIA officers who acted as little
more than liaison officers with local services.

Such weaknesses have a direct effect on the U.S. ability to cope
with the Russian intelligence threat. The failure to handle the Russian menace became so obvious that in late 2004 the White House
National Security Council ordered the FBI, the CIA, the State Department, and other agencies to address the problem. Despite the command, the U.S. intelligence community did little to fix the situation.

But let there be no doubt, the Russian threat remains, and in fact
is growing more severe by the day. In the spring of 2006 the U.S. government finally admitted what it had long denied: that Russia was
not moving in a positive direction under ex–KGB officer Putin. Vice
President Dick Cheney stated the obvious during a speech in May
2006. He warned that "opponents of reform" in Russia were seeking

to reverse the country's post-Soviet democratic changes of the previous decade. Antidemocratic restrictions by Russia's government had "unfairly restricted the rights of her people," while other actions affected Moscow's relations with neighbors, Cheney said. The vice president even acknowledged that Russia might once again become "an enemy."

Putin responded a few days later in a speech of his own. The Russian president described the United States as "comrade wolf" that "knows whom to eat, he eats without listening, and he's clearly not going to listen to anyone." Putin raised the prospect of a new arms race as Moscow seeks to build up its strategic nuclear forces to compensate for its deteriorating conventional military forces. "We must always be ready to counter any attempts to pressure Russia in order to strengthen positions at our expense," he continued. "The stronger our military is, the less temptation there will be to exert such pressure on us."

Putin's frank admission of aggressive intentions should galvanize the United States to action. Of particular interest to U.S. counterintelligence officials was the Russian leader's statement that he intended to strengthen Russia militarily without repeating "the mistakes of the Soviet Union and of the Cold War"—that is, without draining the country's resources. As the Chinese have learned, the most efficient way to build up your weaponry and military strength quickly is to steal secrets from your adversaries.

That's where spying comes in.

The Great Betrayal

To understand the Russian intelligence threat, one need only look at how Moscow handled CIA turncoat Aldrich Ames for nearly ten years. It is a case study in how a foreign government handled a prized agent operating deep within the U.S. intelligence community. Moscow had almost the ideal mole in Ames, since he worked in counterintelligence. More than working in counterintelligence, he actually *ran* counterintelligence operations against the Soviet Union for most of the 1980s and early 1990s. His job at the CIA called for him to study recruited agents and defectors and determine whether they were legitimate—or had been "doubled," meaning they were working secretly for Moscow while pretending to be working for the United States.

Ames began spying for the Soviet Union in 1985. Some details surrounding his initial contacts with the KGB are in dispute. Former KGB counterintelligence official Victor Cherkashin was the case officer for both Ames and Hanssen, and he documented his dealings with the double agents in his 2005 memoir, *Spy Handler.* Cherkashin wrote that Ames first contacted the KGB on April 16, 1985, when he walked into the Soviet embassy in Washington, D.C., and handed the KGB resident a letter. The letter offered to reveal CIA secrets in exchange for $50,000. According to Cherkashin's account, this walk-in identified himself as "Rick Wells" and claimed to be connected to the State Department. But the KGB suspected "Wells" was with the CIA or FBI and was working to recruit Soviet diplomat Sergei Chuvakhin.

The U.S. government's extensive investigation into the Ames case calls into question Cherkashin's account. For several months after Ames's 1994 arrest, officials from the CIA, the FBI, the National Security Agency, and the Defense Intelligence Agency interviewed Ames at length, for some two hundred hours altogether. In 1995, the CIA Counterintelligence Center produced a classified report based on those debriefing sessions. The report, labeled "Secret," is entitled "Counterintelligence Trends: How the KGB Handled Ames." In contrast to Cherkashin's story, the CIA study stated that Ames revealed his true identity to the Russians immediately. The report noted that among the items Ames included in the letter he handed to the KGB was "a telephone list for the CIA Directorate of Operations' Soviet–East Europe (SE) Division." Ames had "highlighted his own name" on the list, so the KGB would have known his identity and his CIA counterintelligence role right away.

The accounts also conflict on the question of what information Ames first gave to the Soviets. Cherkashin said that Ames provided classified documents on U.S. Navy ship movements in the Middle

East, for which the KGB agreed to pay him the requested $50,000 as a "one-time shot" to pay off a divorce and other debts and help him marry his Colombian girlfriend, Rosario. Ames told CIA debriefers a different story. He explained that he intended to pull a "con job" on the KGB by selling worthless information on the Soviets' own double-agent operations. The CIA report quoted Ames telling debriefers that the KGB probably thought "the $50,000 is peanuts in terms of laying [*sic*] back and waiting, trying to turn it into something bigger and real." As the report noted, "Moscow did not have to wait long" for big information.

The KGB used Chuvakhin, the diplomat, to communicate with Ames. On June 13, 1985, Ames met with Chuvakhin for lunch at Chadwicks, a restaurant in the Georgetown section of Washington, D.C. Before the meeting, the CIA report said, Ames "gathered up a bundle of cables and memorandums on the U.S. government's most sensitive Soviet cases, which had accumulated on his desk. He also hand-printed in his office a note on other Soviet assets of the CIA. It gave such information as their parent organizations, job descriptions, location, and place and time of contacts—enough to identify the assets without having their true names, most of which Ames lacked."

The material filled a shopping bag that weighed nearly five pounds. Ames handed it all over to Chuvakhin. Ames thus gave up the identities of virtually every recruited agent working for the United States in the Soviet Union—the most valuable commodities in intelligence.

The June 13 meeting became known as "the big dump." Ames claimed after his arrest that he needed to give up the penetration agents to prevent them from learning that he had become a spy for the KGB. Whatever his motivation, Ames's "big dump" will go down as one of the worst betrayals in the history of espionage. Ames did much more than devastate American intelligence operations in the Soviet Union; by giving up the spies' identities, he put their lives at risk. In fact, Ames's decision "caused the deaths of at least 10 of the U.S. government's most important Soviet assets," the CIA report said. The KGB, reportedly shocked that the United States had penetrated

Soviet intelligence, rolled up the spies quickly. The KGB simply executed these American agents, typically shooting them in the back of the head.

The names of the betrayed agents deserve mention, if only to honor their memory: Leonid Polishchuk, Gennady Smetanin, Gennady Verennik, Sergei Vorontsov, Valery Martynov, Sergei Motorin, Vladimir Potashov, Vladimir Piguzov, Dmitri Polyakov, and Vladimir Vasiliev. These men are heroes who silently fought against the evil system that was the Soviet Union.

Missed Warning Signs

As much as Ames was guilty for his betrayal, the CIA must be held responsible for failing to stop Ames before he could give up the lives of the CIA's elite agents. Ames was a habitual drunk—he consumed at least a bottle of vodka a day—and yet was allowed to continue working within the CIA's Directorate of Operations with impunity. He was a time bomb waiting to go off. Even the KGB apparently felt that Ames's alcoholism would eventually become too much for the CIA to tolerate. During his postarrest debriefing sessions, Ames said he believed the KGB felt his "days were numbered" at the CIA because his drinking caused him to miss many meetings. (Ames also missed three meetings with the KGB because he was so drunk.)

Yet the CIA kept Ames on. And this, remember, was not just any old spy; Ames was the senior agent in charge of all counterintelligence operations against the Soviet Union—at a time when the Cold War was still raging.

How could the CIA keep someone so untrustworthy, who spent most of his life in an alcoholic stupor, in such an important position? It was a sign of the agency's extremely low regard for counterintelligence. The CIA culture was not merely averse to tough counterintelligence; the agency actually hated counterintelligence, viewing it as something that got in the way of intelligence-gathering operations.

There were other red flags besides Ames's drinking. One former

CIA operations officer remembered that Ames had been driving an old used car but showed up at CIA headquarters in a brand-new Jaguar in 1989, after he came back from a visit to South America. Ames claimed that the new car was a gift from his mother-in-law. Ames's mother-in-law at the time lived in Medellin, Colombia. But when the officer questioned the source of Ames's new wealth, counterintelligence officials at CIA dismissed the concerns. "So the Medellin drug cartel had just bought a CIA operations officer and apparently no one cared," the officer said. The CIA did begin a review of Ames's finances, and it showed unusual cash deposits. But even that review got sidetracked because the investigator in charge of the case was sent for a two-month training course.

Much as with the Robert Hanssen FBI case, the failure to thoroughly investigate the agent's finances would prove costly. As it turned out, between 1985 and his arrest in 1994, the KGB paid Ames nearly $5 million for thousands of pages of secret CIA documents. Another $2 million was held in Russian banks for Ames as a way to keep him spying and to keep him loyal to the KGB. Ames told debriefers that Russia's intelligence service sometimes paid him using International Monetary Fund cash and other Western aid money provided to Russia. The United States contributes about a third of all IMF funds.

The very fact that Soviet intelligence swiftly executed or imprisoned so many American recruited agents might also have tipped off U.S. officials that an American agent had betrayed them. Ames himself was scared when the Soviets rounded up the Americans so quickly, fearing that the CIA would then identify him. He later told his CIA debriefers that a KGB handler had even apologized for moving on the American spies right away and had said that the Soviets "fully understood the consequences . . . of having created a very dangerous security situation for their source, i.e., me."

So worried was Ames that he provided the KGB with the names of two CIA officers who had access to the identities of the CIA's compromised agents, so the KGB could use disinformation to try to falsely blame them for the losses. The KGB did try to fool the CIA, planting disinformation to create the impression that the compromises resulted from insecure agency communications.

Ames needn't have worried about being discovered as a result of the Russian spy purge. The CIA did not launch a mole hunt. In 1986, the agency did begin to investigate the compromised cases, but the review went nowhere, even after the FBI joined the probe in 1988. The task force formed to look for a spy was also sidetracked by a CIA reorganization in 1988 that downgraded the counterintelligence function. Amazingly, investigators concluded that the arrests of U.S. agents were coincidental, not the result of a betrayal. When officials finally began to realize the losses could not be coincidental, they first suspected that the KGB had broken into U.S. intelligence communications. Anything was better than believing that there was a spy in their midst. It would take the CIA a full nine years to figure out that one of its own officers was selling secrets to the KGB.

Capture

Richard Haver, a senior counterintelligence official who was involved in the top-secret damage assessment of the Ames case, said that Ames showed no concern about the CIA's internal security system. Believing that the CIA system for catching spies was broken, Ames thought he could spy as long as he wanted and then retire to the south of France. In this regard he was like Robert Hanssen, who had contempt for FBI internal security. "I will tell you for sure," Haver said, "Rick Ames felt the same way about that CIA security system: It would never catch him. Some breach from the other side might turn him in, but it would never catch him because he was inside the system."

Thus Ames "overwhelmed the KGB with CIA documents," thousands of them, according to the CIA's secret postarrest report. These documents contained the most important secrets of the U.S. intelligence community. He communicated with the KGB using old-fashioned tradecraft involving impersonal communications—namely, "dead drops" at remote locations in Washington, D.C. In a dead drop, an agent leaves a package at a prearranged spot; only later does his contact come to the spot to pick up the material. This is how Ames and the KGB exchanged documents and money. Interestingly, the KGB altered its dead-drop methods after seeing an FBI report Ames had supplied. The report showed that the FBI had information on Moscow's dead drops, so for the first time the KGB began using public parks in the Washington metropolitan area as drop-off points. FBI mole Robert Hanssen adopted this technique, too.

Ames also met periodically with his KGB handlers. The meetings took place every six months in South America and Europe. In all, he contacted his handlers eleven times between 1985 and 1993. He spent about forty hours talking to the KGB, which recorded the sessions with a microcassette recorder.

Because of Ames's drinking problem, the KGB resorted to putting meeting schedules in writing, on flimsy yellow paper. Ames's second wife, Rosario, discovered one of the papers years later in an old wallet. That is how she discovered that Ames was a spy. Rosario Ames was no innocent, however. She was arrested at the same time as her husband and was convicted of lesser spy charges.

Ames was finally arrested in 1994, though of course the CIA had had opportunities to detect him many years earlier. The agency had begun to look into Ames's finances after the tip-off about his new Jaguar. One reason the investigation didn't go far was that in August 1990 a KGB defector diverted the hunt. The defector claimed that the KGB had recruited a CIA officer who had served in Moscow, where Ames never served. After more than a year, the agency realized that the information was bogus.

Though the financial review turned up irregularities, CIA investigators decided not to polygraph Ames until 1991, when he was scheduled to receive the test as part of his five-year review. They feared that a polygraph before then would alert him to the probe. When he finally took the polygraph in 1991, he passed, despite his spying activities. By August 1991, a review of cases that were unexpectedly compromised had listed 198 CIA officials who had had access to the failed cases and could have been the mole. Ames was among those 198, but the probe was diverted again in October when a KGB defector said a mole in the CIA was Russian-born.

It was a stunning series of failures that allowed America's worst spy to operate unimpeded.

Finally, in October 1992, Ames's bank transfers were traced to a Swiss account. Only then did the investigation begin in earnest. In 1993, the FBI took over the probe. In February 1994, the Bureau discovered that Ames was planning to travel to Moscow. Fearing that he would learn of the investigation and flee to the Soviet Union, agents swept in and arrested him on February 21. Ames pleaded guilty to spying in a plea deal on April 29, 1994, and for his crimes was sentenced to life in prison without possibility of parole. The plea deal included leniency for Ames's wife, Rosario, who received a five-year prison sentence.

After pleading guilty, Ames issued a statement that said, "In breaking the law, I have betrayed a serious trust. I do regret and feel shame for this betrayal of trust, done for the basest of motives." The motives were indeed base: U.S. Attorney Helen F. Fahey put it bluntly when she said, "He traded people's lives for $2½ million." But money seems not to have been the only motivation. In his statement, Ames said he had betrayed his country because he objected to what he called a "decades-long shift to the extreme right" in U.S. politics and security and foreign policies. Of the CIA intelligence-gathering, Ames said it was a "self-serving sham carried out by careerist bureaucrats" who sponsor "huge and ultimately useless espionage campaigns" against friends and foes.

Some U.S. government officials considered Ames's life imprisonment insufficient punishment for a man who had caused the deaths of so many Russians helping the United States defeat the Soviet empire. Richard Stolz, a former CIA operations chief, expressed the view of many former CIA officers when he said, "As far as I'm concerned, [Ames] got less than he deserves." Another former CIA officer told me, "In our day, we would have sat him down, learned everything he knew, then quietly arranged his death." Congress later passed a law that allows the federal government to seek the death penalty in especially egregious cases of espionage like that of Ames.

Two years after Ames's arrest, I obtained a copy of a private letter Prisoner No. 40087-083 wrote from his isolation cell at the Allenwood maximum-security prison in White Deer, Pennsylvania. In the "dear family and friends" letter (which included a postscript noting that the document was not for publication), Ames revealed his struggle at maintaining his sanity. "Life in prison," he wrote, "with its double meaning for me, has to be coped with, accommodated, resisted and used if I am to stay sane and healthy." The convicted spy said that he didn't expect ever to be released from prison but that he still hoped one day to be free, perhaps through some prisoner exchange—which, if U.S. government officials have their way, will never happen. The letter also provided interesting insights on life in prison. He did not feel in danger, he wrote, and in fact he received "frequent congratulations for how badly I screwed the government." This person who had complained about the "shift to the extreme right" in the United States also noted that his fellow prisoners and the prison staff were "big fans" of conservative talk radio and "especially dote on Rush [Limbaugh] and G. Gordon Liddy."

Moscow's Aggressive Spying

Aldrich Ames is locked away for life, but the problems his case highlighted have not similarly been contained. Counterintelligence official Richard Haver revealed that the CIA has made no fundamental reforms to ensure that a betrayal like Ames's will not occur again. The Ames damage assessment identified numerous problems that led to Ames's betrayal, and still the agency has not acted to address the vulnerabilities. Here again, we see that the failure to reform reflects cultural resistance. "That is part of a culture that has to be attacked," Haver told me. "Change that culture; that's what good counterintelligence is all about."

Attacking the culture is needed more urgently than ever, because the problem of Russian spying against the United States has not disappeared with the arrests of Aldrich Ames and Robert Hanssen. Several classified intelligence reports indicate the scope of Moscow's intelligence operations. One especially eye-opening report came from the U.S. Office of Naval Intelligence (ONI) in June 2000. This 21-page top-secret report noted that there is a "false perception" in the West that Russian intelligence services no longer pose a threat. The continued and regular expulsions of Russian intelligence personnel from around the world showed that this is not the case. Moreover, the report revealed, both the GRU (military intelligence) and the KGB successor agency, SVR, "have a demonstrated interest in acquiring technologies that are in the research and development stage of production. This interest is continuously reaffirmed through defector information and double-agent operations."

The ONI report stated that Russian intelligence agencies were reformed after the collapse of the Soviet Union in 1991 and were given a boost following the failed coup attempt in August of that year. While some elements of the KGB were changed, the SVR emerged "intact" from that period. "The SVR has weathered this period and is back in the business of conducting worldwide intelligence collection operations," the report said. Military intelligence was spared similar upheavals. "In the immediate post-Soviet period, the GRU ascended to the top of the intelligence hierarchy," the report stated. "The GRU maintains its overseas residencies and agent networks as it had during the Cold War. Thus, the GRU has become the dominant foreign intelligence collection threat from Russia."

Russian intelligence services also use "front companies" as a pretext for operating in foreign nations. "Even if the company is not directly involved in intelligence collection, it can provide operational support for intelligence officers," ONI reported. "The current proliferation of businesses and Russian organized-crime cells in North America by Russian émigrés is of interest in light of this." The legitimate business fronts provide facilities, communications, and vehicles for supporting Russian human intelligence operations and networks, the report noted. The companies also launder money and develop operational funds.

Moscow's aggressive spying is not limited to land-based human operations. For example, the ONI report documented an extensive GRU electronic surveillance operation against the United States and allied military forces that kicked off in early January 1999. The GRU Main Intelligence Directorate produced a daily intelligence summary that identified U.S. strategic aircraft at various locations in the Pacific and Indian Ocean regions. The Russians reported the number of B-52 strategic bombers deployed at the U.S. military facility on the island of Diego Garcia, for instance, as well as the precise locations of four U.S. aircraft carrier battle groups. When the United States and NATO launched airstrikes in Kosovo in March of that year, the Russian GRU signals intelligence (SIGINT) center began electronic surveillance. On March 26, the Fifth Radiotechnical Brigade in Severomorsk sent to subordinate military units a summary of foreign aircraft and ships that were capable of conducting spying operations.

It also appears that Russian intelligence got access to U.S. military communications channels, which are generally classified at the highest top-secret level. In late March 1999, the U.S. Air Force global command-and-control system in Europe planned to switch to a new communications frequency; the day before the change went into effect, a GRU SIGINT center in the North Caucusus shifted its surveillance to the new frequency, an indication that Russia had inside knowledge of U.S. SIGINT.

There were other Russian intelligence successes in this period. On March 24, three GRU SIGINT centers and one SIGINT brigade in the Russian Far East stepped up operations in response to the U.S. Pacific Command exercise known as Tandem Thrust '99, a multinational exercise involving forces from South Korea, Canada, Australia, Singapore, and the United States. In May, the Russians spied on a U.S. nuclear command-and-control exercise known as Polo Hat. In July, Russian eavesdroppers conducted electronic surveillance of the U.S. aircraft carrier *Constellation* as it traveled from Pusan, South Korea, to Yokuska, Japan; simultaneously, a Russian intelligence-gathering ship shadowed the carrier. Then, in 2000, nine different GRU electronic eavesdropping stations listened in to a U.S. Strategic Command exercise known as Global Guardian 2000, an annual exercise to test nuclear commands and communication.

All the various electronic spying by the GRU around the world is sent to the GRU's Fifth Directorate, which fuses the information and disseminates it to military units. ONI's review of the GRU's activities showed that Russian military intelligence is "capable of conducting short notice intelligence operations on a global basis—essentially a capability undiminished from the Soviet era." The Pacific activity by Moscow's spies is especially significant in light of recent Russian-Chinese military cooperation. China's first major joint military exercise took place in the summer of 2005 and included a scenario that U.S. officials said was obviously a rehearsal for a joint invasion of Taiwan. The United States was excluded from observing the exercise, despite the fact that several Southeast Asian and Central Asian military representatives were allowed to attend. The cooperation shows that Russia is becoming a supporter of Chinese military plans for conflict with the United States.

The ONI report disclosed that the Russians employ an important but little-noticed espionage method—using merchant ships to collect intelligence in the United States. The report stated that electronic intelligence "conclusively indicates that Russian commercial maritime vessels are reporting on U.S., allied and other naval units in the European theater." The Navy study, based on communications intercepts between February 1999 and May 2000, revealed forty-four different coded communications from Russian merchant ships that spotted foreign naval vessels and reported the locations within ten minutes to thirty minutes of the closest point of approach. The communications were sent to three former Soviet Western Fleet headquarters areas: Northern Fleet, Baltic Fleet, and Black Sea Fleet. "Analysis of these contact reports suggests Russian merchant and fishing vessels continue to provide Russian military intelligence with the location and movement on naval entities and their activities," the report said. "This activity is nearly identical to that which was practiced by the Soviet merchant and fisheries fleets throughout the Cold War."

During the time ONI tracked Russian communications, Russian merchant ships reported scores of reported sightings of U.S., British, Danish, and Italian warships, and even an Algerian Kilo submarine. The report noted that the Russian freighters use a personal computer to encrypt the information and transmit it over high-frequency radio waves. The messages are labeled "urgent" for high-interest targets, such as warships close to Russian coasts. The ship captain is the only one allowed to handle the codebooks used for enciphering the messages.

The ONI report said that the intercepts in Europe were conclusive, but difficulties in collecting and hearing similar communications in the Far East and near North America had made it harder to tell if the Russian ships were doing the same level of espionage there. The report stated, however, that Russian freighters and fishing vessels continue the Cold War practice of taking part in Russian command-and-control military exercises directed by the General Staff, Moscow's centralized military leadership unit, and by the navy main staff. Thus it is very likely that the ships are involved in spying operations against U.S. Navy warships in both the Atlantic and the Pacific. In the past the ships were equipped with special electronic equipment that allowed them to spy on U.S. military exercises.

One Russian merchant ship mentioned specifically in the ONI report was the *Kapitan Man,* which was searched in April 1993 by officials from U.S. Customs and the Immigration and Naturalization Service. The search revealed that the ship carried expendable bathythermographs (XBTs), which are used to collect acoustical environmental data for sonar predictions. A later search uncovered sonobuoys in a booby-trapped compartment; the compartment had been treated with a dog repellent in order to put off law-enforcement canine teams. The sonobuoys are used to track submarines. The ONI noted that the devices were ideal for spying on submarines and other naval vessels.

The report's revelations about the *Kapitan Man* are of particular interest because the ship became notorious for an April 1997 incident in which the freighter's crew fired a laser at a Canadian helicopter that was conducting surveillance of the ship. Only minutes before the laser was fired, the surveillance team had watched the *Kapitan Man* pass a surfaced U.S. nuclear missile submarine as it entered the Strait of Juan de Fuca, near Washington State's Puget Sound. The laser damaged the eyes of the pilots, U.S. Navy Lieutenant Jack Daly and Canadian Captain Pat Barnes, but the incident was covered up to avoid upsetting U.S.-Russia relations. (For a full account, see my book *Betrayal: How the Clinton Administration Undermined American Security.*) Now the ONI report of 2000 had offered still more evidence that the *Kapitan Man* was spying for Moscow.

The Ministry of Maritime Fleets continues to have contacts with both the GRU and the SVR, the ONI report said, noting that "these organizational ties are virtually identical to that established during the Cold War." The difference is in the size of the merchant fleet. Once boasting more than 5,000 merchant ships, by 2000 the Russian fleet had been cut to 362 ships. The ships are an average of twenty years old. The report noted that the decline shows that "Russia is losing its status as a global maritime power." Most of the ships were sold off on the open market. But Putin has sought to reverse the decline in merchant shipping, with support from the military. The report concluded that Russia's commercial fleet is being reorganized to better meet Russian naval intelligence-gathering requirements.

Why would Russia continue to spy on the United States using its commercial ships when Russia desperately relies on Western democracies for economic aid? "In an era where the West is required to provide increasing assistance to Moscow to assist the fledgling democracy from returning to an autocratic (and more volatile) government, the issue of commercial maritime intelligence or any intelligence collection by the Russians makes little sense," the report said. "But the reality of the situation is that Russia's current military and political leadership probably still sees the U.S. and NATO as a threat." Indeed, the ONI observed that "Russian military intelligence (GRU/Naval) maintains a peacetime plot of U.S. and allied global maritime disposition to facilitate military action in the event of hostilities."

Another classified intelligence report confirmed the ONI's conclusions about Russia's use of commercial ships for spying. The CIA Worldwide National Intelligence Daily released on July 14, 2000, stated, "Special intelligence provides the first solid evidence of long-suspected Russian merchant ship intelligence collection efforts against U.S. nuclear submarine bases." U.S. intelligence intercepted two messages from the Russian ship *Kapitan Konev,* a sister ship to the freighter *Kapitan Man,* to Russian intelligence in Vladivostok, where Russia's Far East fleet has its headquarters. The *Kapitan Konev* had sighted a U.S. submarine in the Strait of Juan de Fuca. The first message was sent within minutes of the sighting and a more detailed message was sent seven hours later.

The CIA report noted that the *Kapitan Konev* was not alone, as many other Russian ships "have been involved in numerous incidents in the vicinity of U.S. submarines since 1992, when Seattle and Tacoma ports were opened to Russian merchant ships." The Clinton administration had opened the ports as an effort to improve ties with Russia.

By 2001, the U.S. government had finally recognized Russian spying as a security threat to the Navy. The State Department delivered a diplomatic protest note to the Russian embassy. The United States would now require Russian ships to provide a three-day advance notice of their arrival at all ports where U.S. submarines are based, the letter said. "We remain concerned about continued patterns of unacceptable activity by Russian vessels bound to or from U.S. ports," the note stated. The letter added, "The government of the United States of America would note that if Russian vessels continue to engage in activities that are incompatible with innocent passage, as well as such activities while bound to or from U.S. ports, the United States may find it necessary to take appropriate national security measures to prevent such activities. Such activities might include stricter control over the movement of individual vessels bound for the U.S."

The United States did not demand that the Russians stop spying on U.S. submarines. Diplomats also continued to seek a commercial maritime agreement with Russia.

The warning did not have much effect. The Coast Guard launched a secret program with the U.S. Navy's Submarine Group 9, based in Puget Sound, to check whether the Russian merchant ships were providing advance notice of their arrivals in sensitive ports. A test survey found that the vast majority—thirty of forty-four—failed to give the State Department the proper seventy-two hours' notice.

The United States cannot continue to let diplomatic interests overwhelm efforts to resolve the problem of Russian spying. Doing so only undermines U.S. national security.

A Worldwide Spy Force

As the ONI report indicated, the United States is Russia's most important intelligence target, but it is not the only target. Other intelligence shows that Moscow aggressively spies on America's European allies.

In Britain, for example, Russian spying has reached Cold War levels, just as it has in the United States. Moscow's agents target military and defense industry secrets, and also spy on Chechens who have sought asylum in Britain. A 2005 memorandum from Britain's MI-5 security service alerted government officials that Russian intelligence poses "a SUBSTANTIAL espionage threat to the UK." The Security Service Espionage Alert urged British government officials to report "any chance sighting of Russian diplomatic cars," since Moscow's agents in Britain—roughly eighteen SVR officers and fourteen GRU officers—operate under cover as Russian diplomats. "We are aware that Russian intelligence officers travel widely throughout the UK and that some of the activity undertaken by these officers is intelligence related," the memo said.

Unlike the United States, Britain has aggressive and accomplished counterintelligence units. Thus the MI-5 memo told local authorities to do nothing to stop or question suspected Russian agents. The only directive was to report the Russians to Scotland Yard's Special Branch, which would then pass the information on to MI-5.

German government officials are also coping with the upsurge in Russian spying. While German-Russian relations on the surface appear

close, Germany's intelligence and security services see Moscow's spy
activities increasing sharply. The Federal Office of Criminal Investigation, known by its German initials, BKA, and the Federal Office
for the Protection of the Constitution, which conducts counterintelligence, have stepped up efforts to deal with Russian spying. Moscow
dispatched the spies and spy handlers to gather intelligence on German political parties and their leaders, and to obtain sensitive documents and information from German businesses, including research
and development and military secrets.

"Russian secret service residents have substantially increased their
personnel in Germany," one German counterspy said. "Staffing levels
are now nearly as high as they used to be during the Cold War." By
early 2005, Russia had 130 spies at its embassy in Berlin and at consulates in Bonn, Hamburg, Leipzig, and Munich. "Sixty-five or so officers are on operational assignments," the official revealed. "They
recruit and supervise traditional sources. We are hardly able to keep
them under control. Before agents meet, they drive and run across
town for up to three hours, cleverly shaking off pursuers."

Germany remains vulnerable to Russian spying because the German government has focused on monitoring terrorists in Germany.
"The government in Berlin is not interested in any tough investigations against Putin's spies," a German federal investigator told *Focus*
magazine. "This would only mean foreign policy trouble, so that it is
better to turn a blind eye." In February 2005, German military intelligence officers identified a Russian operation to entrap a German
military official and have him supply Moscow with documents related to the armed forces. The soldier played along and worked with
the German Military Counter-Intelligence Service to counter the Russians. The GRU was not taken in, and its officers were forced to leave
Germany in the aftermath of the spy incident.

Countering the Russian Threat

As many intelligence reports reveal, the United States and its allies
cannot underestimate the threat represented by Russian intelligence.

The fact that the Cold War is over has not brought an end to Russian spying. The Aldrich Ames and Robert Hanssen cases are stark reminders of that truth. And Russia's troubled economic conditions clearly will not prevent Moscow from investing heavily in an aggressive, worldwide spying apparatus.

The United States must make a priority of countering Russia's espionage operations. Continued counterintelligence failures will cause problems for years into the future, if not decades. The Aldrich Ames case shows why this is so.

The stacks of classified information Ames provided to the KGB and the SVR hurt the United States in several ways. First, they allowed Moscow to manipulate U.S. government policies. Russia provided the CIA with disinformation that eventually found its way to the highest levels of the U.S. government, including the White House, the State Department, and the Defense Department. Angelo Codevilla, a former congressional intelligence specialist and a professor at Boston University, told me that Ames thoroughly undermined the reliability of CIA reporting, the fundamental mission of the agency. "In the 1980s," Codevilla said, "when the Soviet Union was collapsing, we had no hints of that from official intelligence channels." He added, "The CIA should look upon all the information we received from human intelligence in Russia as tainted."

Ames's spying had other immediate consequences—most notably, of course, it caused the deaths of those American agents recruited in Russia. In all, Ames revealed more than one hundred covert American operations and betrayed more than thirty sources. Michelle Van Cleave, who served as President George W. Bush's top counterintelligence official until January 2006, said, "He was responsible for the loss of virtually all of CIA's intelligence assets targeted at the Soviet Union at the height of the Cold War." That is why Van Cleave calls Ames "the most damaging spy in U.S. history."

But other damage is less obvious and is being felt only now. The classified report the CIA produced in the aftermath of the Ames case reveals the long-term impact. According to the report, Ames's Russian handlers did not seem particularly focused on processing the reams of extremely sensitive intelligence he provided. Ames concluded that most of the CIA documents he stole "just sort of had to sit in the bottom of the file drawer." The reason was simple: Russian intelligence knew it could exploit the material effectively in the future. The most important priority for the short term was to protect the security of the Russians' prized agent.

Now that Ames and Robert Hanssen no longer work as spies, the Russians have begun the real work of exploiting the U.S. secrets supplied by the traitors. Thanks to the mole operations, Moscow knows the weaknesses of CIA and FBI security, a valuable tool for penetrating the services. It also knows how U.S. intelligence communicates, gathers intelligence, runs double-agent operations, and uses technical operations such as electronic eavesdropping in support of human operations. Ames's spying was particularly damaging because he worked in counterintelligence, so he could provide information on all U.S. intelligence operations and plans, offensive and defensive.

The Ames and Hanssen cases are stunning for the damage they inflicted and the repeated counterintelligence failures they revealed. But we may well see other cases like them. As Richard Haver warns, the intelligence community has put in almost no safeguards to prevent a recurrence of such mole operations.

When one considers that just one counterintelligence failure can damage U.S. national security for years into the future, Haver's warning becomes particularly chilling.

Chapter 6

NORTH KOREA: CRiMiNAL STATE

North Korea has become a *"Soprano* state," a government guided by a Workers' Party leadership whose actions, attitudes, and affiliations increasingly resemble those of an organized crime family more than a normal nation.

—Former State Department official David L. Asher

Future historians will have the luxury of documenting in exquisite detail how the Communist regime in North Korea was among the most inhuman and repressive states to exist in the modern era. But we must understand the true nature of the totalitarian dictatorship now, not at some far-off point. The following will show why Supreme Leader Kim Jong-il's regime in the so-called Democratic People's Republic of Korea (DPRK) must be ended. The only answer is a policy of regime change—not accommodation and appeasement, as so many in Asia and the West advocate. The best method to bring down Kim's brutal dictatorship is a concerted program of counterintelligence operations directed at the North Korea ruling party's intelligence and security services, which serve as pillars upon which the rogue regime has rested for more than fifty years.

Rogue State

It was 6:30 P.M. on November 15, 1977, and thirteen-year-old Megumi Yokota was returning home from badminton practice in the dark. She made the mile-long walk every day down a slope from her junior high school in the suburbs of Niigata, on the northwest coast of Japan's main island, Honshu. But today, as she was about to turn down her family's street, she encountered a team of six men. They were North Korean intelligence operatives from the Operations Department of the ruling Korean Workers' Party of North Korea. One of the North Koreans snatched Megumi and carried her off to the beach on the Sea of Japan, some three hundred feet away. There a small boat was waiting to take the team and Megumi off to North Korea. To her parents, she had disappeared without a trace, leaving them grief-stricken.

Japanese authorities believe the North Koreans mistakenly thought Megumi was an older Japanese woman. Thus a young girl was thrust into the middle of a nightmare. But she has not been the only victim. Since the early 1970s, the North Korean government has abducted as many as forty Japanese to be used in secret training courses for North Korean intelligence officers. Held incommunicado, the kidnapped Japanese have been forced to work as language and culture trainers for North Korean intelligence operatives who need to learn the nuances and customs of Japan. These agents have then been dispatched to Japan as "illegals"—that is, spies who operate outside any formal or informal diplomatic outpost. North Korea also used the Japanese to give the agents what intelligence officials call "legends," or cover stories and identities that would allow them to obtain false identity and travel documents.

The kidnapping of Japanese nationals is the most flagrant use of North Korean government agents for criminal activity. But it is simply part of what North Korea regards as its unique policy of diplomatic and economic self-reliance that it calls *juche,* a derivative of Marxism-Leninism with Korean characteristics under a totalitarian, Stalinist-style system.

North Korea today epitomizes the term "rogue state." Under absolute leader Kim Jong-il, who has ruled as a demigod since his father's death in 1994, North Korea has demonstrated that it can fire a long-range ballistic missile thousands of miles away, as it threatened in June 2006. Kim has fulfilled the goal of his late father, Kim Il-sung, by covertly developing a nuclear weapons arsenal as a way to ensure that the regime stays in power. Intelligence officials told me they have "high confidence" that a series of underground nuclear tests carried out in Pakistan in 1998 included two North Korean devices set off in deep underground shafts.

The North Koreans have admitted to secretly developing uranium-based nuclear arms—in flagrant violation of a 1994 agreement with the United States. During an October 2002 meeting in Pyongyang, the North Korean capital, then–Assistant Secretary of State James Kelly showed North Korea senior official Kang Suk Ju intelligence indicating the covert uranium enrichment. Confronted, the North Korean official told Kelly, "Your president called us a member of the axis of evil. . . . Your troops are deployed on the Korean peninsula. . . . Of course we have a nuclear program." The admission set in motion a crisis that continues. The North Korean nuclear arsenal is believed to include several large bombs that would be delivered not on North Korea's arsenal of missiles but on one of twenty Soviet-era IL-28 bombers.

The North Koreans have built numerous large underground facilities in the north-central part of the country, according to U.S. intelligence sources. Many of the facilities have been built in the past several years and house sensitive research projects. A CIA official who spent years analyzing North Korea told me that these secret efforts will lead to "a North Korea with a nuclear delivery capability to threaten Japan and South Korea at least, and to threaten Russia, China, and the United States as a worst case, within the next four to six years."

Kim Jong-il's regime is unlike that of any other state in modern history. Known to enjoy Chuck Norris action films, Kim was considered a minor figure compared with his father. But he has ruled North Korea with an iron fist. His Communist system is the most regimented society on earth today. North Korea's 21 million people are indoctrinated from the very earliest age with an ideology built on hatred for "enemies"—mainly the United States, the non-Communist government in South Korea, and Japan. A North Korean math book, for example, uses the lesson of throwing a grenade at a group of American soldiers, asking students to determine how many are killed if the grenade lands within X number of feet of the soldiers.

The Communist state is also predicated on indoctrinating the people in "love" for the ruler. Kim is always referred to as the "Dear Leader," and every speech or writing that mentions him must use terms like "great," "benevolent," and "all-knowing." Intelligence officials say Kim's rule has gone beyond personality cult and reached the level of a leader-centered pseudo-religion. Government lies are standard fare in describing Kim's supposed benevolence, wisdom, and concern for the people of North Korea. Official video from North Korea is strictly controlled by authorities and includes images of mass demonstrations in stadiums where tens of thousands of North Koreans use carefully orchestrated cards that create huge images of Kim and his late father.

"Dear Leader" lives in some forty special mansions and houses spread out around Pyongyang and other parts of the country. Like Saddam Hussein in Iraq, Kim rarely spends more than one night at a single residence, fearing he will be assassinated or bombed by the United States. He leads by issuing faxes to his subordinates, who must carry out his directives without question or face execution.

Kim is known to be vindictive. He frequently watched CNN news broadcasts until the cable network aired a report exposing dissidents in North Korea; he quickly prohibited senior officials of the party from watching any CNN broadcasts and made sure none of the network's reporters were allowed to visit. More disturbing, in 1987 he ordered party agents to plant a bomb on a South Korean passenger jet. The blast destroyed a Korean Air Boeing 707 over the Andaman Sea off the coast of Burma, killing ninety-five passengers and twenty crew members. Kim ordered the bombing after finding out that North Korea would not have any role in the 1988 Olympic Games held in Seoul, even though North Korea had built a large stadium and sports complex in Pyongyang. Intelligence sources told me that Kim was especially outraged by the 2004 puppet comedy film *Team America: World Police,* which portrayed him as a mad dictator. Kim reportedly ordered Workers' Party of Korea agents to "take care" of the film's writers, Trey Parker and Matt Stone, creators of the controversial cartoon television series *South Park.*

In many ways North Korea is an intelligence-run state—indeed, a police state. To keep the regime in power, Kim exploits the organs of the Workers' Party of Korea as a combination of intelligence and security services. North Korea's intelligence and security network is a vast political police system modeled on the Soviet Union's KGB, conducting operations abroad as well as squelching even the slightest internal dissent. According to a classified Defense Intelligence Agency report, the State Security Department carries out North Korea's defensive and offensive counterintelligence programs, and functions much like a secret police. It keeps a close watch on political attitudes in the country, tracks defectors and dissidents overseas, monitors foreigners and returnees, and targets "antistate criminals"—a broadly defined term in Kim's North Korea.

Another government organ, the powerful Ministry of Public Security, is in charge of internal security, social control, police functions, and border security. It has up to 144,000 public security personnel.

Kim complements the intelligence agencies with military special operations commandos. One intelligence official told me, "North Korea's 122,000 special operations troops are the world's largest, and a high funding priority for the regime." According to the classified DIA report, their mission is different from that of most other special operations forces: North Korean commandos handle special reconnaissance missions for the armed forces, light infantry operations, and sniper operations. "Snipers conduct assassinations, kidnappings, and interrogations of key civilian and military personnel and members of their immediate family," the report said. North Korea's commandos were also involved in several assassination attempts against South Korean leaders.

Life in Hell

The ultimate purpose of all these intelligence and counterintelligence operations is to keep the Communist regime in power, at all costs. Key to that control function is the regime's attempt to keep the population from knowing what is going on in the outside world.

But that effort is failing. Smugglers from another Communist state, China, as well as from Japan and South Korea, are risking their lives to bring in communications technology ranging from cell phones to compact digital video cameras to VHS-format videotape recordings. "We have smuggled phones inside the country," one defector told CNN in 2005. "Of course, the regime intercepts the calls, they have to, to preserve the dictatorship." Under this police state, a key to regime survival is preventing the population from knowing what is going on in the outside world.

Likewise, the true picture of life in North Korea is beginning to emerge through video smuggled out of the country. And the true picture is a hellish one. Footage shows starving homeless children forced to steal food in markets, crowds combing trainyards for small amounts of fertilizer that they can sell to get food, and diseased people—and dead bodies—lying in the streets. The CNN program that so outraged Kim was broadcast in November 2005. It featured smuggled hidden-camera footage that showed an impoverished nation struggling to cope with a brutal dictatorship. In one scene from March 2005, a crowd of North Koreans is ordered to gather at an open field in an unidentified city in northern North Korea. At another point, a voice is heard on the video: "Carry out the death sentence immediately!" A man, blindfolded and tied to a stake, is shot to death. His heads slumps forward. The scene is repeated in another village square. What crime did these people commit? They had made contact with foreigners in nearby China. They were helping people escape the horror that is North Korea.

Scores of defectors who have managed to escape North Korea are exposing the lies and deception of the Kim regime, as well as the brutality. Some who fled were forced to watch public executions carried out as a lesson to North Koreans not to revolt or flee. Smuggled video has shown the ultimate in dissent within the North Korean police state: dissidents defacing portraits of Kim Jong-il and posting anti-Kim banners on the side of an overpass. Such acts of defiance are punishable by imprisonment or death. The defaced poster carried the words "Kim Jong-il, who are you? You are a tyrant. People will not forgive you and we will bring you down from power. We want freedom and democracy. Open policy is the only way for us to survive."

Dissidents who work against the regime say that Kim is convinced he must kill all his political opponents, at home and abroad, or they will kill him and drive him from power. He has dispatched assassins to hunt down and kill the defectors working against the regime.

Repression in North Korea is widespread. Satellite photographs show that the regime has built vast prison labor camps. The State Security Department controls these political-prisoner detention facilities, which hold up to 200,000, according to the nongovernment organization Human Rights Watch. The North Korean regime reviews families' loyalty to the government, using three categories to classify people: the "core" people, those considered to be "wavering" in their support of the system, and those classified as "hostile" to the regime. The government punishes transgressors by sending entire families—parents, children, and grandchildren—to the prison labor camps. Those "criminals" considered beyond Communist reeducation are sent to the most deadly camps, where forced labor and starvation will kill them in a relatively short period of time. Others are considered capable of being "reformed" and are sent to less severe but still horrific camps.

There has also been widespread famine because the food production and distribution system collapsed in the late 1990s. According to intelligence estimates, the devastating famine that resulted claimed the lives of as many as 2 million people. The Communist regime employs a ration system as a control mechanism, denying food and essentials to anyone who is viewed as not acting in accordance with the government's wishes.

The combination of repression and famine has ensured that

North Korea is one of the few countries whose population is dropping precipitously. Estimated to be 28 million in 1992, the population was believed to be about 21 million in 2005—a loss of 7 million people in less than fifteen years.

Kang Chol-Hwan, who survived ten years in a prison labor camp, is one of the most high-profile defectors to tell his story outside the closed society of North Korea. His 2001 book *The Aquariums of Pyongyang*—copies of which President George W. Bush is known to have given out—disclosed in detail the systematic torture, beatings, public executions, and starvation in his camp. "The people who are at the camps, the [North Korean] government wants to kill them all," Kang told me in an interview. "Instead of executing them, they kill them slowly, making them work in forced labor. That was the hardest part." Kang revealed how prisoners are fed minute portions of corn and salt that make it "impossible to survive" without additional food. Kang and his family managed to survive by eating cooked rats and snakes, and live lizards.

Kang was released from the camp in 1987, but the repression was so overwhelming that in 1992 he risked his life to cross the border into China. Working as a trader, he bribed a border guard to let him go. He told me that his trip across the border was relatively easy compared with what North Koreans face now, since the government has recently set up triple fences and more guards to block the defections. Kang has maintained contact with a network of other defectors and smugglers who continue to provide information on the situation inside North Korea.

North Korea, according to Kang, grows more unstable as food and energy shortages increase. Foreign aid—primarily from China, South Korea, and Japan—keeps the regime from collapsing completely, he told me. Kang said he urged President George W. Bush in an Oval Office meeting on June 13, 2005, to do more to help provide assistance to North Korea without going through channels controlled by the government. "Elites" use the foreign assistance sent by international relief agencies and foreign states to keep the regime in power while most of the population starves. Kang also said he told the president that the United States should provide direct support to North Korean defectors to help counter the fact that North Koreans are "brainwashed with anti-Americanism" from very early ages.

In addition, Kang noted that in recent years the armed forces have assumed an even more prominent position in Kim's regime, ranking in importance only after the absolute ruler himself and the Workers' Party of Korea. "Without the military, the government would collapse immediately," he told me. Thus, a nation of just 21 million people has a military of around 1.5 million troops. The regime must devote vast resources to sustaining that large an army. Without foreign assistance, it would be an unsustainable model, since North Korea's failed economic system could not support Kim's "military first" policies.

Kim also invests heavily in keeping his spy agencies active, diverting foreign assistance for that purpose. "The secret services of North Korea are quite powerful and stable," Kang told me. The intelligence services target South Korea and, especially, the estimated 300,000 defectors hiding in China. According to Kang, North Korea's intelligence service recently purchased high-technology equipment from China and Japan to detect and locate cell phone users in the country, and even to monitor North Koreans who change the channels on their television sets, a crime in the police state. "The government is doing poorly on the economic side but doesn't hesitate to invest in this," Kang said.

All these factors combine to form a system that is near collapse, Kang believes. North Korea's economy, the most centrally planned and isolated in the world, is in a dire state. Industrial equipment and factories are nearly beyond repair because of lack of investment and spare-parts shortages. Only large infusions of foreign aid since 1995 have kept the disaster of food shortages and starvation from growing worse. In this economic crisis, maintaining totalitarian political control has remained the regime's overriding concern. But Kang told me that the ruling elites in the Workers' Party of Korea, the military, and the intelligence services have become desperate and rely heavily on outside assistance to survive and prosper. South Korea's government has adopted a pro–North Korean stance known as the "sunshine" policy, which many critics say has kept the foundering North Korean regime in power. If South Korea and other governments were to cut their foreign aid, the regime would ultimately collapse, Kang believes. He told me the military could overthrow Kim if it failed to get adequate assistance from outside.

Infiltration

Although South Korea has softened its stance on Pyongyang, North Korea continues to target the South Koreans and their allies—including the United States.

Most of North Korea's 1.5-million-man army is deployed within a few miles of the demilitarized zone (DMZ). Moreover, according to an internal U.S. government counterintelligence report produced in 2004, North Korean intelligence conducts electronic eavesdropping on many South Korean and U.S. communications in Northeast Asia. The report noted that "the primary threat posed by North Korean intelligence operations is directed against U.S. forces stationed in South Korea." The North Koreans also rely heavily on human intelligence-gathering. North Korean military intelligence has dispatched commandos to South Korea. "The primary methods of infiltration have been through tunnels under the Demilitarized Zone and seaborne operations involving submarine and high-speed patrol boats as insertion vehicles," the report said. Four of these tunnels under the DMZ were discovered by the South Korean military. They raise particularly disturbing questions about North Korea's ability to devastate the South Koreans using asymmetric warfare. U.S. officials say that the North Koreans may have dug as many as twenty-five tunnels wide enough to drive military vehicles through.

The same counterintelligence report, entitled "Intelligence Threat Handbook," highlighted North Korea's efforts to infiltrate the United States. The report noted that North Korea's operations in the United

States remain limited, but some of the operations that do exist are the most threatening of all—efforts focused on "acquiring nuclear weapons technology."

An earlier classified report confirmed that North Korea sought nuclear secrets from the United States. This report, produced in 1999, stated that prospective nuclear weapons states like North Korea and Iran seek details of first-generation nuclear explosives. An intelligence source told me that a North Korean government agent successfully penetrated the Los Alamos National Laboratory in the late 1990s, posing as a South Korean who had moved to Canada. The agent obtained technology and information that would have been useful to North Korea's nuclear arms program.

The classified report stated that North Korea has "aggressive intelligence programs that place a priority on science and technology collection." While the North Koreans have marginal access to Energy Department facilities in the United States, government agents recruit spies based on cultural ties. "Oftentimes this cultivation process is very subtle and may take many months or years to fully develop," the classified report said. "All U.S. visitors to North Korea are under constant escort and believe all their faxes are copied. In addition, a Department of Energy scientist reports that his escort asked him to discuss 'in private' U.S. and North Korean nuclear weapons complexes." North Korea agents also go through other countries to obtain America's nuclear secrets. "They operate abroad to obtain U.S. nuclear technologies and information related to their needs," the report said. "North Korea has tried to obtain U.S. nuclear-related information or technology from third-country sources."

Echoing the 2004 "Intelligence Threat Handbook," American counterintelligence officials have told me that few North Korean intelligence operations have been detected in the United States. But few does not mean none. Two cases highlight the danger North Korea poses to the United States because of its aggressive intelligence work. The cases also underscore the need to develop an offensive strategic counterintelligence program against North Korea.

Aiding the "Revolutionary Cause"

FBI documents in the case of Korean-American businessman John Joungwoong Yai provide a rare glimpse into the secret world of North Korean intelligence activities in this country. Yai was arrested on February 4, 2003, for failing to register as a foreign agent. Later that year he pleaded guilty to lesser felony charges related to not reporting more than $18,000 to U.S. Customs officials, and was sentenced to two years in prison. But there is overwhelming evidence that he was in fact an agent for the North Korean government, conducting what U.S. officials called "low-level intelligence services" over a seven-year period. Indeed, according to a mass of evidence compiled by the FBI, he had received the $18,000 from North Korean officials as payment for his intelligence reports.

Yai was born in South Korea in 1943 and became a naturalized U.S. citizen in 1980. He also was a spy for North Korea who traveled to China to meet North Korean officials. His main goal, according to an FBI affidavit, was to recruit a subagent who could join the U.S. government in order to obtain top-secret information for North Korea. Between December 1996 and February 2003, the FBI kept Yai under surveillance, intercepting telephone and fax communications; installing clandestine microphones in his Los Angeles office, house, and car to monitor conversations; and secretly searching his residence (but with authorization from a special court in Washington, D.C., under the terms of the Foreign Intelligence Surveillance Act).

"During the period of the . . . surveillance, the FBI found no evidence that Yai was employed by any entity other than the North Korean government," said FBI counterintelligence agent James G. Chang in the affidavit. The FBI detected Yai sending reports to North Korea through China based on information he had obtained from publicly available sources in the United States. In the reports, Yai embellished his reports to make them sound more valuable to his North Korean handlers.

One Yai fax intercepted by the FBI went to a North Korean agent identified as "Mr. Ahn" and discussed the disappearance of a North Korean agent who had defected. Yai claimed to have been in touch with South Korean intelligence agents in the United States about the defection, although the FBI doubts that Yai had any ties to South Korea's government. The FBI traced several of Yai's telephone calls to the North Korean embassy in Beijing and to Shenyang, China, which is located close to the North Korean border and, according to Chang, has considerable ties to North Korea, including a $30 million North Korean–built hotel.

In May 2000, Yai began using e-mail to communicate with the North Koreans in Beijing, sending messages to the e-mail address GreenEarth2000@yahoo.com. After misaddressing one of his e-mails, Yai faxed them to China with a note stating, "For now, I am sending you copies of what I saved in my computer. I could not store 2 or 3 reports after I sent them. Try to look for them in GreenEarth2000 @yahoo.com." On May 29, Yai received a fax, addressed to "Mr. Y," that stated, "I am receiving your proposals that you worked so diligently on. It is busy season right now, so please continue to use the airmail for a while. And about the e-mail, it seems things will be normal when both sides make some more adjustments. But first I must inform you that the e-mail address for Mr. Shin has been changed to Green_Earth_2000@yahoo.com." The fax identifier revealed that it had been sent from a telephone number in Beijing. The FBI learned from cooperation with Yahoo!, the e-mail provider, that the Green Earth e-mail address was created by a subscriber in Shanghai. Yai's son, Dennis, set up the e-mail account Yai used. Dennis used a pseudonym: Denniskim22@yahoo.com.

Over the next year the FBI intercepted a number of e-mails to Yai's North Korean contacts in China. Agent Chang said the North Koreans used China for communicating with its agents because of the extremely limited availability of e-mail access in North Korea at the time. Only a few high-ranking government officials in North Korea, including Kim Jong-il, were permitted to use the Internet.

A clandestine search of Yai's house on April 8, 1998, revealed "code charts" that Yai used to communicate in secret. The charts contained two columns, one for "base" words and one for code words, or, in Korean, "substitution words." The base words and phrases included "the White House," "the State Department," "the Pentagon," "secret operation," "military," "human target," "secret code," "covert surveillance," "top secret," "secret contact," "recruitment," "CIA," "FBI," "nuclear facility," "military exercise," "Korea-US annual security meeting," and "invasion." All indicated targets of North Korean intelligence-gathering in the United States. The code words listed included Yai's cover names—"Won," "Doe," "Adams," and "Paul"—as well as multiple substitutions for the word "headquarters," such as "Chang," "Kang," "Peter," and "James." Two names ("Steve" and "Joseph") meaning "headquarters" were crossed out, indicating that they had been used as code words at an earlier time. Faxes sent from Yai's home in 1999 and 2000 were addressed to names other than those found on the charts, including "Mr. Chi," "Mr. Jefferson," "Mr. Robertson," "Mr. Bill," "Mr. John," "Mr. Oh," "Mr. Ahn," "Mr. Shin," and "Mr. Kim."

Intercepted communications and physical searches revealed that Yai was meeting with North Korean contacts overseas, and receiving money as well. On March 15, 1998, the FBI intercepted a fax to Yai from "Peter Kang," which was code for North Korean headquarters. The fax stated, "I received your itinerary fine. It would be preferable that Mr. Kang [code for 'headquarters'] greet you, but in due concern for the health [code for 'safety'], we have decided not to. Thus, when you arrive and settle in, call these local numbers, 894-2311 or 894-2313, and ask for Kim Chol-yong, and inform him of your location." The telephone numbers provided were for the North Korean embassy in Vienna. A search of Yai's office a few weeks later, on April 8, produced an envelope on which was printed the address "Hotel Erzherzog Rainer Wien, A-1041 Osterreich," which is in Vienna ("Wien" in German). The envelope was filled with $8,500 in cash. According to the FBI affidavit, a stamp in Yai's passport shows that he was in Austria on April 4, 1998.

It seems clear that North Korean agents passed Yai the money during his April 1998 visit to Vienna. This was not the only instance in which the FBI discovered money. On December 16, 1997, FBI agents searching Yai's office had found $3,300 in cash in an envelope on which was handwritten, in Korean, "Embassy in Beijing (Reception) 011-86-10-532-1186 Mr. Koo's telephone number 011-8610-6532-5792 (used also as a fax number)." ("Mr. Koo's" number was, in fact, the main number to which Yai sent faxes to North Korean headquarters.)

Later, in April 2000, Customs agents at Los Angeles International Airport discovered that Yai and his wife were carrying $18,179 in cash. Before the Yais were searched, they had repeatedly affirmed to Customs agents that they were not declaring more than $10,000 in currency. Yai later sent a letter to the Customs Service explaining that he and his wife had saved most of the money and had received some of it as gifts for their twenty-fifth wedding anniversary and had been saving for the special occasion for three to four years and that it was from gifts from children. According to the FBI, that claim was false. The Yais were returning from a trip to Austria and the Czech Republic. Before the trip Mr. Yai had received a coded fax that included the telephone and fax numbers for the North Korean embassy in Prague. The FBI reported that Yai met with North Korean representatives while in Prague and received payment for his reports.

The FBI also concluded that Yai traveled to North Korea on several occasions. He apparently made side trips during visits to China.

According to the Bureau, Yai did more than provide information to North Korean intelligence; he also recruited another American as an agent for Pyongyang. On December 1997, the FBI found a typewritten letter in Yai's office from a North Korean handler. The note stated, "It would be preferable that you find a student inside the church"; the word "church" was code for "Washington, D.C." The following March, the Bureau intercepted a fax from Yai in which he gave his progress report on the recruiting effort. In the fax, Yai stated that he had worked on recruiting someone "for a long time and anguished over it. There are two or three persons whom I have been working on for a while. In Mr. Won's [code for Yai's] opinion, the person has to possess a high quality presence; at least or higher than a U.S. university education, absolutely fluent in English and Korean, young with clear ideology, and has potential to work in the church." He concluded with good news: "I have successfully found an excellent, young high quality person who lacks nothing for becoming a student who has potential for a long range plan."

Over the next several days Yai sent two more faxes to provide more details on his recruit, who is identified only as "Person C" in the FBI affidavit. Yai wanted the recruit to visit headquarters, which he referred to as "pastor Peter" in one fax. "It is better to have the pastor give him the blessing himself, and then give him directions," Yai wrote. In another fax, he told the North Koreans that his "new student" was born in Seoul in 1969, spoke English well, was skilled in the use of computers, and had an ideology that "is beneficial and reliable to our causes."

In May of that year, hidden FBI microphones picked up a conversation between Yai and an associate, whom the affidavit identifies as Person L. Yai explained that "the long term plan is to hook him [Person C] up with his friends in Washington, D.C. who are going to school there." Person L asked if the recruit could get a job as a reporter in Washington, to which Yai replied, "Historically, for spies, if the head leaders fall, everyone falls also." He did not explain this cryptic remark, but it indicates that Yai saw himself as a spymaster for the North Koreans.

The recruit eventually did visit North Korea. On July 20, 1998, Yai sent another fax to North Korean headquarters, reporting on the recruit's reactions to the visit. "He indicated it was a valuable experience, although a nervous one," Yai wrote. "Disciple believes he had a precious experience at Mr. Kim's [code for headquarters]. It was obvious that he had a new outlook in life. . . . Disciple will do well. . . . I think you can trust disciple C. . . . He expressed in several versions how he is so eager to give every bit of effort for the revolutionary cause."

The recruit would best serve the "revolutionary cause" by someday infiltrating the U.S. government, of course.

Yai apparently tried to get at least one other person into the U.S.

government in order to feed secret information to the North Koreans. That individual was his coworker, Person L, whom Yai helped get a job with the Los Angeles district attorney's office. Yai hoped the job would be a stepping-stone to employment at the FBI, according to the Bureau. "They need Chinese speakers and people like me who can speak Korean," the unidentified coworker told Yai, in a conversation overheard by the FBI. "I heard people wait up to five years to be hired by the federal government. So I think I should apply to places in Washington, D.C. as soon as possible." She said that she was seeking employment at the Library of Congress as a researcher in Korean-American crime. "The office I am working for right now is a law enforcement office," she stated. "So I heard it is very easy for me to get hired by another law enforcement agency later on."

Interestingly, for all of Yai's apparent efforts to plant a North Korean spy in the U.S. government, it could turn out that he was the one being manipulated. The FBI spotted Person L getting into a car with South Korean diplomatic tags, meaning it was a car belonging to diplomats at the South Korean embassy and probably the National Intelligence Service. It is possible, then, that Person L was secretly working for South Korean intelligence.

Whether or not Person L was working for Seoul, North Korea clearly indicated in its communications with Yai that it was focused on obtaining top-secret information from inside the U.S. government. This is the most revealing part of the Yai case. On May 5, 1997, the North Korean agency sent a fax to Yai saying that the "company president" thought Yai "has made too many proposals about medicine that is already well known, and the types of goods are not varied enough." ("Medicine" is code for "source," in the sense of "basis of information.") North Korean officials wanted newer and better "medicines," specifically ones that were "a little more interesting and inexpensive"—codes for "undisclosed [not sold to public]" and "top secret," respectively. Another 1997 fax to Yai from North Korean headquarters stated that "it is important to work on medical proposals that are not known," while still another said,

"It was suggested that the items might not be accepted unless the items were inexpensive, interesting, and have a lot of variety."

Yai took the message to heart. In Yai's office, the FBI found notes handwritten in Korean saying, "Do not send anything that has been revealed in the newspaper or radio. (Engage in a lot of conversation with people above [connoting people of a higher rank], and things that we do not see in homeland.)" He also was overheard telling Person L that the North Koreans "are looking for things that are not public. They want about 100 or 150 reports a year. I finished about 160 last year."

Why was there such a premium on fresh information? Apparently the reports were being reviewed by more and more North Korean government officials, going up to the hierarchy of the Workers' Party of Korea. The FBI heard Yai telling Person L that North Korea had "increased the number of people in the analytical section. They are the ones who review the stuff and determine if they are new information or not." Under this system, Yai said, "even if they do not see them [the reports] in Beijing, they might see them in North Korea."

All this evidence pointed to one conclusion, according to the FBI: Yai was a North Korean agent. FBI agent Chang concluded the affidavit by stating, "Yai was working for the North Korean intelligence service, and not any other component of the North Korean government. The coded means of communication, the repeated travel to the homeland (or a closely allied country), the meetings abroad, the payments in cash, and Yai's description of the handling of the information in China and North Korea, are characteristic of an agent of an intelligence service."

Of course, Yai was able to plead guilty to the lesser charges of not reporting $18,179 to Customs. It seems Yai got off easy. Yai's lawyer, William Genego, argued in court that Yai was simply sending newspaper clippings to North Korea to compensate for the lack of free media and Internet access, but the FBI's extensive surveillance calls that defense into serious question.

The Yai case highlights the difficulty of dealing with foreign spies.

U.S. espionage laws require showing proof that a person who spied for a foreign power damaged the national security of the United States. That charge is difficult to prove in court, partly because, as mentioned, the evidence contains classified information. As often happens in spy cases, prosecutors were forced to seek lesser charges. Nonetheless, the case opens a window onto North Korea's aggressive intelligence activities, and reminds the United States why it must learn to counter the threat from Pyongyang.

David Szady, until 2006 the FBI's most senior counterintelligence official, said in an interview that if spies get off easy it is usually because of the complexities of prosecuting the cases in court. "It usually goes to issues of prosecution, DOJ [Department of Justice], everything from jury appeal . . . what are we trying to prove, can we prove it," he told me. Spies are getting "smarter and smarter," Szady remarked, and as a result prosecutors many times are forced to rely on easier-to-prove lesser charges such as failing to register as a foreign agent or conspiracy. "All of them, they're tricky cases," he said.

Nuclear Spying

Another North Korean spy case involved Jong-Hun Lee, an aerospace scientist who worked at the Johnson Space Center in Houston for a NASA contractor from 1990 to 1992. Lee, a Canadian citizen born in Japan, had previously worked for the NASA Ames Research Center in Mountain View, California.

Lee was a specialist in aerothermodynamics, the study of the physical effects of air flowing over vehicles, which is useful for missile research. The FBI had classified information indicating that he supplied missile-related data to the North Koreans. Several years later, in 1998, North Korea flight-tested its first long-range Taepodong-2 missile, which Pyongyang later claimed was a civilian space launcher. The CIA said it was a long-range missile capable of carrying a warhead to the United States.

The North Koreans triggered another crisis in July 2006 when they test-fired seven missiles, including the Taepodong-2, which is capable of reaching the United States. The test preparations had triggered the Pentagon's new Ground Base Interceptor missile defense system, which included nine interceptor missiles in Alaska and two in California. A senior government official told me at the time that shooting down the North Korean missile would be an option if it headed for U.S. or allied territory. As it happened, the Taepodong-2 launch failed forty-two seconds into flight, but the other missiles were fired off successfully in what Pentagon officials said was an impressive display of launch operations for the third-world Communist state. The United Nations Security Council passed a resolution condemning the launches, though China and Russia blocked efforts to impose sanctions against Pyongyang.

Suspicion surrounded Lee well before the 1998 missile launch. His brother lived in North Korea, and Lee had visited there around 1979 to attend his brother's wedding. He had also been in contact with scientists belonging to the General Association of Korean Residents in Japan, known as the Chosen Soren community. Japanese intelligence sources have described the Chosen Soren community, which is made up of ethnic North Koreans in Japan, as an overt North Korean intelligence-related organization that provides logistical assistance to Pyongyang. An underground element is directly linked to the Workers' Party of Korea; according to intelligence sources, an estimated 5,000 members engage in intelligence activities and political influence operations, and help obtain high technology for North Korean weapons programs. By investing in networks of Japanese pachinko parlors (pachinko is a Japanese form of pinball), the association has supplied the North Korean regime with between $600 million and $1.9 billion in hard currency.

Lee claimed that his last contact with the Chosen Soren scientists occurred in 1980 and that all the information he shared with them was in the public domain. But investigators believed otherwise. In 1992 NASA forced him out of his job because of his connections to the Chosen Soren.

In 1994, a federal immigration judge, after reviewing the FBI's evidence, declared Lee a national security threat and ordered him to be deported. Few details of the case have been made public, but in making his decision, the judge cited the fact that North Korea was developing nuclear weapons and noted that Lee had the technological expertise to help Pyongyang develop missiles that carry nuclear warheads. The judge stated that Lee's ties to the Chosen Soren were the issue, acknowledging that there was no direct evidence Lee was spying on behalf of North Korea.

But there was enough evidence to raise serious concerns. U.S. officials said that the judge was shown a report of a polygraph test the FBI gave Lee in 1985, when he was working at the NASA Ames Center. The report stated that "testing revealed deception" to several questions, including, "Are you connected in any way with any non-U.S. Intelligence Service?"

Canadian authorities gave Lee a security clearance and citizenship, Lee told authorities. He began working in the United States on a temporary work visa in 1990. FBI counterintelligence officials said that Lee had obtained a visa by mistake and, because of his North Korean connections, should never have been granted entry into the country.

U.S. officials believed that North Korea could pressure Lee to obtain further missile-related information by threatening his brother in North Korea. Lee denied the spying allegation. "Even under pressure from North Korea, how could I possibly get the information they need?" he said. "I never had any access to that kind of information." Lee claimed that the FBI had pressured him to become a double agent for the United States, and that he came under suspicion only because he refused the request. After his deportation, Lee eventually settled in Tokyo, telling the Associated Press that U.S. officials had "destroyed my career and my life without proper reason."

"Portfolio of Illicit Activities"

The North Korean regime represents a significant threat to the United States and its allies around the world not just because of its aggressive intelligence work and its nuclear weapons program. It also is one of the world's worst weapons proliferators, and it is tied up in illegal drug trafficking, counterfeiting foreign currency, money laundering, and illicit trade in sanctioned items.

The primary goal behind all these activities is the same: to provide an infusion of cash that the regime can invest in its military buildup, its intelligence structure, and its nuclear weapons program. And of course, those investments are linked by the same ultimate objective: to keep the Communist regime in power.

One U.S. official told me, "There's this whole portfolio of illicit activities which they [the North Koreans] engage in to support the regime." Another official said that the evidence of North Korea's dirty dealings is overwhelming, even though it must be pieced together from information from defectors and other intelligence. "You have this catalogue of information that starts to build up and you start to see a pattern develop," the official told me.

David L. Asher, who monitored North Korean criminal activity when working at the State Department, said that all this illicit activity makes North Korea a "*Soprano* state"— a reference to the cable television show about a New Jersey organized crime group. "North Korea is the only government in the world today that can be identified as being actively involved in directing crime as a central part of its national economic strategy and foreign policy," Asher said. The criminal activity provides hard currency for the Pyongyang regime, he reported.

The most threatening of these illegal activities is North Korea's covert arm sales. The transfer of dangerous weapons and related technology represents the most serious danger to U.S. national security today. John Bolton, the U.S. ambassador to the United Nations, has revealed in congressional testimony Pyongyang's indiscriminate arms selling. In 2003, Bolton, then the undersecretary of state for arms control and international security, told Congress that "the North Koreans are the largest sellers of ballistic missile technology to proliferant countries in the world." Bolton was absolutely right about North Korea's extensive arms proliferation, which I documented in detail in the book *Treachery.* According to Bolton, the North Koreans use the money generated from arms sales to "buttress their weapons of mass destruction programs, and, really, to help buttress the elite in North Korea." The earnings, he stressed, did nothing to relieve the "wretched and really horrible lives lived by the 22 million North Koreans who live in poverty."

The CIA official I spoke with told me that North Korea's arms sales are part of a long-range transfer of weapons and technology to Iran, Syria, Libya, Pakistan, and India. These transfers raise serious concerns about North Korea's own covert nuclear weapons program. "There is a fair amount of information, albeit fragmentary, to show that North Korea is and has been using other countries as subcontractors for essential research, especially on their nuclear program," the official said. Most analysts focus on known facilities in North Korea, like the Yongbyon nuclear facility, but "the North Koreans have intensified their use of surrogates and subcontractors to prevent being 'caught' with a smoking gun should the IAEA [International Atomic Energy Agency] and our national collection means discover continued nuclear testing and research going on inside North Korea."

The *Soprano* state also trades in sanctioned items such as conflict diamonds (gems that are traded from areas like Africa and are used to fund rebels), rhinoceros horn, and ivory. According to intelligence officials, the illicit trade in rhino horn produces hundreds of thousands of dollars for North Korea. The North Koreans pay poachers between $100 and $200 in states like Botswana to shoot a rhino and cut off its horn. They resell much of the horn to Yemeni traders who create elaborately jeweled handles for daggers called *jambiyas,* and grind up the rest into a powder to sell in Singapore, Hong Kong, and Macao. Officials told me that with an investment of a few hundred dollars to a poacher, the North Koreans can make as much as $400,000 from a single horn.

North Korean diplomats and intelligence personnel have been engaged in trafficking of heroin and methamphetamine to Russia, China, Japan, and other nations, according to North Korean government defectors. John Bolton also identified Pyongyang's role in the drug trade in his congressional testimony in 2003. Aside from North Korea's arms sales, Bolton said, the two most important "sources of hard currency earnings" for Pyongyang are illegal narcotics exports and dealings with Japanese organized criminal networks.

The North Koreans also make money by selling the right to fly their national flag to merchant shippers and commercial fishermen at three times the normal rate, often bringing in several hundred thousand dollars a year from each of the scores of ships that use the North Korean registry. The shippers prefer North Korean flagging because it often means not having to follow international regulations. They also avoid inspections from many nations' inspectors whose governments fear angering Pyongyang. In March 2006, the North Korean–flagged merchant vessel *Crystal* was stopped at a port in Europe and was found to be engaged in illegal immigrant smuggling. The owner was a U.S.-based company that is incorporated in Delaware. In May 2006, the Treasury Department's Office of Foreign Assets Control banned U.S. and U.S.-based companies from flagging their ships with the North Korean registry.

Another criminal activity North Korea has been responsible for is counterfeiting foreign currency, as the U.S. government confirmed with the arrest of Irish Communist leader Seán Garland. Garland, the head of the Irish Workers' Party—the Marxist-Leninist wing of the Irish Republican Army—was arrested in Belfast, Northern Ireland, on October 7, 2005. Garland and six others had been indicted the previous May for conspiring to buy more than $1 million in high-quality fake $100 bills, or "supernotes," from North Koreans. The indictment stated, "Quantities of the supernote were manufactured in, and under auspices of the government of, the Democratic People's Republic of Korea [North Korea]. Individuals, including North Korean nationals acting as ostensible government officials, engaged in the worldwide transportation, delivery, and sale of quantities of supernotes."

This marked the first time the federal government provided details of North Korea's counterfeiting of U.S. currency. The indictment was not made public until after Garland's arrest; U.S. officials told me that the government did not expose North Korea's counterfeiting until then because it did not want to undermine the six-party talks intended to convince the Communist regime to give up its covert nuclear weapons program.

But U.S. authorities had been investigating the counterfeiting for some sixteen years. The Communist regime is the world's only state producer of the supernote. One U.S. intelligence official told me that North Korea's counterfeit money, including counterfeit Japanese yen and European euros as well as American dollars, is produced at the Pyongsong Science and Research Institute, located about fifteen miles north of Pyongyang. According to U.S. law-enforcement officials, the North Korean government has produced at least $45 million in supernotes since 1989.

To thwart investigators, U.S. officials told me, Garland hid North Korea as the source of the counterfeit notes by limiting those with knowledge to a close circle of associates and telling others that the counterfeits were produced in Russia. As the Workers' Party leader, Garland made official party visits around the world to make arrangements for the supernote purchases.

Garland denied the charges in the indictment. After being set free on bail, however, he fled to the Republic of Ireland to avoid extradition to the United States. And U.S. investigators assembled a pile of evidence linking him to the North Koreans. Informants and electronic wiretaps showed that North Korea used its diplomatic outposts in Russia, Belarus, and Poland to provide the supernotes to Garland and his accomplices. For example, Garland reportedly met with North Korean intelligence officials in Warsaw in 1997 to buy a quantity of supernotes. And one official told me that in Moscow, surveillance revealed that Garland was "picked up by North Korean diplomats, by a North Korean limousine, and taken to the North Korean embassy."

Counterfeiting does not pose as obvious a threat as does arms sales, but it does hurt the United States. The use of fake notes, even a small amount, undermines the integrity of all U.S. money. "If people who use U.S. currency don't believe they can tell the difference between the counterfeit and genuine, all the currency becomes suspect," one law-enforcement official told me. "That's why it's very troubling."

David L. Asher cautions, "Under international law, counterfeiting another nation's currency is an act of casus belli, an act of economic war. No other government has engaged in this act against another government since the Nazis under Hitler."

Like Garland, North Korea's government immediately denied involvement in counterfeiting. The government-run Korean Central News Agency released a statement on October 21, 2005, in which it declared the Garland indictment to be part of a U.S. "smear campaign" against North Korea.

Of course, for decades the North Koreans had denied any involvement in the abduction of thirteen-year-old Megumi Yokota and other Japanese nationals as well. But that denial turned out to be false.

A Belated Admission

In 2002, only a month before U.S. official James Kelly's confrontation with North Korea over nuclear weapons, Pyongyang began holding a series of talks with Japan's government aimed at normalizing relations, which had been on ice since 1948. In one meeting, on September 17, Kim Jong-il dropped a diplomatic bombshell. He admitted to Japanese prime minister Junichiro Koizumi that North Korean government agents had abducted the missing Japanese nationals. At last the North Koreans had admitted what the Japanese suspected. A North Korean "organization with a special mission" had abducted thirteen Japanese from Japan and Europe, Kim told Koizumi, according to Japanese officials who briefed reporters after the meeting. The Japanese government hadn't even been aware that two of the people on the list had been abducted.

Kim Jong-il badly miscalculated in disclosing the kidnappings. He had hoped that by coming clean he would normalize ties with Japan and open the way for hundreds of millions of dollars in foreign aid. But the admission turned public opinion against North Korea like no other issue. Even North Korea's August 1998 firing of a long-range missile over Japanese territory did not create as much widespread anger toward the Communist state. Normalization was now out of the question. Despite Kim's apology and his claim that after he came to know about the abductions, "the persons responsible have been punished," North Korea failed to give Tokyo a full accounting of the matter and dealt deceptively in repatriating the abducted Japanese.

Particularly disturbing was North Korea's handling of Megumi Yokota. It remains unclear what happened to her since her 1977 abduction. After he defected in 1993, North Korean An Myong Jin told authorities in Japan and South Korea that he had seen Yokota in a suburb of Pyongyang on October 10, 1988. The North Koreans told the Japanese that Yokota had married and given birth to a daughter who lives in Pyongyang. Then in November 2004, North Korea returned what it said were her remains. But DNA analysis conducted by Japanese authorities revealed that the bones were not those of the abducted student.

Addressing the Threat

The intelligence unit of U.S. Forces Korea aptly summed up the threat from North Korea. In a statement, the intelligence unit told me, "North Korea poses a dangerous and complex threat to peace and security in the region and throughout the world. The Kim regime maintains a delicate balance of threats to ensure regime survival. They maintain a massive, offensively postured, conventional force that far exceeds the requirements to defend their country. Their continuing weapons of mass destruction programs constitute a substantial threat to Northeast Asia and the world. The Korean People's Army continues to invest heavily in military programs designed to offset our operational superiority. We see no indications the Kim regime will change its 'Military First' policy, brinkmanship, nuclear challenges, missile proliferation, and illegal activities that ensure regime survival. The North Korean people will continue to suffer under an oppressive regime. For the foreseeable future, North Korea remains a major challenge to security in Northeast Asia."

The pressing question for the United States and its allies is just how to deal with North Korea's rogue regime. The U.S. government has tried to resolve the problem diplomatically. Specifically, it focused on solving the nuclear weapons crisis through the six-party talks, refusing to engage the North Koreans in one-on-one negotiations. North Korea walked away from the talks in 2005 and demanded economic and political concessions from the United States before it would return.

The North Korean defector Kang Chol-Hwan warns that the United States cannot focus solely on the nuclear weapons issue, urgent as that problem is. "If the United States pressures North Korea only on the nuclear issue," he told me, "the North Korean government can utilize that to increase the level of anti-Americanism in the country." Kang explained that "Kim Jong-il does not intend to give up all the power he has, so there is no way this country will change by itself." In other words, North Korea will not make democratic reforms on its own. The problem is the system: "The whole country is focused on this one person [Kim], and unless the system changes, nothing will change."

The CIA official I interviewed agrees that U.S. efforts to resolve the problem of North Korea diplomatically will fail. "Take it to heart that Kim Jong-il is not at all gifted in foreign affairs, is totally psychocentric, and will stop at nothing to ensure that North Korea maintains its rightful place in the sun, according to his vision of the world," the official said. "This is [more] dangerous the longer it continues."

One way to deal with Kim and his Communist regime would be to buy him out. Such an arrangement occurred in 1986 with the ouster of Haitian dictator Jean-Claude "Baby Doc" Duvalier, who was forced into exile in France but was allowed to take more than $750 million in stolen funds. A similar ouster might work if Kim were offered exile and cash. Another option would be to engage him through South Korea and Japan in commercial contracts to place more emphasis on economic growth and the development of an entrepreneur class. This is the so-called McDonald's solution.

The U.S. government has taken some small steps to address the North Korean problem beyond engaging in the six-party nuclear

talks. In October 2005, Congress supported efforts to rid North
Korea of the Kim regime, passing the North Korea Human Rights
Act. This act called for more Korean-language radio broadcasts into
North Korea and funding for nongovernmental organizations to promote human rights, democracy, the rule of law, and the development
of a market economy. The act was mostly symbolic, though. More
needs to be done.

A full-scale war with North Korea remains a remote possibility.
But the closeness of Pyongyang's million-man army to South Korea,
and its missiles that can hit targets thousands of miles away, make
this the least attractive option. The fact that U.S. forces are engaged
in Iraq and Afghanistan would also make a war with North Korea
difficult to fight. Still, the Pentagon is building up its forces throughout Asia; the effectiveness of U.S. troops there will increase several-
fold by 2010. And the U.S. military has drafted a North Korean war
plan, known as Operation Plan 5027. The plan calls for preemptive
attacks on North Korean leaders in any conflict. U.S. intelligence
agencies have identified the top one hundred North Korean leaders
who would be key targets in any military operation against North
Korea. The main targets are Kim Jong-il and his immediate group of
Workers' Party advisers.

Though military action is an unlikely and undesirable option, the
United States cannot sit by as North Korea flouts international law
and endangers America and its allies. What is needed to bring down
the regime is a concerted international counterintelligence program
targeting North Korea's intelligence services, which play such a vital
role in maintaining Kim's hold on power.

The problem, of course, is that North Korea is a difficult intelligence target. Few American intelligence specialists know enough
about the North Korean mindset to bring about incremental failures
that will lead first to throwing the Kim regime out of alignment and
ultimately to its downfall from within, without a large-scale war. As
one intelligence official put it, "The North Koreans are still *the* hard
target out there. We can recruit a member of the inner circle in
Tehran with relative ease. We can get into Putin's office with some

difficulty. Getting inside the inner workings of Kim Jong-il is daunting to the extreme."

Part of the problem has been the bureaucratic mindset that has limited the U.S. intelligence ability to penetrate terrorist groups. If you go to the Olympics telling yourself that you will never win a medal, you are not likely to win one. But the United States must overcome this self-defeating mindset to deal with the pressing North Korean threat. As the CIA official said in our interview, North Korea is run as Kim's "personal fiefdom," which means that "we have to get in there and work on the levels of personal avarice and greed, mistrust, and cunning that enable Kim Jong-il to exercise total control."

The Essential Weapon

The North Korean problem can best be solved through a covert action and counterintelligence program that disrupts Kim's regime and ultimately leads to his ouster and a new, democratic North Korea.

This program must, first of all, vastly increase the intelligence database on North Korea, since no program aiming at regime change can succeed if it is not based on thorough knowledge of the system.

Because access to North Korea is so difficult, the initial phases of the program must target North Korean officials overseas. While only a small number of North Koreans are authorized to operate outside the country, these represent the best opportunity for reaching the extremely hierarchical leadership in Pyongyang, which is centered on Kim and his family. U.S. intelligence must find out who travels abroad and why; who is posted abroad for any length of time; who has specific missions abroad and what they are; what happens if they fail; what will happen to their families if they fail. Some officials of the Workers' Party of Korea and North Korean diplomats have defected, but not without great personal sacrifice. The CIA has not recruited any of these officials as agents in place, the ultimate objective.

North Korea has a diplomatic and intelligence presence in Europe, Africa, South Asia, and Latin America. Each mission has a small unit of security professionals who are not technically intelligence officers.

The security officials are usually tasked with preventing defections of mission personnel, or with rounding up recalcitrant North Koreans who have made mistakes or otherwise have failed in the regime's eyes. Overseas officials must also produce "loyalty payments"—payments they are required to make to Kim in order to continue living and working abroad. These officials are often caught selling drugs, passing counterfeit currency, or engaging in other black market trafficking.

U.S. intelligence generally considers recruiting overseas officials to be too difficult. That mindset has to change. These officials should be the focus of major recruitment efforts using all means, including financial incentives and appeals to nationalism. For example, if an overseas official falls behind in his loyalty payments to the North Korean regime, U.S. agents could offer to make up the payments in exchange for his cooperation. In one past case, a North Korean official posted overseas had become distraught after his son was killed in a car accident and North Korean officials refused to allow him to return the body to North Korea for burial (the ruling Workers' Party for some reason regarded the accident as an embarrassment). U.S. intelligence secretly arranged for the burial through a third country and then later "pitched" the North Korean to work for the United States in exchange for the family favor.

In some situations U.S. intelligence could carefully orchestrate matters so it appears that North Korean overseas officials have made mistakes against the regime, and then swoop in to offer to "help out." Since those who offend the Kim regime pay a steep price—often with their lives—North Korean officials would have strong incentive to cooperate. And most important, overseas officials can be convinced, despite a level of near-brainwashing by North Korean ideology, to abandon the brutal regime of Kim Jong-il.

The Workers' Party of Korea has a security apparatus of its own, responsible for enforcing party loyalty. The members of this security force often have direct access to Kim and are handpicked, thoroughly trained, and frequently tested to ensure their loyalty to the regime. They are often sent abroad; for example, their personnel carried out the 1987 KAL bombing over the Indian Ocean, and the bombing of the Rangoon leadership in 1983.

Party security officials are required to make a loyalty promise to Kim, in person, and failure is not an option for them. When they do make mistakes, they seek help from the CIA or the South Koreans. Some evidence indicates that a number of former North Korean party security officials, albeit low-level ones, simply dropped out of sight after making mistakes; they felt they could not return to North Korea. Such officials are potential sources and should be located. It is likely that some of these officials are providing help to human rights groups and defectors in South Korea.

Another special recruitment program should be aimed at North Korea's military intelligence (MI) unit. The MI is made up of special operations forces trained for war against South Korea, Japan, and to a lesser extent U.S. forces in East Asia. The unit also helps protect key military sites in North Korea and some of the primary villas used for leadership residences. MI personnel are involved in obtaining, covertly, Western military hardware and are found in organizations such as the Changgwang Credit Corporation, a military front company. These personnel, when posted abroad—usually to carry out a specific arms acquisition or sale—are excellent potential targets for U.S. counterintelligence. Money is very important to them. Their exposure to things "Western" also makes them vulnerable.

Diplomatically, North Korea has no real foreign service within its Ministry of Foreign Affairs. Those posted abroad are not appointed systematically or promoted through a traditional foreign service structure; most are picked by Kim himself. The CIA has recruited some overseas diplomats in the past, usually by identifying, through both traditional and technical operations, mistakes the diplomats made or ways they might be lured. But the recruiting has never been part of a focused operation of the sort the United States needs to put in place now.

Some recruitment targets are not posted abroad. A case in point is North Korea's Ministry of State Security, the agency most responsible for protecting North Korea against criminal activity. Officials of this ministry run the camps and gulags and are posted at every point of entry into the country. They protect the major government buildings and provide security to most government officials. As an intelligence and security organization, they are regarded more as cops—brutal, harsh, powerful—than intelligence officers. These officials should be targeted for recruitment as part of this regime-change program, precisely because of their role in maintaining and securing the Kim system.

As with any strategic or offensive counterintelligence program, this aggressive targeting of North Korea must involve stringent security procedures to ensure that the United States is not fed false information that will influence policy in the wrong direction. The risk of getting bad information is high in North Korea, simply because the United States does not know enough about how the Communist regime works, despite the fact that North Korea has been an enemy for more than fifty years, since the Korean War. A North Korean who is recruited and discovers that the people he is working for know almost nothing about North Korea will probably respond by feeding garbage to his handlers.

North Korea has not been a key intelligence target because budget and personnel have been sparse. U.S. Forces Korea and the Eighth Army have more dedicated intelligence and counterintelligence assets poised against North Korea than does the entire CIA. Thus the CIA's National Clandestine Service must create a core of officers specifically for this covert action and counterintelligence program. The officers must be steeped in North Korea. Technical intelligence operations can help fill the gaps in our knowledge. The more U.S. intelligence knows about North Korea, the better it will be able to gauge the information provided by recruited sources.

The United States cannot take a scattershot approach in trying to set up a covert-action and counterintelligence program. Covert-action rules require that programs be aligned with general public policy. Therefore it is important to connect this program to a long-term objective rather than simply looking for bits of intelligence, as has been done in the past. So the United States must connect the program to an end goal that can be publicly identified—changing the regime in Pyongyang.

Connecting the counterintelligence program to the goal of ousting the Kim regime will provide focus for recruitment and action. The world is beginning to understand the horror of the Kim regime, through defectors and escapees like Kang Chol-Hwan. The ruthless nature of North Korea's Communist state can no longer be ignored. And the U.S. intelligence community must step up to the challenge of burrowing deep within the North Korean system in order to undermine it.

Penetrating the enemy's services to cause disruptions and then cause a downfall—it's the same approach CIA master counterspy James Jesus Angleton once told me was the key to defeating Communist regimes in the Soviet Union, Eastern Europe, and elsewhere. Counterintelligence—the tool the United States largely abandoned years ago—is the essential weapon in the fight against this key member of the axis of evil.

Chapter 7

COUNTERiNG THE
TERRORiST THREAT

Al Qaeda, its affiliates and other terrorist groups have used official identification, uniforms, or vehicles to gain access to secure
areas in order to carry out attacks overseas.

*—Department of Homeland Security and FBI intelligence report on
preparations for the January 2005 presidential inauguration*

The fact that foreign agents have stolen America's most sensitive
secrets is frightening enough in itself, but it highlights an even
more serious danger—that terrorists will plant agents within the
U.S. government, too. As one senior American intelligence official
told me, "If the Cubans and Chinese can penetrate the heart of our
government, so can terrorists."

Ever since September 11, 2001, the U.S. government's national security priority has, of course, been tracking down terrorists. Shortly
after the 9/11 attacks, Congress issued a joint resolution authorizing
the president "to use all necessary and appropriate force against
those nations, organizations, or persons he determines planned, authorized, committed, or aided the terrorist attacks that occurred on
September 11, 2001, or harbored such organizations or persons, in
order to prevent any future acts of international terrorism against the
United States by such nations, organizations or persons."

Immediately it became clear that U.S. intelligence would play an essential role in the effort to protect the United States from further attack. There was only one problem: The U.S. intelligence community was woefully unprepared to penetrate the dark world of al Qaeda and other Islamist extremist organizations.

In particular, the United States had extremely limited capabilities when it came to human intelligence-gathering—the real stuff of spying. Sadly, these shortcomings remain five years after the attacks of September 11, 2001. U.S. intelligence agencies still have been unable to plant agents in or recruit them from inside the Islamist extremist organizations.

Congressman Peter Hoekstra, Michigan Republican and chairman of the House Permanent Select Committee on Intelligence, told me that many of the problems facing U.S. intelligence are a legacy of President Bill Clinton's administration. "It's ineffective in 2006 because it was gutted in 1996," Hoekstra said. In a period of five to seven years in the 1990s, the Clinton administration severely depleted U.S. human spying capabilities. A global network of CIA case officer training, which involved sending officers abroad to train in underdeveloped countries before sending them to major targets, was lost. Restrictive rules put in place by Clinton administration CIA Director John Deutch that prevented CIA officers from recruiting unsavory spies also hampered the agency, Hoekstra said. The rule led to wholesale layoffs of key sources around the world. "The message that sends is 'Who wants to do business with the United States?'" Hoekstra told me. "Some of these folks put their lives on the line to spy for the United States and then suddenly they get the message, 'Sorry, you're laid off. We don't do business with people like you.'"

Hoekstra said President Clinton damaged U.S. spying efforts further by telling U.S. intelligence that there should be "no risk" in certain nations. "Well, in humint [human intelligence] it's all about risk," Hoekstra told me. The congressman said he was briefed in 2000 on U.S. spying in key targets around the world and "it was pathetic" that there were so few human spying operations under way. "Clinton's stance was 'We don't want any incidents,' and the thing is if you don't want any incidents, you don't do anything, because in humint it's always high-risk and there's always the chance that something is going to go wrong."

President George W. Bush never publicly recognized the problems of U.S. intelligence caused by Clinton's policies. As a result, the president has paid a political price for serious intelligence shortcomings, Hoekstra said.

Indeed, the inability to conduct real intelligence operations against terrorists and terrorist organizations—which should be a major priority in the War on Terror—led to one of President Bush's most controversial decisions: to authorize the NSA, the top-secret electronic intelligence-gathering service, to take special measures to find al Qaeda cells in the United States and get into al Qaeda's decision-making chain of communications.

The controversy would explode years after 9/11.

Tracking al Qaeda

Why did the Bush administration turn to the NSA after the September 11 attacks? For starters, the FBI couldn't deliver the kind of human spying needed in the War on Terror. The Bureau increased its activities, but it had no way to actively investigate Islamist extremist networks linked to al Qaeda or other foreign terrorist groups.

Moreover, NSA had a proven track record within the U.S. intelligence community of providing the best and most important intelligence to policymakers. The agency was there in 1983 when a Soviet MiG fighter shot down a Korean Air jetliner that had strayed into Soviet airspace, killing all 269 passengers and crew. NSA listening posts in Japan recorded the pilot's report that "the target is destroyed," and it was played before the United Nations to prove that the attack was deliberate, albeit mistaken.

Soon after the attacks on the World Trade Center and Pentagon, President Bush and National Security Adviser Condoleezza Rice called on the NSA director, Air Force Lieutenant General Michael V. Hayden, who would later become CIA director. The administration was to begin a highly secret special access program (SAP) aimed at intercepting al Qaeda communications. Only about eight people were authorized to know about the operation, which used special satellites and ground stations to siphon off massive volumes of electronic communications from communications satellites and telecommunications switches located around the United States. The data were sifted for key words and especially for telephone numbers coming from the Middle East, where al Qaeda was active. The operation intercepted calls from cell phones, satellite phones, and land-line telephones that had been identified by foreign intelligence services as linked to al Qaeda or its shadowy support network. It also intercepted e-mail messages and culled them for intelligence on al Qaeda communications.

An NSA employee working within this small group decided the program violated the key rule that governs all NSA electronic eavesdroppers: U.S. Signals Intelligence Directive 18 (USSID 18). The directive —first issued in 1978 by NSA Director Vice Admiral Bobby Ray Inman and revised most recently in 1993—outlines NSA procedures governing electronic spying involving Americans or U.S. institutions. It is designed to protect Americans' Fourth Amendment right to be free from unreasonable government searches and seizures while still allowing the intelligence apparatus to collect foreign intelligence on spies and terrorists. According to the directive, which is partially classified, "intelligence operations and the protection of constitutional rights are not incompatible."

To protect the privacy of Americans, NSA is generally prohibited from collecting communications between Americans unless a court order is obtained from the court created under the Foreign Intelligence Surveillance Act of 1978 (FISA). The USSID 18 states that the FISA court must authorize "the intentional collection of the communications of a particular, known U.S. person who is in the United States, all wiretaps in the United States, the acquisition of certain radio communications where all parties to that communication are located in the United States, and the monitoring of information in which there is a reasonable expectation of privacy." In "certain limited circumstances," the directive states, the U.S. attorney general may provide authorization.

The NSA employee took the concerns about the SAP to a reporter for the *New York Times* in late 2004. After a year of discussion within the newspaper, including appeals from President Bush not to disclose the existence of the NSA intercept activity, the *Times* revealed the program on December 16, 2005. The sensational front-page report, quoting more than a dozen intelligence officials who apparently opposed the program, suggested that the warrantless intercept program was illegal because it had bypassed the FISA court.

Partisan opponents of the Bush administration seized on the disclosure. Democrats and several Republicans voiced concerns about the legality of the intercept program. Senator Jay Rockefeller, the highest-ranking Democrat on the Senate Intelligence Committee, released a July 2003 letter he had sent to Vice President Dick Cheney questioning the secret NSA program. He had stated in the letter that because of the secrecy surrounding the program, he was "unable to fully evaluate, much less endorse these activities." Rockefeller said he had received no reply from the White House on the letter.

Such complaints were exposed as raw politics by the fact that none of the critics called for the program to be ended.

The Bush administration's justification for the program was outlined in a letter to the House and Senate intelligence oversight committees from William E. Moschella, an assistant attorney general. Moschella stated that "the NSA intercepts certain international communications into and out of the United States of people linked to al Qaeda or an affiliated terrorist organization. The purpose of these intercepts is to establish an early warning system to detect and prevent another catastrophic terrorist attack on the United States."

Moschella argued that the president had constitutional authority to institute the intercept program, given that Article II of the Constitution makes the commander in chief responsible for protecting the nation from attack. He emphasized that Congress had recognized this constitutional authority in its joint resolution of September 18,

2001, which stated that the president "has authority under the Constitution to take action to deter and prevent acts of international terrorism against the United States." Moschella declared, "This constitutional authority includes the authority to order warrantless foreign intelligence surveillance within the United States, as all federal appellate courts, including at least four circuits, to have addressed the issue have concluded."

The letter also explained that the intercept program was consistent with FISA. Moschella argued that FISA contains an exemption for certain electronic surveillance authorized in other statutes. Congress's post-9/11 authorization to use force trumped the FISA court requirement, the administration argued. Moschella added that the intercept program played an essential role in protecting the nation from further attacks, and that it was necessary to work outside of the FISA court system to create an early-warning detection system. "FISA could not have provided the speed and agility required for the early warning detection system," he wrote. Moreover, the president could not seek legislation specifically authorizing the intercept program, because that "would have tipped off our enemies concerning our intelligence limitations and capabilities."

Though many members of Congress were now speaking out against the Bush administration for the intercept program, Moschella revealed that congressional leaders had been briefed on the program more than a dozen times since its launch. He also noted that the administration had reviewed and reauthorized the NSA program every forty-five days to make sure it was legal.

President Bush publicly defended the program. "The NSA program is an important program in protecting America," he said on January 1, 2006. "We're at war, and as commander-in-chief, I've got to use the resources at my disposal, within the law, to protect the American people. And that's what we're doing." The NSA spying "is one that listens to a few numbers, called from the outside of the United States and of known al Qaeda or affiliate people," he said. "In other words, the enemy is calling somebody and we want to know who they're calling and why."

Left unsaid in all the debate about the NSA intercepts was this key element: The Bush administration might not have needed to rely on the program so heavily, and risk infringing on civil liberties, if American counterintelligence were not so weak. The administration needed to take extraordinary measures to track down al Qaeda cells. And even those haven't done enough. Despite the communications intercepts program and increased FBI activity, U.S. intelligence has been unable to find any al Qaeda cells in the United States, although the group is believed to be planning future attacks.

The key to addressing the terrorist threat is to develop better counterintelligence techniques. The case of U.S. Army sergeant Asan Akbar, a Muslim terrorist, offers an important lesson in why that is, and why the United States must move swiftly to improve.

Under Attack

Asan Akbar was a thirty-two-year-old African-American soldier from Los Angeles who had graduated from the University of California–Davis with an engineering degree. He was also a Muslim who studied at the Masjid Bilal Islamic Center, a predominantly African-American mosque in South Central Los Angeles. Before he converted, he was known as Mark Fidel Kools.

He joined the U.S. Army in April 1998, surprising his friends. In March 2003, he was deployed with the 326th Engineering Battalion, part of the storied 101st Airborne Division based at Fort Campbell, Kentucky. He had been sent to Kuwait against the recommendations of some of his fellow enlisted men who recognized that as a Muslim, he posed a security risk to U.S. forces then preparing to go into Iraq to oust the regime of Iraqi dictator Saddam Hussein.

Sergeant 1st Class Daniel Kumm later testified during a hearing that Akbar was unable to lead soldiers. "I did not want him to deploy," Kumm said. "And if there was a job for him back in Fort Campbell, that is where I would prefer him to be." Kumm was overruled by senior officers. "I was told, 'You will take him. We need the numbers, and we need to take full strength into Kuwait and Iraq.'"

Soldiers who worked with Akbar said he was stressed in the weeks before the attack and had been seen walking aimlessly, talking to himself, and laughing for no apparent reason. He had had trouble sleeping and often walked in his sleep. He had been caught sleeping in training rooms and inside military vehicles.

Sergeant Billy George Rogers testified that Akbar had called him once at Fort Campbell asking if U.S. soldiers planned to "rape and plunder" Muslims in the Middle East. Rogers tried to disabuse Akbar of the notion. But it obviously had little effect.

At around 1 A.M. on March 23, 2003, days after the launch of military operations in Iraq, Akbar turned off the generator that ran security floodlights in Camp Pennsylvania, an American base camp twenty-five miles from the Iraqi border in Kuwait. Nine minutes later he took four grenades that he had stolen from a supply tent and rolled them into two tents where officers and senior enlisted soldiers slept. When the explosions and fire forced soldiers out of the tents, Akbar opened fired with his M-4 assault rifle. He shot Captain Christopher Scott Seifert in the back, killing him within minutes. Later, Air Force Major Gregg L. Stone would die from burns and shrapnel wounds. Fourteen other soldiers were wounded.

Soldiers initially believed they were under enemy attack. Only after the brigade initiated emergency accountability procedures did the Army realize Akbar was missing. A major found him hiding in a concrete bunker, overpowered him, and took him into custody. As he was being taken away, Akbar said, "You guys are coming into our countries and you're going to rape our women and kill our children."

Akbar's terrorist attack forced the Army to change the way it treated Muslims ordered into combat. In early April 2003, shortly after Akbar's attack, the DIA warned in a classified report that Akbar's action may not be an isolated incident and that American Muslims in the military should be considered a security risk regarding U.S. military operations in the Middle East. Military counterintelligence agencies launched an investigation into Muslim soldiers both in the Persian Gulf region and around the United States to determine whether there were other Asan Akbars who were preparing attacks. There were no other major attacks by Muslims in the armed forces in the next three years, but the incident forced the military to tighten its counterintelligence procedures against terrorist attack.

The real problem was that the military had put security aside in favor of political correctness. The armed forces view their soldiers, sailors, airmen, and Marines as Americans first, and they made no effort to single out any religious group. The problem was accentuated during the Clinton administration, which made so-called diversity a major component of all government agencies, including the military. Under this mandate, it was politically incorrect even to suspect that Muslims in the armed forces might be considered security risks. The military at the time of Akbar's attack had more than 4,100 Muslims.

Investigators said Akbar's fellow soldiers should have reported his predeployment behavior. The military's failure to detect any problem was yet another counterintelligence breakdown. And it cost two officers their lives.

The So-Called Moderate

Asan Akbar was not the Army's only counterintelligence failure. A Muslim radical linked to al Qaeda was another.

Abdurahman Alamoudi, an Eritrean-born naturalized American citizen, helped found the American Muslim Armed Forces and Veterans Affairs Council, one of two organizations the Defense Department designated to certify Muslim military chaplains. U.S. intelligence linked him to the other organization as well, the Islamic Society of North America. That group receives funding from Saudi Arabia and has set up a network of Wahhabi Islamic centers. Wahhabism is the militant strain of Islam that condones the use of violence to propagate the faith; numerous al Qaeda terrorists subscribe to it.

In July 2004, Alamoudi pleaded guilty to three criminal offenses, including concealing hundreds of thousands of dollars he had received from Libya. That money was intended to support al Qaeda and other terrorist activities, investigators concluded. Court papers in the case reveal that Alamoudi conspired with Libyan government officials in a plot to assassinate Saudi Arabian leader Crown Prince Abdullah, who had argued with Libyan leader Muammar Qaddafi at an Arab summit meeting in Sharm el Sheik, Egypt. Alamoudi received nearly $1 million from the Libyans; the assassination was to be carried out by Saudi dissidents based in London, according to court records.

New intelligence information surfaced after Alamoudi's plea bargain that identified him as a major al Qaeda financer. In a statement issued on July 14, 2005—just days after the London subway bombings—the U.S. Treasury Department revealed that Alamoudi had given approximately $1 million to a British-based Saudi opposition group that had close ties to al Qaeda. According to Treasury, the Movement for Islamic Reform in Arabia (MIRA) provided ideological and operational support to al Qaeda–affiliated networks, and the MIRA website had posted messages from al Qaeda leaders Osama bin Laden and Abu Musab al-Zarqawi. According to the Treasury statement, "the September 2003 arrest of Alamoudi was a severe blow to al Qaeda, as Alamoudi had a close relationship with al Qaeda and had raised money for al Qaeda in the United States."

How had the U.S. government failed to recognize Alamoudi's al Qaeda connections, which dated back to the mid-1990s? Not only had the U.S. armed forces trusted him with the Muslim chaplain program, but as director of the American Muslim Council he had met with top FBI and U.S. government officials, and had even sat in on White House meetings. Alamoudi was viewed as a moderate because for years he had encouraged Muslims to be more involved in U.S. politics and society. He had also denounced the September 11 terrorist attacks.

It was good cover—a cover the FBI and CIA didn't pierce because they did not have a strong counterintelligence program to investigate extremist Muslims. Even today, the intelligence approach remains passive.

Radicals in the Ranks

A senior Army official told me that the mindset allowing Alamoudi such access to the U.S. government and military is pervasive. The

Muslim chaplain program was a major security failure, the official said. The problem began a decade before the 9/11 attacks, when the U.S. military invited Saudi clerics to preach Wahhabi Islam to large numbers of American soldiers based in Saudi Arabia after the 1991 Persian Gulf War. As a result, as many as 3,000 U.S. soldiers converted to Islam in a short period of time.

Such programs in all likelihood have enabled radicals to infiltrate the armed forces, the Army official told me. One military officer who converted to Islam in the early 1990s, Army Captain James Yee, came under suspicion for terrorist links. Yee was charged with espionage, accused of passing secrets to al Qaeda from inmates held at the military prison in Guantánamo Bay, Cuba. He was himself a chaplain who worked with inmates. Yee was later found to be innocent. He had aroused suspicion because he allegedly showed feelings in support of the captives.

Court documents showed that another soldier, Air Force Senior Airman Ahmad I. Halabi, an Arabic translator, opposed the holding of prisoners at Guantánamo and U.S. policy in the Middle East. Halabi, a Syrian-American who worked as an Arabic translator at Guantánamo, was accused of trying to deliver written messages from Guantánamo prisoners to an unidentified Syrian. He eventually agreed to a plea deal in which the spying charges were dropped. The senior airman admitted to taking two photographs in Guantánamo, wrongfully transporting a classified document to his living quarters, lying about taking photographs, and conduct prejudicial to military discipline.

Another translator, Ahmad F. Mehalba, was arrested in 2003 after he returned from a trip to Egypt carrying classified information on a computer disk. In 2005, Mehalba, an Egyptian-born U.S. citizen, pleaded guilty to unauthorized possession of classified material and lying to federal investigators.

These and other cases have raised concerns that Muslims may place loyalty to their coreligionists above loyalty to their country. The Akbar case, in particular, has led officials to worry that some Muslims will not take up arms against other Muslims, or in fact may feel compelled to assist Muslim extremists. More troubling is the belief that al Qaeda is recruiting American Muslims to its cause.

Such concerns raise the question of how the U.S. military should approach Muslims. Officially, the armed forces treat Muslims equally. But after the Akbar and Alamoudi cases, military officials suspect that there is an enemy within. "Who knows when a moderate Muslim decides to become radicalized or is a plant?" the senior Army official told me.

The concern is not misplaced. At least one known al Qaeda member has served in the U.S. Army. Ali Mohamed reached the rank of sergeant in the Special Forces. In 2000, he pleaded guilty to conspiracy charges related to the 1998 embassy bombings in Kenya and Tanzania; he admitted to helping Osama bin Laden plan the attacks.

The potential problems resulting from having Muslims in the ranks are not confined to the armed forces. Counterintelligence experts worry especially about U.S. national security officials who receive security clearances. For example, the U.S. government has hired a large number of Arabic translators in recent years. After the September 11 terrorist attacks and through the military operations in Afghanistan and Iraq, both the FBI and the Defense Department set up translation centers to work through the hundreds of thousands of pages of Arabic-language documents obtained from the Middle East and South Asia. The need for translators was so desperate that, according to one U.S. military enlisted soldier, the government had no vetting process to speak of. In many cases, Arab immigrants were given quick, interim security clearances without benefit of background checks. In at least one case, a translator had ties to Muslim extremists in Pakistan. "They were hiring cab drivers in Washington, D.C., who spoke Arabic with almost no vetting procedures," the soldier told me.

The senior Army official I interviewed argued that Alamoudi was able to penetrate the U.S. military because the Army, as an institution, "was not culturally aware." The lack of awareness when it comes to Muslim teaching and culture is a point that U.S. intelligence officials have made repeatedly. For example, one military intelligence report, produced by the United States National Intelligence Cell in

Sarajevo, Bosnia-Herzegovina, stated, "Intelligence operations and law enforcement investigations requiring the cooperation of Muslims will encounter theological, legal, and cultural obstacles. The source of this conflict is the difference between two cultures. The Western culture recognizes the separation between church and state; Islam does not. When a Muslim is called upon by a non-Islamic government to participate in an investigation against other Muslims, he is being called upon to betray his values."

Islamic scholars also say that Muslims "should lie to people of the book [Christians and Jews] to protect their lives and religion," the intelligence report noted. This authority has implications for Islamic press reporting and a wide range of other activities. In addition, Muslims are permitted to deny Islam to escape punishment from nonbelievers who are their captors. That has implications for trusting double agents, a key tool used by counterintelligence agencies. According to the intelligence report, too, Muslims are permitted to lie and deceive "as a subterfuge to gain acceptance by nonbelievers for the purposes of cover for assassination and covert operations."

The report concluded that the use of two moral standards, one for Muslims and one for non-Muslims, poses unique challenges for intelligence specialists. "The analyst seeking accuracy and truth from Muslim sources on sensitive Islamic issues may be confronted with an Islamic mandate to conceal, lie, and mislead," the report said. "The analyst should be aware that Islam jealously protects its flaws and, that when pursuing subjects potentially embarrassing or uncomfortable to Islam or Muslims, the analyst must take the additional analytical step of double-vetting or double-checking his sources. Failure to do so surrenders the strategic initiative to the target of analytical inquiry and the analyst risks incorporating flawed information from deliberately deceptive sources."

The FBI's Failure to Reform

The United States has experienced numerous counterintelligence failures in recent years, but no failure would be greater than one that allowed Islamic terrorists to penetrate the upper reaches of the U.S. government, military, or intelligence community. The government has finally taken some steps to counter the threat of penetration. The case of Ana Belen Montes, a Cuban spy in the Defense Intelligence Agency (who is discussed in the next chapter), awakened the Pentagon to the fact that the United States remains basically defenseless against foreign spies.

In February 2002, responding to the Montes case, the Defense Department set up the Counterintelligence Field Activity (CIFA). Just days before leaving office, President Clinton had signed an executive order to reorganize counterintelligence with the aim of identifying, understanding, prioritizing, and counteracting the intelligence threats. The emphasis, according to a White House fact sheet, was to be "predictive, proactive" and to "provide integrated oversight of counterintelligence issues across the national security agencies." The Bush administration created CIFA in order to coordinate all this counterintelligence activity across numerous agencies and departments. The idea was to detect and neutralize espionage in order to protect critical personnel, resources, critical information, research-and-development programs, technology, and so forth.

Unfortunately, CIFA was doomed from the start. It had no direct operational authority and could not conduct the operations needed to stop spies and terrorists. The organization was limited to being a "principal adviser" on operations and policy—shorthand for being another bureaucratic layer over a number of counterintelligence agencies that had direct authority to go after spies and terrorists. Without operational power, CIFA became another cog in the bureaucratic wheel of intelligence and counterintelligence agencies.

By 2005, the Bush administration had recognized CIFA's limits and had given the agency a greater role to investigate crimes such as treason, foreign or terrorist sabotage, and economic espionage. The Pentagon sought changes in intelligence law to allow the FBI and others to share information on U.S. citizens with the Pentagon, the CIA, and other intelligence agencies. The goal was to better arm the services to deal with terrorism and the spread of weapons of mass destruction. Much like the NSA intercept program, however, this initiative raised the ire of civil liberties advocates. The Pentagon defended the changes, with a spokesman saying, "In the age of terrorism, the U.S. military and its facilities are targets, and we have to be prepared within our authorities to defend them before something happens." But ultimately the effort was blocked by government officials who opposed strong counterintelligence measures.

The Defense Department has made other moves to shore up U.S. defenses against spying. The Pentagon set up two intelligence centers under the newly created U.S. Northern Command, or Northcom. These centers, which house some 290 analysts in Colorado and Texas, pull together reports from CIFA, the FBI, and other intelligence agencies.

Beyond that, the military intelligence and security services have begun gathering data on possible terrorist attacks on military facilities. For example, the Air Force Office of Special Investigations set up Eagle Eyes, which calls on service members to report information.

The Pentagon has sought all these changes primarily because the FBI has shown itself to be totally incapable of conducting counterintelligence and counterterrorism operations successfully.

The FBI guidelines for national security investigations, those related to both terrorism and foreign spying, are contained in a secret order signed by Attorney General John Ashcroft in October 2003. The order authorized the FBI to "conduct investigations to obtain information" related to international terrorism, foreign espionage and intelligence, foreign computer intrusions, and other activities not spelled out. Additionally, the FBI was authorized to collect foreign intelligence and assist U.S. intelligence agencies in conducting strategic analysis. Reversing earlier restrictions that prohibited the FBI from even gathering newspaper clippings on suspected domestic terrorist groups, the guidelines also allowed the FBI to "retain and disseminate" information it gathers.

Noticeably, the guidelines contained no reference to domestic intelligence collection. The Bureau's law-enforcement culture vehemently

opposed any domestic intelligence role for the FBI. Bureaucrats in the
FBI viewed intelligence work as too difficult and only wanted to conduct activities, like arresting criminals, that could provide them with
measurable results.

The guidelines also contained a loophole for terrorists or spies. It
barred the FBI from spying on U.S. "persons" solely for the purpose
of monitoring activities protected by the First Amendment or other
rights in the Constitution or other U.S. laws. So all a terrorist or foreign intelligence operative needs to do to avoid investigation is to use
some type of cover related to protected legal actions, such as that of
a news reporter.

The new guidelines were intended to remedy FBI weaknesses in
countering terrorists, which had been exacerbated during the Clinton
administration. Under FBI Director Louis Freeh, experienced counterintelligence specialists were forced into retirement and some of the
best-trained officials were relegated to menial tasks such as conducting background checks. Freeh and his key aides considered intelligence something that the CIA did. He believed it was the job of
the G-men to catch bank robbers and other criminals. Terrorism was
looked at as simply another type of crime. The FBI emphasized
catching terrorists after they attacked rather than stopping them before they could strike.

That all changed after the September 11 attacks. The new guidelines were meant to "change from a reactive orientation to an orientation emphasizing early intervention and prevention of terrorist acts
before they occur," a fact sheet released by the Justice Department
stated. "The guidelines," the statement said, "are intended to allow
the FBI to use all lawful investigative techniques to protect the American people from international terrorism and espionage." For instance, the reoriented FBI would provide threat assessments, meaning
that the Bureau would now focus on trying "to identify terrorist
threats and activities" instead of "waiting for leads to come in
through the actions of others."

The new guidelines did not have their intended effect, however.

One problem was that bureaucrats within the FBI opposed the move toward more aggressive counterterrorism and counterintelligence investigations.

David Szady, the FBI's senior counterintelligence official, lamented the Bureau's problems with counterterrorism and counterspying in a candid speech he gave to a group of private and government security officials in May 2002. Szady noted that counterterrorism and counterintelligence go hand in hand—"you can't separate the two anymore." He explained: "Prior to every terrorist act there's an intelligence operation. The expertise that we have in intelligence operations can be used in working terrorism threats also. We need to put our resources together to do that." Unfortunately, he revealed, the FBI had no joint counterintelligence task forces. Meanwhile, the Bureau had established special Joint Counterterrorism Task Forces in all of its fifty-six field offices. There wasn't enough work to go around for the counterterrorism task forces, simply because the FBI wasn't set up to do the kind of investigative work necessary to find terrorists. The Bureau was relegated to sending paid informants into mosques to conduct "walk-arounds," looking for Muslims who might be terrorists.

Another problem is that the FBI never bothered to change its training to teach agents how to be intelligence collectors. Szady disclosed that agents receive only sixteen hours of training in counterintelligence during sixteen weeks' training at the FBI Academy in Quantico, Virginia. Szady proposed beefing up counterintelligence training to last four weeks and to include instruction in such techniques as recruiting informants, running double-agent operations, and working with the FISA court.

Szady opposed suggestions to strip the FBI of its counterintelligence role and create a separate agency, but he said he understood the motivation behind that proposal. "The issue is that people are thinking that way because they feel at times the FBI is not taking counterintelligence seriously," he said. He vowed that the FBI was going to reform, that training would change, and that the focus would shift.

Szady also proclaimed that the Bureau would do away with the incompetence that had characterized the Wen Ho Lee spy case. "We're never again going to have a case happen like the Lee case," Szady said. "What we did there and what we didn't do. You can't have incompetent agents working a case with incompetent or inexperienced supervisors with unengaged executive management and with inexperience and incompetence at headquarters. Those are formulas for disasters." He even said that he had told FBI Director Robert Mueller, "If I'm going to get fired and that's okay, you can fire me, but I want to have my hands in the reason I got fired. I want to fire myself. I don't want somebody I never heard of working the case do something that causes me to get fired."

Of course, as we saw in Chapter 1, Szady himself was involved in the problems that plagued the Katrina Leung case. When it came to Katrina Leung and J. J. Smith and his old friend Bill Cleveland, Szady, who took part in assessing the damage for the FBI, appeared to look the other way. His hands were in it from the beginning to the end. And he was never held accountable for the obvious conflict of interest.

That is emblematic of the FBI's overall failures in recent years. Despite Szady's claim in 2002 that the FBI had gotten "serious" about counterintelligence and counterterrorism, nothing changed. The FBI resisted. The law-enforcement mindset was too strong among the top FBI officials, including FBI Director Mueller.

It would take a presidential commission to begin to change the way the Bureau did business—and even then, the FBI bureaucrats continued to resist reform.

"The FBI Is Out of Control"

The Commission on the Intelligence Capabilities of the United States Regarding Weapons of Mass Destruction (commonly referred to as the WMD Commission) was organized in 2004, in the aftermath of Operation Iraqi Freedom. The presidential commission, headed by federal appeals court judge Laurence Silberman and former senator Charles Robb, Virginia Democrat, examined how and why the U.S. intelligence community failed to properly assess Iraq's nuclear, chemical, biological, and missile weapons programs. The panel also looked beyond the Iraq case to explore the overall capabilities of U.S. spy agencies. And it revealed just how inept the FBI had been in conducting counterintelligence and counterterrorism programs.

The WMD Commission's report, issued in March 2005, included a section on "intelligence at home." It said that the FBI had made some strides in becoming true collectors and analysts of intelligence but still had "a long way to go." Though FBI officials had trumpeted the creation of fifty-six Field Intelligence Groups, the commission's report said that the FBI had acknowledged that its intelligence-gathering capabilities "will be a work in progress until at least 2010." In other words, the United States will have no adequate domestic intelligence capability until nearly a decade after the September 11 attacks.

Unlike the 9/11 Commission, which had issued its report in the summer of 2004, the WMD Commission was not influenced by the FBI. Bureau officials had lobbied the 9/11 Commission not to recommend changes, preferring to continue operating how they pleased. Thus, despite the fact that FBI intelligence failures were the main contributing factors to the September 11 attacks, the 9/11 Commission made very few recommendations for improving FBI intelligence capabilities against terrorism. The WMD Commission, in contrast, offered hard-hitting criticisms of FBI intelligence capabilities and serious recommendations for reform.

But it was not as if the FBI didn't try to influence the WMD Commission as it had the 9/11 panel. In fact, the Bureau was caught attempting to plant an agent inside the commission to steal information and influence the panel's work. Apparently the FBI has no problem with domestic spying as long as it involves spying on its intragovernment enemies, not foreign terrorists and spies.

The female FBI agent, whom commission officials did not identify by name, was fired from the panel in late 2004. She had improperly removed from a secure vault a highly classified CIA report produced for the panel that criticized the FBI for its failures on weapons-related intelligence gathering. When Szady, the senior FBI counterintelligence officer, called the commission to complain about the CIA report, the panel investigated to learn how he had gotten hold of the document. The investigation led to the female agent. The woman admitted removing the report and was dismissed with a recommendation from the commission that she also be fired from the FBI. But the FBI took no disciplinary action and simply reassigned her to another post within the Bureau. This decision indicated that senior FBI officials approved of her actions. Responding to the incident, one government intelligence official told me, "The FBI is out of control."

The WMD Commission's report made no mention of the covert action by the FBI agent. Still, it proved highly critical of the FBI's intelligence deficiencies. The report noted that the "biggest challenge" was making the FBI part of the intelligence community. "This is not just a matter of giving the Bureau new resources and new authority," the report said. "It must also mean integrating the FBI into a community that is subject to the [Director of National Intelligence's] coordination and leadership."

In response to the 9/11 Commission, the FBI had created an intelligence-analysis division within its headquarters, but it made sure that the division had no authority to tell special agents what to do. The WMD Commission exposed the emptiness of this reform. "Currently the directorate has no authority to initiate, terminate, or re-direct any collection or investigative operation in any of the FBI's 56 regional field offices that are scattered throughout the nation or within any of the four operational divisions (Counterintelligence, Counterterrorism, Cyber, and Criminal) at FBI Headquarters," the report said. Without direct authority, tasking agents were doing nothing more than "asking," the report pointed out. The commission thus called for the creation of a National Security Service that could fully manage, direct, and control all FBI resources used in countering terrorists, spies, and other threats to U.S. national security.

The report highlighted other FBI failures. For example, it called for breaking down the bureaucratic wall between foreign intelligence and domestic law enforcement, which had helped the September 11 terrorists avoid detection and capture. And it declared that the FBI needed to move past its decades-old, bitter rivalry with the CIA, which was preventing the agencies from complementing each other's efforts in the War on Terror.

A bigger-picture problem remained, the WMD Commission noted: an FBI culture that resisted reform. "Past efforts to build a strong intelligence capability within the FBI have foundered on this resistance," the report said. "In 1998 and 1999, similar reforms failed in quick succession as a result of strong resistance from the FBI's operational divisions and an intelligence architecture that could not defend itself inside the bureaucracy." The law-enforcement investigators did not want to become spies. They argued that "bin Laden is never going to Des Moines."

Sure enough, the FBI fought the WMD Commission's reform recommendations. Most notably, FBI Director Mueller argued, at meetings of the National Security Council, against the proposal of a National Security Service. He said the FBI did not need a new service and he was opposed to anything remotely resembling Britain's MI-5 security service. Mueller even persuaded Attorney General Alberto Gonzalez to oppose the new service, a move that upset some national security officials at the White House. They had expected Gonzalez to support the president, since he had been the White House counsel before moving to the Justice Department.

President Bush overruled Mueller and Gonzalez, and on July 11, 2005, during a speech at the FBI Academy in Quantico, he announced the creation of the National Security Service within the FBI. He said it would "more completely integrate the Bureau's work with the intelligence community" and would make the FBI "more capable to stop the terrorist acts before they happen."

Even after the president's announcement, the FBI continued to resist. It finally relented in September 2005, creating what it now calls the National Security Branch (NSB), combining the counterterrorism, counterintelligence, and intelligence-analysis divisions in one section. Gary Bald, the FBI's executive assistant director for counterterrorism and counterintelligence, was appointed the new director. Bald was a career law-enforcement investigator with little intelligence experience. His selection was a clear sign that the FBI would oppose building a tough, aggressive counterterrorism and counterspy capability.

Bald told me in an interview that the FBI had embraced the new service and was working to make it successful. He said a substantial number of the 12,000 FBI special agents were working for the service, although the actual number remains classified. All of the 1,720 intelligence analysts are part of the NSB. Bald bristled at the suggestion that the FBI opposed reform and had a cultural aversion to improving its intelligence-gathering capability. "When you talk about the culture of the FBI when you're talking to an FBI agent, it's a culture of complete dedication to our mission, working around the clock, being called in on weekends and nights and not getting paid extra, and really doing everything you can to protect our nation. That is internally what we refer to as our culture." He also highlighted new initiatives the FBI had undertaken, such as the Investigative Data Warehouse (IDW). The IDW, which he called the "backbone" for FBI investigations, replaced the Bureau's failed case-management computer system, known as the Virtual Case File, which had been scrapped after costing the taxpayers $170 million.

Still, Bald acknowledged the FBI's opposition to the NSB, telling me that the new service "was not something that was an original thought within the Bureau." That was a remarkable admission. Bald also admitted that not everybody in the FBI supported the reforms. "The focus of what we're doing has changed over our history a number of times," he said. The NSB, he indicated, was simply the latest in a series of priority changes imposed on an unwilling FBI. "This is the most significant, no doubt. But it's just the latest." Bald said that as in any large organization "you aren't going to have every single person in the organization happy about it."

He voiced other concerns about the NSB. Specifically, he said the problem came in getting the FBI to change its institutional viewpoint that the Bureau is its own "primary customer of information." He said he feared what would happen if sensitive FBI investigative information leaked out and damaged the reputations of people under investigation who may be found to have done nothing wrong. "Now what we're in is a realization that not only are there other services that benefit from our intelligence, but other services can provide value to our investigations as well, intelligence and law-enforcement investigations," Bald said. "We understand that. The challenge is developing the processes that make that efficient, and the technology challenges that we've had, and in the training aspect of it and in hiring reports officers; that is new to us. . . . It's not the embracing or the understanding of the need to do it, it's getting us efficient at something that we've not had a long experience at doing."

The fact that the person in charge of the NSB had doubts about its mission was a clear sign that it would not be successful.

Vulnerabilities

As the Iraq War began in March 2003, FBI Director Robert Mueller said in a press release that the FBI had put in place "extraordinary measures" to stop terrorism during the war. "We are bringing to bear the full weight of our resources, expertise, and partnerships. We are running down every lead, responding to every threat, coordinating with every partner, and doing our utmost to keep terrorists from striking back. . . . The FBI is working around-the-clock to protect this nation—gathering intelligence, quickly investigating tips and leads, and taking actions against those who may do us harm. Every agent and every resource necessary has been put into service."

The reality, however, was different.

By the spring of 2006, the FBI did not have under way a single active investigation of al Qaeda or another Islamist extremist terrorist group anywhere in the United States. Al Qaeda is not the only threat in the United States. The FBI believes that the Lebanese-based Hezbollah has terrorist cells in at least ten U.S. cities. The Iranian government has backed Hezbollah to the tune of $100 million. John Miller, the FBI's assistant director for public affairs, told me that the Bureau is concerned that Iran could activate a network of Hezbollah terrorists in the United States if the international community takes action to stop the Iranian nuclear program.

As described in the Introduction, counterintelligence reform also foundered within the new Office of the Director of National Intelligence (ODNI), which was set up in the aftermath of the September 11 and Iraq weapons-of-mass-destruction failures. The National Counterintelligence Office was subsumed into the ODNI in 2005, but its functions and powers remained limited. Two top officials of the National Counterintelligence Office, Director Michelle Van Cleave and Deputy Director Kenneth deGraffenreid, left in quick succession. Van Cleave and deGraffenreid had great hopes for the National Counterintelligence Office and the new national strategy for counterintelligence they'd drawn up. But even with the newly empowered office and a presidential strategy document, they could not implement tougher counterintelligence. Opposition within the national security bureaucracy won out.

The new ODNI quickly became dominated by State Department officials with little intelligence experience. Congressman Peter Hoekstra, the House intelligence committee chairman, has noted that when they answer the phone at the office of the Director of National Intelligence, former ambassador John Negroponte, it is "Ambassador Negroponte's office"—not "Director Negroponte," as the top intelligence official should be called.

The intelligence officials who were detailed to the ODNI were many of the same people who had botched the Aldrich Ames case. One of them, Mary Margaret Graham, was head of the CIA Counterintelligence Center before being appointed as a senior intelligence collection official under Negroponte. Graham opposed Van Cleave's aggressive, independent counterintelligence program, favoring instead a program that would be limited to checking the reliability of recruited agents.

Counterintelligence, or a lack of it, has made the jobs of our armed forces more difficult in the War on Terror. The problem is that in many cases the military services themselves have woefully inadequate counterintelligence. For example, U.S. Army Special Forces, which have been called upon to lead the effort in Afghanistan, have experienced major intelligence failures. According to U.S. officials,

Afghans working as cleaners, construction workers, and interpreters
on U.S. military bases stole classified information on small computer
flash drives and walked right out the front gates with it. The stolen
material included secret intelligence reports disclosing how the U.S.
military searches for members of the Taliban, al Qaeda, and other
terrorist organizations operating on the Afghan-Pakistani border, as
well as documents revealing the identities of U.S. military personnel
working in Afghanistan, assessments of targets, descriptions of American bases and their defenses, and U.S. efforts to limit the activities of
certain Afghan government officials. A *Los Angeles Times* reporter
discovered the flash drives for sale and alerted U.S. authorities in
spring 2006.

These compromises had a devastating effect. Less than a week
after the data showed up in Afghanistan, authorities in Pakistan
came across a gruesome discovery: the beheaded body of a man in
the village of Manzarkhel. Next to the corpse was a note that said the
man had been a spy for the U.S. military in Afghanistan and warned
that anyone working with the United States would meet the same
end. According to U.S. officials, more than one hundred people in the
same area, including tribal elders, had been killed after they were accused of spying for the United States or supporting the Pakistani government. Without good counterintelligence, recruiting agents and
supporters in local populations who can provide information on terrorists will be nearly impossible.

The lack of counterintelligence has also exacerbated the problem
of bringing stability to post-Saddam Iraq.

Defense Secretary Donald H. Rumsfeld has noted the difficulty of
ferreting out terrorists and insurgents in the Iraqi government and
armed forces. "You start an intake that enables you to go from zero
to 131,000 Iraqi security people in a matter of four or five or six
months, you've got to know that some of those folks you're ultimately not going to want in there," he said during a visit to South
Korea in November 2003. Rumsfeld said the Iraqis were being
checked through a database and by public vetting—for example, an-
nouncing that an Iraqi has been appointed to a certain position and

seeing whether any derogatory information surfaces about past connections to the Ba'ath Party in Iraq or terrorists.

A senior military officer who took part in setting up the Iraqi security forces told me that preventing enemy agents from infiltrating the forces proved challenging. In some cases Islamist extremists or former members of Saddam Hussein's regime got jobs within the military and government system simply by paying bribes to Iraqi officials. Many times the cover was that an Iraqi was simply trying to get a relative a job. The Iraqi police proved to be a big challenge because the hiring of police in late 2004 was done so rapidly. The senior officer told me that, using documents recovered from the Saddam regime, the United States had uncovered more than one hundred enemy agents trying to get positions in the Iraqi police. The question remains: How many enemy agents—from the former regime, from Iranian intelligence, and from the terrorist network led by Abu Musab al-Zarqawi—got inside the organization? U.S. and Iraqi military and intelligence forces scored a major success in June 2006 when they tracked and bombed Zarqawi. In the process, they uncovered what one U.S. general called a "treasure trove" of documents on Zarqawi's deadly group. The document coup led to other successes against al Qaeda in Iraq. But such successes have come too infrequently.

Once more, the United States is left in a reactive mode because of its severe counterintelligence deficiencies. Whether it's enemy agents penetrating the Iraqi security structure or terrorists infiltrating the U.S. government and military, the threat is grave. And we will remain this vulnerable until we dramatically reform our intelligence and methods. Double-agent operations, planting spies inside organizations, and using human-intensive spying—all these and other classic counterintelligence strategies will be essential to protecting our fighting forces overseas and citizens at home.

Chapter 8

CUBA'S MOLE iN THE PENTAGON

I believe our government's policy towards Cuba is cruel and un-
fair, profoundly unneighborly, and I felt morally obligated to help
the island defend itself from our efforts to impose our values and
our political system on it.

—*Ana Belen Montes, a Cuban mole inside the Defense
Intelligence Agency, at her sentencing for espionage*

FBI agents arrived at the Defense Intelligence Agency headquarters
at Bolling Air Force Base on September 21, 2001, and arrested
one of the agency's most senior analysts. The arrest was over-
shadowed by the terrorist attacks of September 11, but it highlighted
the extent to which America's enemies have infiltrated the U.S. government and stolen valuable secrets.

The high-level DIA analyst, you see, had been spying for Cuba's
Communist government for sixteen years. As the U.S. government's
most important and trusted intelligence official on Cuba, Ana Belen
Montes had a line to White House national security officials and had
influenced U.S. policy in favor of Fidel Castro's ruthless regime.
Worse still, since the 1980s she had provided the Cubans with a
passkey to America's vital intelligence secrets—secrets that Cuba fed
to America's enemies, including the Chinese and the Russians.

And once again U.S. counterintelligence completely missed the spying for years. It was yet another counterintelligence failure that will haunt the United States for years into the future.

In 2005, long after Montes had been convicted of espionage, the Office of the National Counterintelligence Executive produced a classified damage assessment of the case. The report revealed that Cuban intelligence officers had been so contemptuous of FBI spy-catching capabilities that they met openly with Montes at Washington-area restaurants more than a hundred times. Montes admitted meeting with her handlers "as often as twice a week," the report added, a rate "much more frequent" than that of the typical spy. The Cubans understood that FBI counterintelligence had targeted their "official" intelligence officers, who posed as diplomats working at the Cuban mission to the United Nations and at the Cuban Interests Section of the Embassy of Switzerland. So instead they reached out to Montes using their extensive network of spies who used nonofficial cover, posing as businesspeople, academics, or students, for example.

U.S. intelligence officials determined that Montes had been spotted by the Cubans while she was a graduate student in the early 1980s. The Cuban Directorate of Intelligence, known as DGI, had carefully prepared her to burrow deep within the U.S. intelligence community, directing her to seek a job at the DIA. "Ana Montes was Castro's deep mole and intelligence resource inside DIA," a DIA official familiar with the case told me. "She was recruited by him before she became a civil servant." One of the many indications that the FBI mishandled the Montes investigation is that it failed to capture the spymaster who recruited her or any of her other Cuban intelligence handlers.

The damage Montes did has largely been hidden from public view until now. The Montes case is, in fact, one of the most damaging spy cases for the U.S. government, because Montes had almost unlimited access to U.S. secrets, including data on the identities of American intelligence personnel and information that defectors provided to U.S. intelligence.

A senior U.S. counterintelligence official familiar with the damage assessment told me, "As a career analyst with high-level security clearances, [Montes] had access to virtually unlimited amounts of sensitive data from a number of intelligence community organizations." She actually turned down several promotion opportunities to remain as a DIA analyst and keep her access to secrets. The counterintelligence official said that Montes commented during one debriefing session that she had access to "just about all the information there was about Cuba." And not just about Cuba. Montes networked extensively with other civilian and military intelligence officials and agencies, allowing her "to obtain information that was not readily available to the typical analyst," the official said. She sat on a special interagency intelligence group known as the Hard Target Committee, which would meet to discuss all the intelligence operations under way in the most difficult places, including Iran, China, and North Korea. Over the years she had access to hundreds of thousands of intelligence reports, many of which she could re-create because "she had an extraordinary, almost photographic memory," according to the counterintelligence official.

The NCIX damage assessment concluded, "Montes was the first national-level analyst from the intelligence community known to have turned traitor and the most damaging Cuban spy arrested to date." The report added that Montes "was able to effectively inform the Cubans of the United States information gaps and served as a feedback loop for the Cubans that potentially would facilitate the formulation and execution of a robust denial and deception program at U.S. intelligence."

The counterintelligence official said, "Her damage was especially grave and affected every major intelligence community organization. She compromised numerous sensitive intelligence collection activities and provided Havana with a unique window into Washington that undoubtedly helped the Cubans chart their tactics and strategy in dealing with Washington." U.S. officials also believe that information she provided to the Cubans led to the deaths of Nicaraguan anti-Communist Contra rebels and possibly of American agents as well.

Michelle Van Cleave, who was the national counterintelligence executive until January 2006, said that although Montes was "lesser known" than notorious double agents Robert Hanssen and Aldrich Ames, she was "no less damaging." Other counterintelligence officials told me that Montes actually did more harm than Ames and Hanssen did. Whatever the case, the damage inflicted was severe.

It is fitting that Ana Montes was arrested after 9/11, for she warns of a dire threat the United States faces in the War on Terror: the ideological enemy. Whereas Ames was a traitor for cash and Hanssen was motivated by the money as well as the intrigue that came with betraying his country, Montes was driven by her opposition to the United States and her sympathy for Cuba's Marxist-Leninist system. "She did not fit the profile of a typical spy," a counterintelligence official said. "She was not motivated by greed, revenge, or romantic entanglement with a foreign national." In fact, she received little money for the volumes of sensitive secrets she gave Havana; she was merely reimbursed for her expenses. She later said that she had felt "morally obligated" to spy for Cuba's Communist regime. Montes, a U.S. citizen of Puerto Rican descent, claimed to debriefers that she was not a Communist herself, only a sympathizer with Cuba's "socio-economic" values as well as those of the Communist Sandinistas in Nicaragua. The counterintelligence official said, "Montes established a relationship with the Cubans as a way to aid the Sandinistas. Following the electoral defeat of the Sandinistas in 1990, helping Cuba became her priority." She was the ultimate example of the anti-American leftists who former United Nations ambassador Jeane Kirkpatrick once described as the "blame America first" crowd.

In the clash with foreign governments and terrorist organizations that despise America, the threat from such ideological opponents keeps growing.

The Cuban Threat

Although Cuba's Communist regime does not receive much attention as a national security threat, the Ana Montes case and other recent spying cases remind us that Cuba poses a significant danger to the United States and the free nations of Latin America. Cuba has significant intelligence capabilities that it inherited from the former Soviet Union, which helped Castro seize power.

Soviet intelligence files, made public in a 2005 book, show that Fidel Castro and his brother, Raul, worked with the KGB for several years before taking power in Cuba. The book, entitled *The World Was Going Our Way*, is based on documents that former KGB archivist Vasili Mitrokhin took with him when he defected to Britain in 1992. According to the book, KGB officer Nikolai Leonov became "firm friends" with Raul Castro in Prague in 1953 and then worked with Fidel from 1956 until after he took power in 1959. *The World Was Going Our Way* also revealed how Moscow sought to defeat the United States during the Cold War through large-scale disinformation and influence operations in the developing world. Mitrokhin died in 2004, but his coauthor, Cambridge history professor Christopher Andrew, told me, "The KGB really believed they could win the Cold War in the Third World." That is why the Soviets invested so heavily in Cuba. As Mitrokhin's documents demonstrate, the KGB even helped set up Cuba's intelligence service, the DGI.

Cuban intelligence remains quite advanced. Cuban affairs specialist Manuel Cereijo, a specialist on Cuba and analyst for the group NetforCuba International, describes Havana as skilled at all the various intelligence disciplines, including imagery, signals intelligence, human intelligence, signals-and-measurement intelligence (which measures foreign weapons and related systems signatures), and open-source intelligence. "Cuban intelligence operations against the United States have increased in sophistication, scope, and number, and are likely to remain at a high level for the foreseeable future," Cereijo said in a report.

Cuba's government has also maintained close contacts with Russia's intelligence services. Until recently Moscow operated a major electronic eavesdropping post at Lourdes, Cuba. And Havana is developing closer ties to Communist China's military, having hosted visits by several high-level Chinese generals. A DIA official told me that U.S. intelligence harbors deep concerns that the information Montes supplied to Cuba was passed on to Moscow or Beijing. "If [the Cubans] thought it was worth anything to Russia, China, or anybody else, [they] would have no doubt passed it on," the official said. Other intelligence officials confirmed to me that intelligence obtained by Russia and China originated in Cuba.

U.S. officials believe Cuba used the thousands of pages of DIA intelligence reports gathered from Montes to barter for other goods and means of support from Russia and China. The DIA official told me that Fidel Castro could have "leverage[d] U.S. intelligence information for his own purposes." Castro's regime could have taken the intelligence from Montes "to go to the Chinese, for example, and say, 'Give me three million bucks and I'll tell you what U.S. intelligence knows about your nuclear weapons.'" Other U.S. intelligence officials tell me they believe that is exactly what happened.

"The Go-To Person on Cuba"

Ana Belen Montes was born on February 28, 1957, at an American military base in what was then West Germany. After leaving the Army, her father, who was born in Puerto Rico, became a Freudian psychoanalyst, settling in the Baltimore suburbs in 1967. According to U.S. counterintelligence officials who investigated Ana's background, her father was a harsh disciplinarian who sought to instill conservative values in his four children. Her mother worked as an investigator for a federal employment antidiscrimination office and was active in local Hispanic groups.

Ana graduated from the University of Virginia in 1979. In 1982, she moved to Washington, D.C., where she attended Johns Hopkins University's School of Advanced International Studies. She focused on Latin American affairs, earning a master's degree. While in Washington she went to work as a clerical assistant at the Justice Department, where she received her first security clearance. She moved to the DIA in 1985.

Why would Cuban intelligence dispatch Montes to work within the U.S. intelligence community? Aside from the obvious benefits of having a mole in the Pentagon, the Cubans could learn details about the CIA's support for the Contra rebels in Nicaragua who opposed the pro-Castro government there. Even after Daniel Ortega's Sandinista government was swept out in 1990, Montes fed the Cubans valuable information about Nicaragua. In 1990, Montes was one of several U.S. military intelligence officials who briefed the new Nicaraguan president, Violeta Chamorro, on Cuban intelligence operations in Nicaragua—and she secretly passed along details of her meeting to the Cubans.

Montes's influence extended far beyond the Nicaraguan situation. Once installed at DIA, she became widely known in Washington foreign policy circles. She achieved such influence that in 1998 she traveled to Latin America with two senior staff members of the Senate Foreign Relations Committee. The committee was headed by the staunch anticommunist Senator Jesse Helms, who was a vocal critic of Castro's regime in Cuba. "For the U.S. government, she was the go-to person on Cuba," one official told me.

Montes was a good, disciplined spy. Cuban intelligence trained her to steal secrets without being caught. She even traveled to Cuba twice—once as an employee of the Justice Department, once unofficially for the DIA—without arousing suspicion. Coworkers described her as an efficient, no-nonsense intelligence analyst who guarded her political views. "She was not a warm, gregarious person," one official who knew her told me. "She would do her work and that was it."

The usual indicators that tip off counterintelligence officials—unexplained affluence, money problems, or criminal behavior—were absent in Montes's case, said a DIA official who provided a briefing to me on the condition of anonymity. Not only did she live modestly, but she also performed her DIA job well enough to earn praise and numerous awards for her intelligence analyses. According to U.S. counterintelligence agents, officials who are performing poorly in their duties—think Aldrich Ames—are much more likely to turn to espionage. "Somebody that was as good as she was at what she did is always a concern," the official told me. Her ability to fly under the radar for so long highlights a vulnerability in American counterintelligence. According to the DIA official, "The mechanisms that are available to us as counterintelligence and security professionals are relatively limited, unless something pops up which allows us to focus on an individual." Of course, Montes met openly in Washington restaurants with her Cuban handlers and still wasn't detected.

These are weaknesses America's enemies have learned to exploit.

Incalculable Harm

Ana Montes may have done even more damage to U.S. national security than the more infamous Aldrich Ames and Robert Hanssen did. The reason is simple: She had access to more vital intelligence secrets than either of those double agents had.

Montes had access to a treasure trove of classified information from her office in the Defense Intelligence Analysis Center at Bolling Air Force Base. Not only had she penetrated DIA, but she could tap in to virtually any classified U.S. intelligence database outside the agency. Notably, she could retrieve information from the U.S. intelligence community's top-secret desktop computer system known first as SAFE and later as the Corporate Information Retrieval and Storage system (CIRAS). The database was an "all-source" network that included information from almost every available intelligence producer, including the CIA, the State Department Bureau of Intelligence and Research, embassies, the National Security Agency (NSA), and the FBI.

"She did great damage and a lot of our enemies were getting a great deal of information," an intelligence official told me.

Court papers in the case show that Montes gave the Cubans classified information on the identity of numerous U.S. intelligence officers. For example, she notified Cuba's DGI when undercover American intelligence agents visited Cuba, compromising the agents' contacts on the island. Thanks to Montes, the Cubans determined who was spying on them and thus prevented the United States from knowing exactly what the Communist regime was doing, how it was trying to spread Marxist-Leninist revolution in the hemisphere, and the true nature of the threat it posed to the United States and our Latin American allies. Intelligence officials told me that Montes compromised at least four agents in Cuba who had agreed to work with the U.S. government against the Castro regime. Those four were not executed, but it is not known whether they were imprisoned.

Montes also passed along details of U.S. military exercises and what U.S. intelligence had picked up about Cuba's armed forces. A DIA official told me, "It would appear that because of her position, she could tell the Cuban government what we know about their military, what we knew about their positions, and perhaps even more important, what we didn't know, whatever the gaps might be."

Montes's clearance gave her access to information classified at the most secret levels—sensitive compartmented information (SCI) and special access programs (SAPs). In a message investigators later obtained from Montes's home computer, she told a DIA coworker that one particular SAP, which involved electronic intelligence-gathering operations, was so secret that she and one other agency employee were the only ones in her office who knew about it.

As in the Katrina Leung case, it was the compromise of these secret U.S. electronic eavesdropping systems that did the most damage. In 1999, Montes visited the NSA's Medina Regional SIGINT Operations Center at Lackland Air Force Base in San Antonio. During two days of briefings, she learned about every single NSA eavesdropping program targeted against Cuba and Latin America. She almost immediately passed the information on to her DGI handlers, who met her during the visit. It is even possible, officials told me, that she clandestinely carried a video camera and recorded everything she saw and heard at Lackland.

In another instance, as a senior analyst on Cuba and Latin America intelligence operations, Montes took part in long-range strategy sessions for the Future Imagery Architecture intelligence planning program. With that access, she would have been able to provide the Cubans with the most intimate details of current and future U.S. electronic spying systems, the targets, and the methods used. The information would be an intelligence windfall not just for Cuba but also for China and Russia, two nations that are major targets of U.S. electronic spying operations.

Such disclosures did incalculable harm to U.S. national security. "I think she probably did more damage than Hanssen did at the FBI," one official familiar with the case told me. "I don't think Hanssen had the same analytical and intelligence tools at his desk that Montes did at hers."

Disinformation

The Cuban regime, like all Marxist-Leninist regimes, has an overriding goal: to preserve the system. Montes's access to U.S. intelligence secrets furthered that goal, as it allowed Havana to know secret information that the U.S. government used to set policies toward Cuba. Most important, by granting Cuba full knowledge of electronic spying operations against the island, Montes enabled the Communist regime to strategically provide disinformation to the United States.

The Cuban Communists worked very hard to change U.S. policy and perceptions toward Havana. The goal, according to U.S. officials, was to portray Cuba in a nonthreatening way, with the ultimate objective being to convince the United States to lift economic sanctions. It appears that Montes herself contributed to this effort.

In debriefings after her arrest, Montes denied that she had deliberately presented false and slanted reporting on Cuba. But the counterintelligence damage assessment looked at the hundreds of reports Montes wrote during her years at the agency and concluded that she had supplied disinformation.

One report to which Montes contributed contained disinformation that led the Clinton administration to take a softer line on Cuba. The report was identified in 2002 by John Bolton, the undersecretary of state for arms control, who later became U.S. ambassador to the United Nations. In a speech to the conservative think tank the Heritage Foundation in Washington, D.C., Bolton revealed that the U.S.

intelligence community had ignored or "underplayed" the threat from Cuba's Communist regime, including its biological weapons program. He cited an official U.S. government report from 1998 that reached the astonishing conclusion that Cuba did not represent any significant military threat to the United States or the region. According to the report, "Cuba has a limited capacity to engage in some military and intelligence activities which could pose a danger to U.S. citizens under some circumstances."

That conclusion was apparently too much for President Clinton's defense secretary, the former Republican senator William Cohen. The secretary added a note of realism in his preface to the report by stating, "I remain concerned about Cuba's potential to develop and produce biological agents, given its biotechnology infrastructure." Cohen also cited Havana's intelligence activities against the United States and its human rights abuses.

Bolton revealed in his speech that Montes, who by that point had pleaded guilty to spying for Cuba, "had a hand in drafting the 1998 Cuba report." Thus, he said, the report was so unbalanced largely because of Montes's spying and, more broadly speaking, Cuba's aggressive intelligence activity against the United States.

Army Lieutenant Colonel Joseph C. Myers, who was a senior DIA military analyst for Colombia at the time the controversial report was published, agreed with Bolton's analysis. Myers said that Montes "took the lead in crafting" the report. And he challenged the soft line Montes took in the 1998 report: "There is no doubt that Cuba poses a significant, dangerous, and hostile intelligence threat to the United States—and Ana Montes herself embodied it."

Myers said that when he later learned a DIA analyst had been arrested as a spy for Cuba, he immediately knew it was Montes. "I remember telling this guy, 'She's an ideological recruit,'" Myers recalled.

Despite Defense Secretary Cohen's addition to the 1998 report, the Clinton administration favored Montes's benign view of Cuba. President Clinton suspended enforcement of the provision of the Helms-Burton Act, which blocked foreigners from doing business in

Cuba. The soft-line approach sought to advance democracy but only bolstered the Communist regime.

John Bolton's speech noted the cold realities the Clinton team downplayed or simply skipped over: that Cuba is a "totalitarian state"; that it has been a major violator of human rights; that based on intelligence analyses and reports from Cuban defectors, "Cuba has at least a limited offensive biological warfare research and development effort"; that Havana has for decades provided safe haven for terrorists and remains on the State Department's list of state sponsors of terrorism; and that Castro views terrorism as a legitimate tactic to advance revolutionary objectives, and has visited other terrorist-sponsoring states, including Iran, Syria, and Libya. Indeed, Bolton noted that during a 2001 visit to Tehran University, Castro declared, "Iran and Cuba, in cooperation with each other, can bring America to its knees. The U.S. regime is weak and we are witnessing this weakness from close up." Castro subsequently stepped up his anti-U.S. rhetoric, claiming in 2006 that the United States was preparing to invade Cuba.

An earlier classified DIA report also contained disinformation from Montes. She is identified as the author of the Central American section of the 1991 report entitled "Special Operations Forces of the USSR, Eastern Europe, and Selected Third World Countries." She wrote that Cuban special forces were linked to the DGI (her own clandestine master), not to the Soviets. "Although their influence on Cuban special purpose forces has been noted, the Cubans should not be characterized as Soviet surrogate SPF [Special Purpose Force] forces," Montes wrote. This was false. The Cuban special forces were in fact surrogates for Moscow and continued operating as such until the collapse of the Soviet Union. She also said Soviet commandos trained with their Cuban counterparts on a "very limited scale"—another false statement.

The U.S. intelligence community did not challenge these statements. Instead it presented Cuba's Communist regime as a nonthreatening entity.

Montes also peddled the soft line on Cuba in a 1993 paper, as former CIA analyst Brian Latell documented in his 2005 book *After Fidel*. According to Latell, Montes spent a year investigating the Cuban military for the CIA, and she even traveled to Cuba as part of the study. She had been chosen by CIA Director George Tenet to participate in what the agency called the Director of Central Intelligence Exceptional Analyst Program. But the only thing exceptional about Montes was that she was working for the Cuban DGI and against the United States.

"If Montes did in fact visit Cuba that year," Latell wrote, "her handlers no doubt took advantage of the opportunity to provide her specialized training in espionage and countersurveillance tradecraft with no fear of being detected."

Whatever happened on her trip to Cuba, her final report put forward the position of Cuban intelligence. "The [Cuban] armed forces believe that improved relations with the U.S. are a necessary component of Cuba's future economic stability and will continue to jump at the chance to improve communications with the U.S.," she wrote. "The Cubans will be anxious to improve cooperation on operational issues, almost certainly would like to exchange military visits, and likely would accept U.S. military lectures at [their National Defense College]." The Cubans were no doubt taking their cue from the Clinton administration's zealous desire to court Communist militaries, especially exchanges with the Chinese People's Liberation Army (PLA). The PLA gained valuable military intelligence on U.S. warfighting doctrines and methods from these exchanges, even as Beijing blocked Pentagon visitors from seeing Chinese military facilities.

Latell noted that Montes's soft-line views on the Cuban military were "iconoclastic, to say the least." He concluded—only in his book, not while working alongside Montes as a top Cuba analyst—that no intelligence analyst could have reached the conclusion she had reached based on the available evidence. "Some of her language in that passage, and throughout the paper, so faithfully, even adoringly reflected Cuban policy that it is surprising in retrospect that she did not come under suspicion earlier than she did," Latell wrote. "The study is replete with pandering to the official Cuban line that ought to have at least raised eyebrows in the American security and counterintelligence circles."

Suspicion and Arrest

But Ana Montes's 1993 report did not raise many eyebrows in the U.S. intelligence community. As Latell noted, Montes operated unmolested until years later and caused "terrible damage to American interests." The DIA was thoroughly fooled.

How could this happen?

U.S. counterintelligence actually had an opportunity to catch Montes as early as 1994. A DIA official told me that she originally came under suspicion because electronic intelligence secrets had been leaked and the surveillance systems had been compromised. Montes, of course, had access to top-secret intelligence reports based on electronic intercepts. U.S. counterintelligence conducted an inquiry. Ultimately, after two years of investigation, security officials gave her a polygraph. On the test, she was asked directly whether she was a Cuban spy. She replied "no"—and passed the test. U.S. counterintelligence officials believe the Cubans had trained her in techniques to fool polygraph machines and investigators. Montes's fooling of the polygraph demonstrates why U.S. counterintelligence agencies should not be relying on the test to the great extent that they do.

Since U.S. counterspies could not prove that Ana Montes was engaged in espionage, she continued passing secrets to Havana.

Typically she exchanged secrets with Cuba's DGI using coded computer contacts, telephone calls, and meetings. These techniques became particularly important once U.S. officials arrested a group of Cuban agents working in South Florida in 1998. Her meetings with her DGI handlers became less frequent after that point. In her apartment on Macomb Street in northwest Washington, D.C., she would monitor high-frequency, encrypted transmissions from Cuba on a Sony shortwave radio. The Cubans used a so-called numbers radio station, which would broadcast a series of 150 five-figure groups. Court papers reveal, for example, that at 7 A.M. on Saturday, February 6, 1999,

Montes tuned to frequency 7887 kHz and took down a list of numbers. The transmission began, *"Atención!, Atención! tres cero uno cero siete, dos cuatro seis dos cuatro* [30107 24624] . . .," and lasted about forty-five minutes. She then keyed the numbers into her laptop computer and decoded them using a special decryption software program. Finally, Montes went to a pay telephone, called a long-distance pager number that the Cubans had provided her, and keyed in a series of prearranged signal numbers that let her Cuban intelligence handlers know she had received the message. It was spy tradecraft 101.

She did not come under suspicion again until 2000. Counterspies detected "anomalies" in intelligence reports from overseas, indicating that U.S. intelligence information had leaked out. Specifically, Cuban counterintelligence discovered a U.S. agent working in Cuba as part of a top-secret special intelligence program. American counterspies investigated, focusing on the small circle of U.S. intelligence officials, including Montes, who had been "read in" to the special program. Montes drew further attention to herself when she showed up uninvited at an interagency intelligence meeting. "Her presence there seemed unusual," the DIA official told me. A DIA analyst talked to FBI counterspies about the incident. The agency also blocked her appointment to CIA Director George J. Tenet's National Intelligence Council before her arrest.

The FBI began clandestine surveillance of Montes. One day in 2000, agents followed her to the National Zoo in Washington. There they observed her going to a pay phone and making a call to her Cuban intelligence handlers. It was the first breakthrough in exposing how Montes communicated secrets to the Cubans.

The investigation continued for more than a year. It might have lasted longer had it not been for the terrorist attacks of September 11, 2001. The FBI had intended to keep monitoring Montes in hopes of catching her in the act of meeting with Cuban agents and passing classified documents to them. Now, as the United States prepared to take military action in Afghanistan, officials realized they didn't have the luxury of waiting to arrest her. The DIA official I interviewed explained that the Pentagon could not risk having a Cuban spy helping to pick bombing targets in Afghanistan and possibly providing the information to U.S. enemies. "After September 11, somebody in her position would have been involved in a task force on Afghanistan targeting issues," the official told me. "To attempt to exclude her from that would have been unusual . . . and probably [would have] tipped her off."

Ana Montes had fooled U.S. officials for years, and most of her colleagues as well. Many of her coworkers were shocked when she was arrested, in fact. A Navy officer who worked in a booth next to Montes at DIA cried for two days. "It really devastated people," one official told me.

In March 2002, as part of a plea agreement, Montes pleaded guilty to passing defense secrets to Cuba. In October 2002, she was sentenced to twenty-five years in prison.

The Failures Continue

Though Ana Montes did the most damage, she was but one of a string of spies who betrayed the United States by supplying secrets to Cuba. Montes herself tried to recruit others inside the intelligence community. U.S. officials told me that one she attempted to recruit was her boyfriend at the time of her arrest, Roger Corneretto. Corneretto was a civilian employee with the Joint Intelligence Center in Miami of the U.S. Southern Command (Southcom), the military command that would be in charge of a conflict with Cuba. The FBI interrogated Corneretto but eventually cleared him. Investigators also questioned Montes's siblings—a brother who was an FBI agent and a sister who worked for the U.S. Immigration and Naturalization Service, which later became part of the Department of Homeland Security. They determined that these family members were not involved in the spying.

Other U.S. officials were spying for the Cubans, however. One apparent spy had been a high-level Pentagon official, serving as a deputy assistant secretary of defense under President George H. W. Bush. Alberto Coll was chairman of the Strategic Research Department at the U.S. Naval War College in Newport, Rhode Island, when his spying was uncovered in 2005. In that position he held a top-secret security clearance. Officials told me that Cuba's intelligence service had recruited Coll, who was born in Havana, in part by using a female agent to seduce him.

A conservative Republican, Coll shifted away from his anticommunist position in the late 1990s and began advocating that the United States lift the embargo against Cuba. After his eighteen-year-old daughter was killed in a car crash in the summer of 2003, Coll was devastated emotionally. His father also became terminally ill, adding to his problems. He was distraught. At this point he traveled to Cuba, noting on his visa application that he planned to visit his aunt. He also had an affair with a Cuban woman.

According to U.S. officials, a government electronic screening system used on travelers discovered that Coll had taken the unauthorized trip to Cuba. That trip, along with the secret liaison with the Cuban woman, raised suspicions about Coll. And when counterintelligence investigators questioned him about the trip, he denied that it had taken place.

Coll was never arrested but was allowed to retire quietly after his unauthorized travel to Cuba was discovered. He eventually pleaded guilty to making a false statement on a federal form and left the War College. He received the minimum penalties: a $5,000 fine and a one-year probation. His law license was suspended for one year. A senior FBI official declined to provide details but said "there is more to that case."

Another notorious Cuba spy ring was headed by Gerardo Hernández, a captain in Cuban military intelligence. The group he oversaw, known as La Red Avispa, or the Wasp Network, included Cuban nationals and Cuban-Americans who fed information to Cuba on anti-Castro Cuban exile groups in south Florida and U.S. military installations. On September 12, 1998, the FBI arrested ten people linked to the ring—eight men and two women. It was these arrests that led Ana Montes to cut back on her contacts with her Cuban handlers.

The case provided valuable insights into Havana's intelligence operations. First, it revealed the identities of several senior Cuban intelligence officers, including Hernández. It also showed how the

Cubans targeted the U.S. military, since La Red Avispa sought to infiltrate the U.S. Southern Command headquarters in Miami, MacDill Air Force Base near Tampa, and the Boca Chica Naval Air Station in Key West. Havana tasked the spies with documenting the activities, exercises, and trends at the bases. The main objective was to get advance warning of a U.S. attack on Cuba so Castro could take preemptive action.

Five people arrested in the case—Alejandro Alonso, a boat pilot at Boca Chica; the married couple Nilo and Linda Hernández; and another couple, Joseph and Amarylis Santos—accepted a plea bargain and cooperated with the prosecutors, providing information about the others. The remaining five defendants eventually went to trial, and were convicted on all counts on June 8, 2001. Gerardo Hernández and Ramón Labañino, both Cuban nationals, and Antonio Guerrero, an American citizen who monitored and reported aircraft landings and takeoffs at Boca Chica, were convicted of conspiracy to commit espionage and were sentenced to life in prison, although they did not collect or compromise any classified information. Two other Cuban nationals, Fernando González and René González, received sentences of nineteen years and ten years, respectively, for conspiracy and for acting as unregistered agents of a foreign power. The five American citizens who reached a deal with prosecutors pleaded guilty to one count of acting as unregistered agents of a foreign power, and received lesser sentences.

The South Florida case showed that Cuba poses a major intelligence threat to the United States. The fact that the Cuban agents operated for six years indicates that the United States needs to direct more efforts at thwarting Castro's spies.

An even more damaging intelligence failure occurred in the CIA. Counterintelligence officials were shocked to discover that all of the CIA's recruited agents in Cuba were double agents loyal to the DGI. A Cuban intelligence officer, Florentino Aspillaga, blew the whistle on the spying when he defected in June 1987. His revelations prompted the Cuban government to go public with the embarrassing story of how thoroughly it had penetrated the CIA's network of agents in Cuba, with the government-run newspaper *Granma* publishing photographs of eighty-three CIA officers working undercover as diplomats on the island.

The CIA had been fooled into thinking that its agents were working for the United States, but in the end they all had been doubled by the Cubans. The situation calls to mind Angelo Codevilla's comment that it is better to have no intelligence agency at all than to have one that is penetrated. But the agency merely shrugged off this debacle, and actually promoted the woman case officer responsible for the failure. It was typical of the CIA's lack of accountability and oversight.

Indeed, in that same period every single CIA officer recruited in East Germany was in fact a double agent working for the Communists, as was later revealed by intelligence files from the Stasi, the East German Secret Police, released after the fall of the Berlin Wall. The spies in East Germany "were either double agents from the beginning or were turned [into double agents] after a short time," a U.S. intelligence official told me at the time. Codevilla, the former Senate Intelligence Committee staff member, called the disclosure "a bombshell, but not a surprise" because of the earlier failure in Cuba.

Such intelligence failures were bad enough, but even more disturbing was the fact that U.S. intelligence did nothing to shore up its problems. With Cuba specifically, the Clinton administration in 1994 decided to give up on human spying altogether, rather than regroup and launch new operations against the Cuban Communist regime. The administration, led by pro-Cuba national security adviser Anthony Lake, banned all U.S. intelligence agencies from conducting human spying operations in Cuba. Instead the United States relied on electronic eavesdropping—which, as we later learned, Cuba knew all about, thanks to Ana Montes's betrayal.

The Clinton administration failed to recognize one of the keys to effective counterintelligence: penetrating the enemy with spies before the enemy can penetrate you. This was a lesson the British learned well in fighting their clandestine war against the Provisional Irish Republican Army, a Marxist terrorist group.

Chapter 9

STAKEKNiFE

Follow me, and I will make you fishers of men.

—*Jesus, Matthew 4:19*

Recruiting agents to operate as spies inside foreign organizations or terrorist groups is the acme of intelligence work. It is difficult and often involves betrayal, certainly deception, and always risk. And it will be essential in the battle against international extremism.

Unfortunately, U.S. intelligence agencies have had great difficulty penetrating terrorist organizations and other foreign threats. The failure reflects the CIA's risk aversion, its poor structure, and the many restrictions that have hamstrung the agency. Despite the rosy progress reports Porter Goss delivered during his nineteen months as CIA director, the fact remains that the CIA has not penetrated our most dangerous enemies, meaning that we don't know al Qaeda's plans, or about Iran's nuclear weapons program, or about the North Korean threat, or about China's massive military buildup. As one agency official put it, "The CIA's problem can be summed up in two words: no spies."

In fact, by 2005 the CIA's number of case officers had dropped below one thousand. And several hundred of those were deployed to Baghdad to build the new Iraqi intelligence service. Most were restricted to operating inside the Green Zone, the secure area in central

Baghdad, limiting their effectiveness in recruiting agents and collecting intelligence on the insurgency. How could the agency have so few spy handlers and recruiters even today, five years after 9/11? Because, regardless of recent reform efforts, the CIA remains wedded to the view that it cannot achieve the goal of planting agents inside al Qaeda and other extremist groups.

The defeatist CIA bureaucracy would do well to look at the success Britain's intelligence and security services have had at getting inside terrorist groups. Case in point: For decades a British military intelligence agent—code-named Stakeknife—worked inside the Marxist-Leninist terror group the Provisional Irish Republican Army. The IRA was considered as lethal a terrorist organization as any that has appeared in modern times. The British penetration will go down in intelligence lore as one of the great counterintelligence coups of the modern era, and is a model for the kind of spying operations that need to be conducted in the global war on terrorism. But the operation also reveals that running an agent in a terrorist organization is a dirty business, full of moral dilemmas and profound difficulties. And getting a spy inside an Islamist extremist organization will be even dirtier than having an agent in the IRA.

Penetrating the IRA

The Stakeknife story began during the violent conflict in Northern Ireland known as "The Troubles," which started in the late 1960s and continued (with some interruptions) through the summer of 2005, when the IRA formally ordered a halt to its campaign of bloodshed and terror. Britain's government remains officially silent on the Stakeknife case as part of its policy of not discussing operational intelligence matters. But my interviews with former officials, along with news reports and books on the subject, have revealed the details of this fascinating and important case.

The IRA's campaign of violence, intended to force unification of the Republic of Ireland with the counties of Northern Ireland that are part of Great Britain, claimed the lives of between 1,800 and 2,300 people over the course of some thirty-six years. More than 17,000 civilians were injured between 1971 and 1982 alone. The Marxist-Leninist group targeted loyalist Protestants using traditional terrorist techniques such as bombings and the shootings known as "knee-cappings." It also went after leadership targets; most notably, in 1979, an IRA-planted bomb killed Lord Admiral Louis Mountbatten, uncle of Queen Elizabeth II, as a warning to British leaders. The organization funded paramilitary and terrorist campaigns through bank robberies, racketeering, and other criminal activities. The IRA had received weapons from Libya's Muammar Qaddafi.

It has now become clear that British intelligence did an extraordinary job of penetrating the IRA, and not just with Stakeknife. The British planted as many as forty agents inside the organization between 1969 and 2005. British military counterintelligence also landed agents inside the Protestant paramilitary groups that sprang up in response to IRA terrorism. But none of these spies was as significant as Stakeknife.

This incredibly important agent's real name, according to former British military intelligence officials and published reports, was Freddie Scappaticci. Scappaticci was the son of Italian immigrants who settled in Belfast in the 1920s. He was republican (opposed to a divided Ireland) and an expert soccer player. Known as short-tempered and a fighter, he was imprisoned in 1970 during a riot. While in prison he met up with other IRA members, including Gerry Adams, the head of Sinn Fein, which is considered the IRA's "political" arm. Released in 1974, Scap, as he was called, became a trusted member of the Provisional IRA. He volunteered his services to British military intelligence in 1978.

What prompted Scappaticci to become a British military intelligence informant? The answer is not clear. One theory is that he went to the British military after suffering a beating at the hands of some IRA members. One British agent who knew Scappaticci, Martin Ingram—a pseudonym the former intelligence officer uses because he is now on the run from British authorities—wrote in his 2004 book *Stakeknife* that his British handler had revealed this to be Scap's motivation.

Or possibly Stakeknife sought revenge against IRA leader Martin McGuinness. Scappaticci referenced McGuinness in an unusual television interview he gave in August 1993, when he was still an active spy. Using an assumed name, "Jack," Scappaticci told reporters for the ITV program *The Cook Report* that McGuinness was more than simply a Sinn Fein political leader, as he was identified in British news reports, but was the operational commander of the IRA Northern Command. In essence, Scappaticci was revealing that McGuinness was the terrorist commander of the IRA. (A video of this interview became available on the Cryptome website in April 2005.) To give a public interview was an extraordinary and risky move for an active spy. Scappaticci clearly felt an urgent need to take such a drastic step. Years later, after Stakeknife's identity was revealed, ITV reporter Sylvia Jones revealed that Scappaticci had contacted them directly, upset that a *Cook Report* story on McGuinness had been too soft on the Sinn Fein leader.

Stakeknife was handled by Britain's ultrasecret military intelligence group in Northern Ireland, the Mobile Reconnaissance Force, which in 1980 was renamed the Force Research Unit (FRU). The military unit included mostly enlisted men from the Royal Army, Navy, and Air Force, as well as special forces troops, including those from the elite Special Air Services. Counterspy recruiters and handlers like Ingram made it through an intensive ten-week training program from which only about three of every ten students emerged. According to Ingram, the FRU was dedicated to recruiting, developing, and controlling spies who could assist the covert war against the IRA. Its motto said it all: "Fishers of men."

In the early 1970s, the unit had run an extremely successful operation known as the Four Square Laundry. The group sent young women into Catholic areas of Belfast, Northern Ireland, to offer special discounts on laundry services. Using special equipment in the back of the shop, the women scanned clothes for traces of explosives or precursor chemicals and gunpowder. The explosives residue allowed British intelligence to identify many IRA terrorists. According to an official familiar with the operation, the IRA later discovered that the laundry was a cover for the British. In response, it attacked one of Four Square's delivery vans, killing an undercover British Army soldier.

Still, the intelligence unit had gotten a peek at how the IRA worked. And Stakeknife would give the British a much longer look. Scappaticci's position as deputy director of the IRA's internal security unit provided the ideal cover for a spy. The internal security unit was responsible for finding spies inside the organization—and killing them. (The brutal unit became known as the "nutting squad," because the IRA put bullets into informants' heads, or "nuts.") Scappaticci had wide latitude to ask questions that for anyone not involved in spy hunting would raise immediate suspicions. He conducted investigations of suspected informants, focused IRA internal investigations on false threats (ensuring that the IRA executed other members of the group rather than actual British agents), and debriefed IRA members who had been released from custody. Stakeknife's position allowed him to feed the British extremely valuable information about the IRA's leadership personalities, its weapons acquisitions and storage, and its plans for attacks. He also acted as a talent spotter for the FRU. In the counterintelligence business, there is no better place to have an active agent than the position Stakeknife held.

Beyond taking advantage of Stakeknife's position as internal security investigator, the British made sure their agents weren't caught as a result of too obvious tactics. They subtly used the intelligence they were being fed. For example, the British military thwarted bombings and blocked weapons pickups by setting up checkpoints; they arranged the checkpoints based on intelligence their agents secretly provided, of course, but it appeared that the British benefited from nothing more than good luck in catching the terrorists at their checkpoints.

By the early 1990s, British military intelligence had penetrated not just the IRA but the Protestant terrorist groups as well. The most notable agent on the Protestant side was Brian Nelson, a senior officer in the paramilitary group the Ulster Defence Association. Nigel West, a British historian and intelligence specialist who is well connected to U.K. intelligence and counterintelligence agencies, told me that the FRU's recruiting of both Stakeknife and Nelson was like secretly recruiting the captains of two opposing soccer teams. "And then for good measure they recruited the referees as well," he said, referring to the fact that the British even put agents inside the Northern Ireland police force, the Royal Ulster Constabulary (RUC).

Using information provided by Stakeknife and the other penetration agents—many of whom Scappaticci recruited—the British government thwarted an astonishing 80 percent of the IRA's attacks and identified or jailed 40 percent of the group's leaders. Stakeknife also fed intelligence to the British that allowed police to rescue two businessmen whom IRA terrorists had kidnapped. Another notable success occurred in 1987, when the British, given advance warning, captured a shipment of Libyan arms intended for the IRA. Also in the late 1980s, Special Air Services commandos ambushed and killed a series of IRA members, setting back the organization's terrorist campaign.

There were other important but less visible achievements. The FRU used inside intelligence to identify arms caches located in remote farmhouses, where surveillance was difficult. It then tagged the IRA weapons and placed sensors in the caches to identify IRA members and prevent the arms and explosives from being used. Operatives inside the loyalist paramilitary groups tipped the FRU off to a planned hit against Sinn Fein's Gerry Adams and several IRA members, allowing the British to replace the ammunition with less powerful rounds. It saved the lives of Adams and the others who were needed for talks.

Of course, along with that success came moral dilemmas that are still being played out in special inquiries in Britain. Families of victims of IRA terrorism now claim that the British government was complicit in the IRA's murders because its penetration agents were aware of the operations in advance and did not stop them. Although published accounts of FRU personnel reveal that recruited FRU agents

Stakeknife

working inside the IRA did divert some attacks and killings, it's clear that important British agents like Stakeknife had a good deal of blood on their hands. Such dilemmas are an ugly reality of the dark world of spies and counterspies.

The Dark Side of Intelligence

Ethical dilemmas are not unusual in intelligence. Consider one of the great intelligence triumphs of World War II, Britain's decoding of German military communications. This intelligence coup allowed Allied forces to stay one step ahead of Hitler's Wehrmacht throughout the war. Early in the war, in 1940, British codebreakers informed Prime Minister Winston Churchill that German bombers would conduct raids on Coventry. Though Churchill knew that casualties would result, he deliberately did not order the evacuation of the city or the beefing up of air defenses. Doing so would have alerted the Germans that their secret military communications were being intercepted and decoded in real time. In wartime, he needed to protect the strategic pipeline into the enemy's military command structure.

Nor are problematic sources unusual in the spy game. And Freddie Scappaticci, valuable as he proved to be, posed problems for the British. Martin Ingram said that he first learned of Stakeknife in 1982, after Scappaticci was arrested for drunk driving. The FRU told the police to do nothing to the prized informant, and Scap was released. It was only later that Ingram learned that Stakeknife was the most important agent within the IRA—the "jewel in the crown" of British intelligence, as Ingram put it, who produced "high grade intelligence" that went to the top levels of the British government, including prime ministers Margaret Thatcher, John Major, and Tony Blair. Ingram said that Scappaticci's handler was willing to take risks to protect him because Stakeknife was so valuable a source.

Drunk driving was the least of the problems that came with Scappaticci. The agent was intimately involved in IRA kidnappings, tortures, assassinations, bombings, and other illegal acts. Also, through his work with the IRA's internal security unit—the infamous nutting squad—Stakeknife was responsible for the murder of IRA informants. Ingram believes that Scappaticci was involved, directly or indirectly, in the torture and execution of some thirty-five IRA members.

Some of Scappaticci's statements about Martin McGuinness in the 1993 television interview might have been cover for his own viciousness. In the interview, he claimed that McGuinness had killed another FRU informant in the IRA, Frank Hegarty. But according to Ingram, Scappaticci had told his FRU handlers that he, not McGuinness, was the trigger man. Stakeknife reportedly killed Hegarty to maintain his cover.

Scappaticci's FRU counterpart in the Protestant Ulster Defense Association, Brian Nelson, also had blood on his hands. On January 22, 1992, Nelson pleaded guilty to five counts of conspiracy to commit murder. Investigators suspected that during his two years as an FRU agent he was involved in at least fifteen murders, fifteen attempted murders, and sixty-two conspiracies to kill.

Clearly, the British could not control everything in their penetration operation. British military intelligence in Northern Ireland was taking on a terrorist enemy and did not fight by the Marquis of Queensbury rules. They were engaged in a dirty war and were playing to win.

The FRU's war against the IRA should not be taken out of context. The counterintelligence techniques used against the IRA were classic tradecraft. Nigel West, the historian and intelligence specialist, told me that the FRU created suspicion about certain IRA members and thus disrupted the group's activities. For example, the FRU would identify a target IRA member and work with the Northern Ireland police to have him arrested and interrogated. Then after a short period, say forty-eight hours, the target would be released. The authorities would then round up the target's friends, neighbors, and relatives for questioning. To the IRA, it would appear as though the target had provided the names of other IRA terrorists. The target might have been an IRA loyalist, but as a result of the suspicion aroused, he would be excommunicated or even killed as a suspected turncoat. Freddie Scappaticci played a key part in these British deception operations. In fact, many of the supposed turncoats Ingram believes Scappaticci helped murder were probably not informing on the IRA.

These were difficult trade-offs the British chose to make in order to maintain a real-time sense of how a terrorist group was operating— and to thwart the vast majority of the group's attacks. Such trade-offs are an inevitable part of intelligence and counterintelligence.

Exposed

The secrets of British counterintelligence operations in Northern Ireland began to seep out in 2003, as part of an official British government investigation that began in 1989. Sir John Stevens, the head of the Metropolitan Police in London, led the investigation. Stevens had been chosen to investigate claims from victims' families that British security forces were somehow linked to IRA killings. Stevens uncovered information that implicated British agents in the 1989 murder of Belfast lawyer Pat Finucane, who was killed by members of the Ulster Defence Association for defending IRA members in court. The FRU claimed it had been unaware of any plans for the killing. But reports revealed that Protestant loyalist paramilitaries had asked Brian Nelson to compile a dossier on Finucane and that the information for the dossier had come from British military intelligence databases. Nelson died in 2003, and Stevens eventually charged an agent with the RUC Special Branch, William Strobie, in connection with the murder. Strobie was killed by loyalist terrorists before he could stand trial. In 2004, loyalist terrorist Ken Barrett pleaded guilty to killing Finucane.

The Stevens inquiry and information from Nelson showed that the Ulster Defence Association had planned to kill Stakeknife, who they believed was merely a senior IRA member. When Nelson told his FRU handlers, they suggested that the loyalists target another IRA member besides Scappaticci. They did: On October 9, 1987, operatives from the Ulster Defence Association shot and killed Francisco Notarantonio of the IRA.

In the course of the Stevens inquiry, Stakeknife was unmasked. British newspapers identified Scappaticci as Stakeknife on May 11, 2003. British intelligence sources told me they believe that former FRU agents, including Martin Ingram, leaked the information to the press to protest the handling of the Stevens inquiry. They felt they were being unfairly treated after working for years against the IRA and were being taken to task simply for doing their jobs. Stevens said in a brief statement capping fourteen years of investigation that British authorities had colluded with loyalist terrorists.

Scappaticci at first denied that he was anything more than a republican Irishman and a humble construction worker. He told the online publication Irelandclick.com that he had nothing to do with British intelligence: "To suggest that I was at the heart of the peace process, doing this Machiavellian stuff, that I had the ear of Gerry Adams— the Mr. Big, in there for British intelligence, pushing the peace process one way, pushing it another to suit a British agenda. It's so ridiculous that it's just unbelievable." Sinn Fein, for its part, claimed that the British had invented the allegations that Scappaticci was an FRU agent to discredit the unification movement and to divert attention from British intelligence collusion with the loyalist terror groups.

In 2004, however, Scappaticci's 1993 interview was made public, and both the IRA and the RUC, renamed the Police Service of Northern Ireland, changed their tune, fearing what Stakeknife might reveal. The IRA, facing pressure from the families of murdered operatives falsely accused of being turncoats, eventually admitted that Scappaticci was the real traitor to the organization. One Sinn Fein leader, Martin O'Muilleoir, told a republican newspaper, the *Anderstown News,* that "there's no getting away from the fact that the majority of our readers, who have been given the full story, are starting to reach their own sad conclusion" that Scappaticci worked for British military intelligence. As news of the British cooperation with the IRA went public, members of the FRU and other intelligence organizations fled the country, fearing they would be persecuted for doing their jobs.

Ingram believes that those British intelligence agents who were involved in the terrorist activities will eventually receive amnesty, as will the intelligence officials who ran agents inside the IRA. "At that point guys like Freddie Scappaticci will be able to avail themselves and tell their stories," Ingram told me. What Ingram fears most, however, is that the amnesty will allow the authorities to cover up the government's role.

Destroying Lives, or Fostering Peace?

After Stakeknife was exposed in 2003, Sinn Fein leader Gerry Adams said that the case showed the British government and its intelligence agencies to be "up to their elbows in killing and in destroying people's lives."

In reality, Britain's extensive penetration of the IRA contributed to the terrorist group's decision to seek a peaceful settlement. That settlement came on July 28, 2005, when the IRA formally announced that it was ending armed struggle and instructed all IRA units to give up their weapons. The group said it would henceforth work to unite Ireland and end British rule exclusively by peaceful, political means. But the statement also made clear that the IRA would not disband and that it viewed armed struggle as "entirely legitimate." It made no apologies for past terrorist actions and atrocities.

The White House accepted the appeal cautiously. "This IRA statement must now be followed by actions," a spokesman for President Bush said. The White House statement noted that the IRA "must show its unequivocal commitment to the rule of law and to the renunciation of all paramilitary and criminal activities."

British intelligence remains vigilant. In December 2005, Denis Donaldson, Sinn Fein's head of administration and a member of Northern Ireland's main Catholic party for more than thirty years, admitted that he had been a spy for the British authorities. Donaldson was expelled from Sinn Fein.

There is good reason to keep an eye on the IRA, given its connections to international terrorists. In 2005, pipe bombs found in a Palestinian outpost in Jenin were identified as identical to pipe bombs produced by the IRA in Northern Ireland. In 2001, an investigation by the House International Relations Committee revealed IRA links to terrorists in Colombia, specifically a long-standing connection with the Revolutionary Armed Forces of Colombia (FARC). The committee found that at least fifteen IRA terrorists had been traveling in and out of Colombia since 1998 and that the IRA was paid some $2 million to train FARC members in bomb-making. Two IRA explosives experts and a member of Sinn Fein were arrested in Bogotá in August 2001; they were traveling with false identity papers and were found with traces of explosives on their clothes and luggage. And former IRA member and admitted double agent Sean O'Callaghan revealed in his book *The Informer* that the IRA worked with Russian military intelligence, Syria, Libya, the PLO, and North Korea.

The Need for Human Intelligence

What can the United States learn from the Stakeknife case and, more broadly, Britain's experience in penetrating terrorist groups with intelligence agents? The Stakeknife case may not seem directly applicable to planting spies in tight-knit Islamist extremist organizations, but the United States must apply the same principles to achieve similar successes against al Qaeda and its offshoots.

Most important, the U.S. intelligence community must discard its risk aversion and emphasize human spying. This was certainly the mandate Porter Goss was given when he became CIA director in late 2004, but he had made little progress by the time he resigned in May 2006. The new emphasis on human spying will be a struggle to achieve. Martin Ingram, who has worked with both the CIA and the FBI, told me that U.S. intelligence agencies are ill suited to conduct human penetrations of terrorist organizations. The British, he noted, are "excellent" at the practice. According to Ingram, British counterintelligence successes arose out of sheer necessity. "We didn't have the money to throw at big electronic spying operations," he said, "so we had to do humint"—human intelligence gathering.

The United States has not faced that need. "Americans rely extensively on technical spying," he told me. "They have very little experience in dealing with humint. They also have inherent difficulties with different cultures that make it hard to actually deal with agents or empathize with target groups." For U.S. intelligence, the electronic spying operations that can snatch valuable secrets out of almost any type of electronic communication are impressive but limited, Ingram said. Also, he noted, U.S. spies have for too long relied on "things coming in over the transom"—that is, through defectors or volunteers. Ingram described that approach as working from an "analyst's point of view as opposed to getting your hands dirty and getting inside an organization."

Ingram said that human spying is "something you have to learn. The skills to do it don't come overnight." Adding to the difficulty of penetrating terrorist organizations is the lack of diversity within the spy services. "We can all run agents in the comfort of London or New York," he said. "But try running them in Lebanon or Iran and it's very, very different."

Beyond broad principles, the United States could pick up specific pointers from Britain's Northern Ireland experience. Nigel West explained that a key lesson for the United States in Iraq is for U.S. troops to limit the time a vehicle checkpoint is set up to no longer than twenty minutes. The Brits learned that IRA terrorists could locate a military checkpoint in ten minutes and then would take ten to fifteen minutes to get their weapons and explosives and launch an attack. Moving to another site quickly makes checkpoints much less vulnerable to terrorist attack. This is a critical lesson for U.S. forces grappling with a dangerous insurgency in Iraq.

The success of British counterterrorist and counterintelligence activities cannot be underestimated. The penetrations forced the surrender of the Provisional IRA, as Nigel West reminded me. But what about the moral dilemma of running counterintelligence operations? Ingram, for one, now has doubts about the lengths to which Stakeknife's handlers went to stop the IRA. He acknowledged that British intelligence operated in a very difficult environment in Northern Ireland, but he said the FRU handlers took "fantastic risks" by continuing to run agents inside the IRA. In retrospect, he said, the moral compromises were so substantial that it was "not an accept-able means of operating."

How do you monitor such operations? When do you decide that getting information is not worth the cost of allowing deadly activities to continue? "There aren't any rules," Ingram told me. He then cor-rected himself: "There are a set of rules. It's do anything you like but don't get caught. And if you do get caught, we'll distance ourselves."

The CIA and other U.S. intelligence agencies have long resisted entering the murky world of spies and counterspies, for fear of resur-recting charges of being renegades that plagued them in the 1970s. But given the extraordinary threats to America and its allies around the world, U.S. intelligence cannot remain paralyzed, and must embrace aggressive counterintelligence operations and make them a priority.

Certainly our enemies—dangerous states like North Korea, China, or Russia, or deadly terrorist groups like al Qaeda—will not pull back from stealing our vital secrets and, if need be, attacking us. In the fight to protect Americans, the U.S. government must use all the weapons at its disposal. Counterintelligence could be an invaluable weapon for the United States.

If only we chose to use it aggressively.

Conclusion

DEFENSELESS

Since the 1970s, the fifteen U.S. government agencies responsible for intelligence activities have been severely restricted in trying to stop the danger posed by foreign spies and terrorists. The problems have been identified in tens of special commissions and reports, most following damaging spy cases or intelligence failures.

Richard Haver, a former special assistant for intelligence to Defense Secretary Donald Rumsfeld, has taken part in numerous damage assessments of major spy cases since the 1980s. Haver believes there is widespread resistance within government, and especially within intelligence agencies, to making the kinds of important reforms that are needed to protect the country from foreign spies and terrorists.

"We've studied every one of these cases to death," Haver said. "Study the recommendations and then look at what we actually did. Take a look at what reforms actually went into effect. I'm afraid you'll see that we have a very low batting average. We do the things that are easy, we do the things that are cosmetically appealing, that make the system feel better, and that perhaps satiate the critics in Congress and placate the media and make it look as though we're really changing."

Real changes—fundamental changes—have not taken place. Changes in procedures or from within agencies are easy. And politicians are very willing to spend money on simple rewiring of existing agencies to make it appear that they have been restructured to perform their missions better.

Haver believes that the most necessary reforms have nothing to do with money or agency-wiring diagrams. "They have to do with culture," he said. "They have to do with the way these bureaucracies view themselves, the way they work with each other."

In the case of Moscow spy Robert Hanssen, the FBI was unwilling even to look for a spy in its midst, and thus Hanssen operated for years without being caught. The CIA, Navy intelligence, and other intelligence agencies gave free rein to spies because there was, and is, a cultural aversion to protecting the organization against foreign penetration, Haver said. "That is part of a culture that has to be attacked," he said. "Change that culture, that's what good counterintelligence is all about."

Haver maintains that the most important element for developing good counterintelligence is shifting from a reactive approach to an aggressive one. "The best defense is a good offense," he said. "If you are sitting back, waiting for the enemy to attack you, it will happen. If you want effective counterintelligence, the principal element of that is the capability of your system to attack the adversary intelligence service before they attack you."

Good counterintelligence gets you inside the foreign intelligence system and reveals what your enemy's plans are even before they are executed. The key to success against foreign agents lies in developing the human spying capabilities needed to reveal the identities of spies and terrorists, their intelligence targets, their methods of operation, their support networks, and how much they are willing to invest in their operations against the United States. That last point is essential, for all foreign spies and terrorists have finite resources to use against the huge target that is the U.S. government. Raise the cost of those operations to prohibitive levels and the problem will diminish significantly.

That's why aggressively deploying counterintelligence operations is the only way the United States can mount effective defenses against spies and terrorists. Taking this step will, as Haver suggests, require a major cultural change within the intelligence community and the government national security system. The current culture is predicated on rules compliance. In effect, as long as government officials comply with the letter and spirit of the directives that guide their work—the rule book—the employees are not responsible even if other people in the organization, even large numbers of people, turn out to be agents of foreign powers. The officials followed the rules—that's all that matters.

U.S. intelligence needs a culture of accountability. Government agencies that collect and disseminate intelligence must be accountable for what happens in the operations they conduct and for the information they disseminate. If the information is bogus, they should be held accountable for getting it wrong.

There's another aspect to the cultural problem: In America there exist certain taboos against people becoming informants, like the schoolyard notion of tattletales. This too has hurt the U.S. intelligence community's ability and even willingness to proactively seek information from inside the enemy's networks.

U.S. Counterintelligence: "Fractured, Myopic, and Marginally Effective"

Fixing these problems will not be easy. The first step the government must take is to reexamine U.S. counterintelligence the way the WMD Commission looked at "positive" intelligence capabilities and the need for reform. This will require a joint congressional–executive branch commission to focus exclusively on U.S. counterintelligence. The commission would examine counterintelligence failures and shortcomings and recommend much-needed solutions.

The WMD Commission, while acknowledging that many facets of the counterintelligence problem were beyond the panel's charter, did include a section that provided a good overview of America's counterintelligence shortcomings. The commission's final report noted that even though both adversaries and so-called friends of the United States were ramping up intelligence activities against the country, "our counterintelligence efforts remain fractured, myopic, and marginally effective." The report stated bluntly, "Our counterintelligence philosophy and practices need dramatic change, starting with centralizing counterintelligence leadership, bringing order to bureaucratic disarray, and taking our counterintelligence fight overseas to adversaries currently safe from scrutiny."

In particular, the commission called for the CIA to conduct counterintelligence activities outside the United States. The report stated that the agency "does not systematically or programmatically undertake the counterintelligence mission of protecting the equities of other U.S. government entities, nor does it mount significant, strategic offensive counterintelligence operations against rival intelligence services." The bureaucrats who dominate the CIA's operations directorate have long refused to take on these important tasks, not wanting to force spies to perform difficult missions that run counter to the culture. To focus on aggressive overseas counterintelligence would also conflict with the defensive approach that took hold after James Jesus Angleton was forced out of the CIA in the 1970s. The backlash against aggressive counterintelligence has taken a heavy toll, as the WMD Commission report observed. "CIA's current approach to counterintelligence is in contrast to its approach during the Cold War, when CIA case officers routinely targeted Warsaw Pact officials, an effort that led to a considerable number of successful counterespionage investigations," the report said.

The WMD Commission also recommended that the Pentagon's Counterintelligence Field Activity (CIFA) take a more operational and investigative role in coordinating and conducting counterintelligence on behalf of the Defense Department and the military services. Pentagon counterintelligence has been limited to protecting military services. The Defense Department remains vulnerable to foreign spies because there is no counterintelligence organization that protects the department as a whole. This is yet another reform that has encountered opposition from government agencies that refuse to cede authority.

The WMD Commission's recommended reforms will not be sufficient to address America's counterintelligence flaws. Indeed, the commission's key recommendation was more of the same: more bureaucracy for an already overbureaucratized intelligence system. The commission called for making the national counterintelligence director the "mission manager" within the Office of the Director of National Intelligence. The mission manager would "provide strategic direction" for counterintelligence throughout government.

The problem is not that counterintelligence lacks strategic direction. It is that counterintelligence agencies are hamstrung from doing their jobs by decades of restrictions that were imposed to limit domestic intelligence-gathering. For too long intelligence bureaucrats focused on law enforcement over intelligence collection.

The U.S. government must institute sweeping change, and quickly, for as the WMD Commission noted, the threat from America's enemies grows. "Enthusiasm for spying on the United States has not waned since the Cold War," the report said. "Quite the reverse. The United States is almost certainly one of the top intelligence priorities for practically every government on the planet." The report added, "While our enemies are executing what amounts to a global intelligence war against the United States, we have failed to meet the challenge. . . . Today, we mostly wait for foreign intelligence officers to appear on our doorstep before we even take notice." Highlighting the need to go on the offensive with counterintelligence, the commission remarked that "the lion's share of our counterintelligence resources are expended inside the United States despite the fact that our adversaries target U.S. interests globally."

Given how fiercely the CIA, the FBI, and other intelligence agencies resist reform, the only way to truly fix America's glaring counterintelligence problems may be to create a new strategic counterintelligence service. The foundation for such a service was established by the new National Counterintelligence Strategy that President George W. Bush approved in March 2005. The strategy calls on the U.S. government to change its approach from a reactive, defensive model to an offensive, aggressive effort. As a nation at war facing a growing and dangerous threat, the United States desperately needs "a proactive response utilizing all of our counterintelligence resources," as the strategy put it. Yet many bureaucrats within the intelligence community have sought to downplay and even ignore the new strategy, making it urgent that the president take action personally.

Taking Action Against Our Enemies

America's enemies have caused untold damage by penetrating U.S. intelligence and government agencies. Taking advantage of America's severe counterintelligence deficiencies, spies like John A. Walker, Aldrich Ames, Robert Hanssen, Ana Montes, and Katrina Leung have significantly weakened U.S. intelligence and defense capabilities. China and Russia have stolen our most sensitive technology on a massive scale. Stunningly, enemies have penetrated every single U.S. national security agency except the Coast Guard. Our opponents have purloined nuclear weapons data, U.S. cryptographic codes and procedures, the identification of U.S. intelligence sources and methods, war plans, and much more. The United States also remains vulnerable to political influence operations, such as the one Communist China conducted in the 1996 presidential campaign, when it covertly channeled Chinese money into Democratic campaign coffers.

Americans must understand that our nation faces threats not just from one or two main adversaries but from any number of dangerous enemies, all of whom aggressively spy on the United States. Our enemies include the traditional intelligence powers, China and Russia, which use both official and nonofficial cover officers to target American interests. And then, of course, there are the nonstate actors who could pose an even greater danger to the United States—terrorist organizations like al Qaeda and Hezbollah. These Islamist extremist groups carry out intelligence operations in the United States and abroad to support their goal of bringing about a worldwide caliphate under the precepts of their brand of Islamist extremism. The terrorists who executed the September 11 attacks conducted detailed intelligence operations before they struck, including reconnaissance of targets. Unfortunately, the CIA and other U.S. agencies have almost no knowledge of the terrorists' intelligence practices.

For all the counterintelligence failures documented in this book, the greatest has been the lost opportunity to take action against the enemy. Counterintelligence must be reoriented toward manipulating foreign intelligence activities to our strategic advantage.

The September 11 attacks are rightly regarded as a reflection of staggering U.S. intelligence failures in the years leading up to the terrorist strikes. What's most frightening about America's counterintelligence failures is that they have become even more pronounced in the years *after* 9/11. In the five years since September 11, government agencies have actually made counterintelligence less of a priority, when it should be at the core of our efforts to protect U.S. national security.

Without good counterintelligence, there is a greater likelihood that the United States will need to resort to the use of military force to deal with such problems as North Korean and Iranian nuclear proliferation and the spread of deadly weapons to terrorist groups. If U.S. intelligence agencies had any inside knowledge of how Islamist terrorist organizations operate, they would be able to mount counterintelligence operations, penetrating the groups and neutralizing their plans—before they can strike at our homeland and at Americans overseas.

The WMD Commission made a striking observation about American counterintelligence in its final report. The commission noted that counterintelligence remains a "second-class citizen in the intelligence profession."

Until the United States makes aggressive changes to elevate the status of counterintelligence, America's national security defenses will be only second-rate.

Appendix

ENEMY SPIES UNMASKED

The following pages present clear evidence that enemy spies are burrowing deep within the U.S. government, stealing vital secrets, and conducting highly effective deception and influence operations. And frighteningly, the documents shown here—which include classified U.S. intelligence reports—also reveal how America's repeated counterintelligence failures have opened the doors for enemy spies. The cases discussed in these pages include some of the most damaging spy cases in recent American history. Until we fix the gaping holes in our defenses, America will remain highly vulnerable to our enemies.

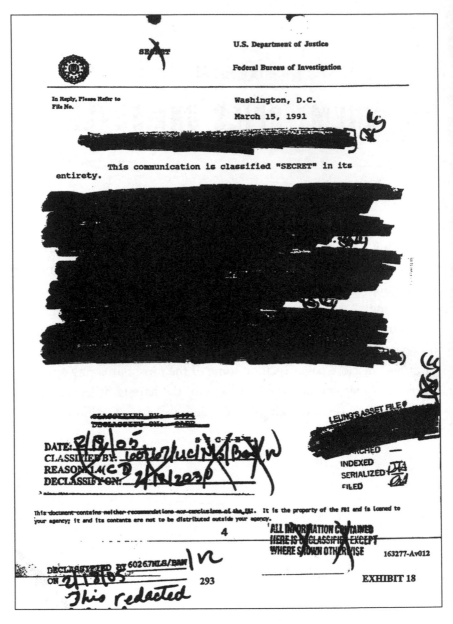

This declassified 1991 FBI intelligence report reveals details of a visit to Beijing by Katrina Leung, a Chinese agent in the FBI. The document shows that senior Chinese leaders discussed plans to conduct a covert influence operation in the Republican Party by making cash donations through Leung. *(pp. 250–253)*

said, the Republican Party is forming a new campaign group in the next few months and a man named Yeutter will head it replacing a man named ATWATER who is very ill. JOHN SUNUNU was the head of BUSH's campaign committee the last time however, he will be replaced as he is currently the president's Chief of Staff. I was hoping you would give me the full name of "MARK."

Source said, MAO's response was very low key. MAO commented, I said his first name was "JAMES" or something but I tried to locate the file and it is not there. Maybe my boss (Minister JIA) or someone else has it. If there will be a new campaign group formed, forget this guy. Source responded, okay. (Source commented, MAO's low key response was a cue to the source not to pursue this topic.)

MAO said, next year is an election year. How can you actively participate in this election? Source said, I vote every year and contribute to individuals but I am not active. Based on my personal knowledge this is the situation: Most people start at the state level. A person could participate as a "major member" if you donate about $10,000 to the Republican Party. Then you are in the inner circle. Then you can become inner circle at the national level of the party. Of course once you are invited to the inner circle you are automatically invited and expected to donate lots of money at various fund raisers. These fund raising parties would include parties for the President, Senators, Congressmen and other state politicians. All of these people would look you up. Even people from out of state. And they would have their hand open for donations. It is all a very involved process.

MAO asked, when will this process start? Source said, a year before the election actually takes place. MAO asked, if we want you to be involved you should start early, right? Source said, yes. MAO said, we will have an answer on how involved we want you to be before you leave.

On March 4, 1991 between 7:00 and 8:00 AM the source met with General Secretary of the Chinese Communist Party JIANG Zemin, Minister of the Ministry of State Security JIA Chunwang and MAO (supra) in secretary JIANG's usual meeting room at Zhongnanhai. A number of topics were discussed in the meeting. One of which is as follows:

S E C R E T
2

5

Secretary JIANG asked, what are President BUSH's chances of being reelected. Source responded, the Democrats cannot compete with the Republicans. His chances for reelection are excellent. Source commented, it seems as though everyone I talked to in China are so very concerned about his reelection. JIANG said, of course we care because we don't know if a new president would be as friendly as BUSH. He asked, will you actively support the Republican Party? Source said, what do you mean? I vote during every election. I do not have the time or the money to be involved in politics. I am into Chinese community work.

JIANG said, we do not expect you to go into politics but we take every opportunity to support people we like because we do not have an organized lobbying effort. It would be nice to have friends like you (pro-China) to be involved in U.S. politics. Every little thing adds up. You could be involved at various levels. If your involvement makes you a friend of the Republican Party at the local, state or congressional level then we have one less enemy. I am sure we will give you the support you need.

MAO said, source is not sure but believes $10,000 will make the source a "major member" of the Republican Party. The source and I will talk further on this.

Source noted that during this conversation MAO did not mention "MARK" who was the topic of discussion in the prior conversation. MAO briefed secretary JIANG on the source's comments regarding the new head of the Republican Party Mr. YUETTER who was replacing Mr. ATWATER.

After leaving Zhongnanhai, MAO accompanied the source to the source's hotel where they talked during the period 10:00 AM until 2:00 PM in order to "tie up loose ends." MAO said I have the approval for you to make contributions to the Republican Party. If you are correct about $10,000 making you a major member of the Republican Party, we want you to join as a major member. I want you to find out if the amount is $10,000. Source said, $10,000 will get me in but I will need a lot of money to sustain the effort over a long period of time. MAO

3

6

163277-Av012

EXHIBIT 18

SECRET

responded, I know. $10,000 is nothing to the Republican Party or
to us. We do not expect you to manipulate anyone with $10,000.
One of the reasons we want you to go ahead is that it would
enhance your image and heighten your profile so that you might be
in a better position to handle other things. I clearly
understand that once you start this process it is a never ending
series of donations. If $10,000 is a reasonable amount to get
you in and if it takes a reasonable amount of money to continue
then we will support you. Source said, define your terms. What
is reasonable to you? Give me a budget and I'll work with it.
MAO responded, I have this approved in principle I have no
details.

Between 5:00 and 9:00 PM on the same date source was
hosted by Minister JIA in room 17, a presidential suite in the
hotel. Minister JIA arrived at the hotel at 5:30 and was
escorted to the room by the Executive Director and Controller of
the hotel KANG Ming STC 1660/2494. He had a serious upper
respiratory infection and insisted on sitting at least 5 feet
away from the source and he covered his mouth with a napkin when
he talked. During dinner he ordered hot water only. Source
insisted he try an old Chinese student flu remedy, boiled Coca
Cola with lemon. Minister JIA responded, you should take better
care of MAO he is too skinny. MAO replied, yes that is true I
have a duodenal ulcer and the source said me too and then
compared symptoms.

One of the current PRC government themes in Beijing is
representing by a slogan: "Be like LEI Feng." Source said you
probably think I am too young to remember LEI but I do and I
remember the song that was written about him and sang a portion
of it. JIA thereafter sang the song in its entirety to
everyone's amusement.

A number of topics were discussed during the meeting
including their request of the source to join the Republican
Party. Minister JIA said, I am sure MAO told you that once you
establish a budget to join the Republican Party, we will give you
the money. Don't worry there is no special tasking from us. I
think it would do you a great deal of good to have a higher
profile which gives you more protection. If anything good comes
your way for China so much the better. (Comment: Source believed
JIA was referring to political influence not information.)

4±

7

163277-Av012

296   EXHIBIT 18

05/22/2004 09:22   8854987338   TOM POWERS   PAGE 01
JJ Smith

Subject: JJ Smith
Date: Fri, 21 May 2004 17:19.29 EDT
From:
To:

This was forwarded to me by a high school classmate of J.J.'s. FYI. Charlie

---

Subject: Jim Smith (JJ) tells his story
Date: Fri, 21 May 2004 06:53:17 -0700
From:
To:

OK, here's the story with gory details:

Since I was arrested a year ago I was in a major sweat about losing my government benefits including retirement and medical [valued at over 80K per year].

I am worried about other things too so this was one of many. My lawyers kept telling me, don't worry about it........I did anyway. All along the government kept suggesting I enter a plea and get this over without mentioning a plea to the Gross Negligence charge results in a loss of benefits.

Several months ago the government superceded the indictment and added Section

1001 [Lying to a federal offical about the affair]. The lawyers told me that was a clear indication the government wanted me to plea to this charge and oh, by the way, you wont lose benefits if you do plea.

We went forward with motions to attack the Wire taps [Patriot Act] and we wanted more classified information declassified to demonstrate that I had ample reason to trust Katrina. Knowing they would lose in a motions hearing before a liberal judge and not wanting set any precedents regarding the Patriot Act, the government called a week ago this Friday and said they had a John Ashcroft approved deal: If I would enter a guilty plea to section 1001, and "cooperate"

with their prosecution of Katrina they would drop the Gross Negligence, Wire Fraud, Mail Fraud and Dishonest Services charges–take it or leave it. After some minor changes, all three lawyers said it wouldn't get any better than this –-take it. So I signed off on it and the judge had room for a plea the following morning at 9:30 AM.

Let me add that the sentencing guidelines came into play here. If I take responsibility for my actions which I will, it drops me into Category A - level 4.

of2   5/21/04 6:21 PM

EXHIBIT 2

Former FBI special agent James J. Smith sent friends this e-mail after his arrest in the Katrina Leung case. (He carried on an affair with Leung for years.) Smith ridicules the idea of cooperating with the FBI in unraveling the spy case—one of the most damaging in U.S. history, according to many officials. *(pp. 254–255)*

My lawyers are saying this almost guarrantees a minimal sentence probably [hopefully] probation. I, being skeptical and cynical will wait and see. With my luck the judges' husband just ran off with his thirty year old secretary and I'll get five years breaking rocks–– in stripes.

So it was Kafka-esque the next day. Gail and Kelly went with me and watched while I had to state for the court the factual basis for my plea- "I entered into an unauthorized intimate relationship with Katrina and then lied about it to my employer". Argh!

So the upshot is that I can not own a gun, vote, hold public office or serve on a jury. I started the "cooperation phase" with my former employer and antagonists last Monday and will do that for awhile–– meaning several months. They will then decide if I could be a valuable witness against Katrina and will keep me on a leash till her trial is over. They set an actual sentencing day for January 10th '05. I can't leave the Central Judicial District till then and of course Judge Cooper can do what ever she damn well pleases in January.

So, the good is that I retain my government benefits and I am no longer preparing for trial where I could lose and go away for a long while. And the meter is not running for three exceptional and expensive lawyers. I can also start working on my tattered relationship with Gail, Kelly, family and high school classmates.

The bad, is that, I am near broke, my relationships are shattered [see above], I have to "cooperate" with the same people who not so gently arrested me on April ninth, I remain tethered to the Central District of California and will perhaps have to testify against someone I believed in for eighteen years and she will go away for a long time.

Personally I have learned alot about myself and others; things I wish I had learned at 18 or 20 or 30 or 40. First, I have lost just about everything that believed in and I am still standing so I fear nothing including death. Second, I have the freedom to define the rest of my life. Third, I wake up every morning [a gift in its self] and believe it is going to be a great day–like a blank canvas and I can fashion a masterpiece.

Feel free to forward this to anyone who has been interested my misery.

Any questions, ask and I'll answer if I can.

JJ

How the KGB Handled Ames (U)
Henry Bradsher, Foreign Intelligence Organizations Branch

Summary

According to what KGB spy Aldrich H. Ames told US Intelligence Community de-briefers, Russian intelligence used old-fashioned tradecraft to handle him. Moscow directed the operation, usually using cutouts, deaddrops, and simple meeting arrange-ments for talks with Russian counterintelligence (CI) experts. No modern, high-tech-nology methods were employed. Ames said he understand that KGB residencies transmitted material, unopened, from him to KGB headquarters; his handlers were unfamiliar with documents that he passed, underscoring efforts by Moscow to com-partment the operation. (S)

Money was the driving factor. After Ames made "the big dump" identifying the US Government's most sensitive Soviet assets, the KGB promised to pay him $2 million. Later, the KGB and its successor SVR also paid Ames $10,000 a month, despite wors-ening economic problems in Moscow. (S)

Meetings were infrequent. During the nine years Ames worked for the KGB, its CI offi-cers met Ames 11 times: in Bogota, Rome, Vienna, and Caracas. Other meetings were scheduled, but Ames missed three of them, because he confused arrangements as a re-sult of his heavy drinking. (S)

While his KGB handlers came to meetings with some topics to discuss, most of the time was spent letting Ames talk about whatever he chose. Ames described meetings as un-structured and informal, with surprisingly little specific tasking or followup require-ments from the handlers. Nonetheless, the KGB did give Ames some generalized task-ing, with the emphasis always on CI matters. According to Ames, Moscow was pri-marily interested in Russians spying for the CIA and in US-directed double-agent operations against them. (S)

Ames was given emergency meeting arrangements, including a fallback "iron meet-ing," at which a KGB officer would appear once a year at a site in Bogota. But, while inquiring repeatedly about his security, the Russians voiced relatively little concern—other than some words of caution—about Ames's drinking and money handling. They never tried to direct him into particular CIA jobs. When he missed meetings—usually by forgetting the locations—he was never chastised or given a pep talk on his security habits and tradecraft, Ames said. At the next meeting his handlers just acted glad to see that he was still safe. (S)

1

The portions of the classified CIA Counterintelligence Center report shown here reveal some of the damage done by CIA turncoat Aldrich Ames. Moscow's KGB, the report shows, stored many of the U.S. secrets for future use. The Russians have only begun the real work of exploiting those secrets. *(pp. 256–260)*

While getting a lot of information, the KGB gave little. Ames said that, "by kind of implicit, unspoken, mutual agreement, they didn't tell me anything . . . that wasn't absolutely directly related to what I was doing, and I'm sure they perceived very early on that I observed that [same restraint] myself in terms of never straying in terms of questions that I would ask . . . [so] they would never interpret me as fishing for anything." (S)

Selling Secrets for the Drawer

Ames overwhelmed the KGB with CIA documents. While Mechulayev and Karetkin were familiar with material in Ames's notes and oral reports, neither seemed to have read all the CIA documents that Ames had delivered through cutouts or deaddrops since the last meeting. The sealed bundles of new CIA documents that Ames turned over at meetings were not opened by the handlers. Neither handler later asked followup questions about the documents or gave any feedback on them. Perhaps the reason was the KGB's tight compartmentation of the Ames case. (S)

Both Mechulayev and Karetkin mentioned that "the massive quantity of documents that I had given them . . . was so highly compartmented [by the KGB that] they didn't have a huge bunch of people sitting working on the case," Ames said. "The clear implication was . . . [that] most of it just sort of had to sit in the bottom of the file drawer." Breaking it out, analyzing it, and using it "either as intelligence information or as operational leads would have required so much work in terms of sanitizing it and sourcing it all somehow so that it wouldn't represent any danger to the compartmentation of the operation, but basically they couldn't handle it," Ames concluded. (S)

Moscow's Tasking

Ames depicted Mechulayev and Karetkin as being "strikingly passive" about what he chose to tell them. He said meetings were "not terribly structured." Sometimes the handler would raise a topic for discussion, but then the meeting would be turned over to Ames. "It was mostly my initiative," Ames said. "I always felt that they had confidence in my judgment" of what to tell them. Mechulayev or Karetkin just asked clarifying or related questions. (S)

Moscow did do some tasking, however. The KGB's message to Ames in Rome in June 1989 said, "We do believe that you are well aware of our operation and information priorities/interests." Nonetheless, the message listed eight subjects on "which we would be always waiting" for information:

1. "The Soviet agents of the Agency" or other US intelligence services, with names, "how, where, when, and by whom they were recruited, how are paid, commo plans, how often and where are they met, what info do they provide, etc."

2. US double-agent operations.

23

3. "Planned important and dangerous political and economic actions against the USSR, including desinformation [*sic*] and CA [covert action] ops . . . ."

4. CIA personnel "who are under suspicion . . . ."

5. "Leads on the officers of the Agency, whom we could contact."

6. "The most important info on military-strategic problems."

7. "Changes in structure, strategy, and MO [modus operandi] of the Agency, first of all in the CIC [Counterintelligence Center] and SE [Division] and on the chiefs of departments and the key stations."

8. "Any info, ideas, suggestions and comments, which could be used first of all to your benefit, for instance, to divert possible attention of CI from you." (S)

Ames commented that he found these points so generalized that they were of little value as guidance. (S)

After the dissolution of the USSR in 1991, Ames said, Moscow also stressed its interest in learning what the CIA was doing in former Soviet republics. A few times it asked specific questions. For example, at the first personal meeting in Bogota in 1985, Mechulayev asked if the CIA had direct communications with agents inside the USSR. Two years after "the big dump", he asked Ames followup questions about some of the cases—although by then people whom Ames had betrayed had been executed or imprisoned. Ames was also queried in Rome about some of the pre-1985 cases that he had recollected and passed in notes via Chuvakhin before leaving Washington. Ames was later given the name of a KGB officer and asked "to find out if this particular person were the object of any particular scrutiny by Vienna Station, by the CI unit there, . . [but] I never made any inquiries." (S)

In Rome, Khrenkov passed him written questions from Moscow. In addition to followups on old cases, at least one query dealt with a current CIA case in an Asian country. It is unclear whether Ames had earlier called this case to the KGB's attention or if Moscow had other sources. Ames wrote answers on his home computer and passed the printouts back through Khrenkov. (S)

As CI specialists, Mechulayev and Karetkin "were very interested in double-agent cases," Ames said. Anything he knew on the subject was "over the threshold" that Ames himself set on what to pass. Ames made a special effort to collect material on the US Intelligence Community's double-agent operations and pass it. He also tried to educate the KGB on how to run its own double agents. "Look," he recalled telling a handler, "if you can smooth your processes of clearing classified information for passage, you're going to be able to make double-agent operations work a lot better." But the handler conceded that it was a problem getting clearance through Moscow's tight system. (S)

24

"Never Holding Back"

In most subject areas, what Ames chose to pass to the KGB depended primarily on what turned out to be available in his various jobs. His handlers "never referred to a particular category of stuff and said, 'Don't waste your time on that'," Ames reported. "I had given them all kinds of stuff," he added, "and I was never holding back . . . ." (S)

Yet, without holding back, Ames insisted to skeptical Intelligence Community debriefers that he had not told the KGB a number of things that it would logically have been expected to want to know—and there is no way to test the accuracy of his debriefing statements. (S)

Ames commented that he was surprised at the failure of his handlers to debrief him in detail, to bring other specialists into meetings to question him on particular subjects, or to read specific, detailed questions that seemed to have been prepared by specialists. As an example of things he could have told them, but said he did not because he was never asked, Ames mentioned identifications of CIA officers in particular places other than his place of assignment. (S)

"There's a lot . . . that I had access to and didn't give them . . . ," Ames said, "They didn't see me as a vacuum cleaner. They weren't interested in seeing that I, you know, picked up everything possible to give them." Besides, his impression that the KGB failed to utilize much of what he was passing left him with little incentive to deliver even more. When he came up with some of the KGB's own book cables that had been provided to the Agency by defectors, his handlers "were actually resentful that I had gotten and passed those." (S)

Ames left unanswered questions in US debriefers' minds by his professed forgetfulness about some details of what he told the KGB or what documents he delivered. Moscow has more aggressively sought to direct some assets' collection of material and to debrief them than Ames admitted to having been tasked or answered questions. (S)

Security Concerns

The KGB CI officers who ran Ames acted as if his security was their first concern. After beginning meetings by reviewing communications and future meeting arrangements, they always discussed Ames's security. They asked if he had detected any security problems, and they repeatedly warned him to be careful spending the KGB's cash. They were worried that his Headquarters conversations might make people think he was prying into compartmented information, thus drawing dangerous attention. They repeatedly expressed apprehension that material he called up on his office computer could be traced, and they warned him to be selective. (S)

Ames felt the KGB was "always superconservative in terms of what they wanted me to do." Although Ames had fully committed himself to helping Moscow in any way possible, his handlers were cautious. "Every time I talked about what I could get" for them from Headquarters jobs, "they would say, 'You know, there are security measures, and you have to be very, very careful about that . . . . Don't do [anything] unless you're absolutely sure that it doesn't cause a problem'." Ames added, "They also were quite aware of the limitations to my access." They never tried to steer him into seeking particular jobs within the CIA, he said. (S)

Overall, Ames's debriefings added up to a picture of a cautious, patient KGB that used well tested, low risk, simple handling methods. It tried to keep its asset productive for as long as possible without trying to squeeze the maximum value from him. But, Ames thought in retrospect, for some time before his arrest, Moscow might have felt his days were numbered because of his alcoholism and communications failures. (S)

26

```
┌───────────────────────────────────────────────────────────
│           S E C R E T  NOFORN  WNINTEL
│
```

TEXT: 1. *IN APPROXIMATELY 1985 THE GRU BECAME INTERESTED IN THE
CONCEPT OF COMPUTER NETWORK EXPLOITATION. SOME GRU OFFICIALS HAD*

*RECOGNIZED THE VALUE OF COMPUTER NETWORKS AS AN INTELLIGENCE TARGET
WELL BEFORE THAT TIME, HOWEVER, PERSUADING THE GRU BUREAUCRACY PROVED
TO BE DIFFICULT. THE PRIMARY OBSTACLE WAS THE LACK OF PASSWORDS AND
ROUTES. IN ABOUT 1988, THE GRU OBTAINED A PASSWORD FROM ONE OF ITS
AGENTS IN EUROPE WHICH ENABLED IT TO PENETRATE A NATO COMPUTER
LIBRARY AND OBTAIN CLASSIFIED CHARACTERISTICS OF NATO MILITARY
AIRCRAFT AND VARIOUS OTHER DOCUMENTS (NO FURTHER DETAILS). A GROUP
OF COMPUTER SPECIALISTS AT THE ALL-UNION INSTITUTE OF SCIENTIFIC AND
TECHNICAL INFORMATION (VSESOYUZNYY INSTITUT NAUCHNOY I TEKHNICHESKOY
SECRET*

SECRET

PAGE 03
*INFORMATSII - VINITI) USED THE PURLOINED PASSWORD IN A DEMONSTRATION
TO A GROUP OF SENIOR SOVIET GENERAL STAFF OFFICERS, TO PROVE THE
VALUE OF SUCH OPERATIONS AND TO PERSUADE THEM TO ALLOCATE MORE FUNDS
FOR COMPUTER EXPLOITATION. THE SUCCESSFUL DEMONSTRATION, WHICH
CLEARLY ESTABLISHED THAT WITH AN APPROPRIATE PASSWORD CLASSIFIED
WESTERN COMPUTER NETWORKS COULD BE PENETRATED AND ACCESSED FROM
MOSCOW, SURPRISED AND EVEN SHOCKED SOME OF THE SENIOR OFFICERS
PRESENT. AFTER THE PENETRATION OF THE FILE, THE AGENT WHO HAD
SUPPLIED THE PASSWORD WAS PLACED "ON RESERVE" FOR AN UNKNOWN LENGTH
OF TIME UNTIL THE GRU COULD DETERMINE WHETHER THE PENETRATION COULD
BE TRACED (NFI). ACCORDING TO SOURCE, THE ALL-UNION INSTITUTE OF*

*SCIENTIFIC AND TECHNICAL INFORMATION WAS A "THINK-TANK" OF SORTS,
STAFFED IN PART BY RETIRED GRU OFFICERS.*

2. *AS A RESULT OF THE DEMONSTRATION, THE GRU BEGAN TO TASK ITS
OFFICERS ABROAD TO RECRUIT COMPUTER NETWORK SPECIALISTS WITH ACCESS
TO PASSWORDS AND ROUTES THAT WOULD ENABLE THE PENETRATION OF U.S. AND
NATO NETWORKS, CONCEAL THE ENTRIES, AND IF POSSIBLE, TO GAIN ACCESS
TO THE MAIN COMPUTERS. GRU OFFICERS WERE TOLD THAT THEY WOULD BE
DECORATED FOR SUCH RECRUITMENTS. THE GRU ALSO CREATED A TEMPORARY
COVER SLOT IN AT LEAST ONE EUROPEAN COUNTRY FOR A GRU COMPUTER
SPECIALIST WHOSE SOLE FUNCTION THERE WAS TO DEVISE MEANS OF
PENETRATING COMPUTER NETWORKS. THE GRU PLANNED TO HAVE THE COVER
POSITION CONFIRMED FOR REGULAR INCUMBENCY. THE GRU BELIEVED THAT IT
WAS UNNECESSARILY RISKY TO CONDUCT ILLICIT ENTRY INTO U.S. COMPUTER
NETWORKS FROM INSIDE THE U.S., AND THOUGHT THAT IT WAS SAFER TO
EFFECT PENETRATIONS INTO U.S. NETWORKS FROM ABROAD, OR EVEN MOSCOW,
SECRET*

SECRET

PAGE 04
WITH THE APPROPRIATE PASSWORD.

3. *ATTEMPTS TO INTERCEPT AND DECIPHER ELECTRONIC EMANATIONS
FROM U.S. OR NATO COMPUTERS WAS A NEW FUNCTION, WHICH THE GRU*

*CONCENTRATED ON THE PENETRATION OF NETWORK SYSTEMS VIA THE SOFTWARE.
(HEADQUARTERS COMMENT: FOR FURTHER INFORMATION FROM ANOTHER SOURCE
ON THE SUCCESSFUL PENETRATION OF A NATO COMPUTER NETWORK, SEE FIRCI-
K-312/03141-90, DATED 31 DECEMBER 1990.)*

```
┌───────────────────────────────────────────────────────────
│           S E C R E T  NOFORN  WNINTEL
│
```

This 1991 CIA report, stamped "Secret," provides revelations from a defector who worked in Moscow's GRU military intelligence service. It shows that the GRU recruited computer specialists who would help the spy agency break into U.S. and NATO computers.

ZNY SSSSS ZOC STATE ZZH
VPF8478
OO RUEHC RUEHMO
DE RUEHC #8478 0321616
ZNY SSSSS ZZH
O 011613Z FEB 01
FM SECSTATE WASHDC
TO AMEMBASSY MOSCOW IMMEDIATE 3951
BT

S E C R E T STATE 018478
E.O. 12958: DECL: 1/31/11
TAGS: EWWT, RS

SUBJECT: DEMARCHE ON RUSSIAN MARITIME ACTIVITY

1. (S) CLASSIFIED BY SETH WINNICK, DIRECTOR, EUR/RUS, FOR

REASONS 1.5 (A), (C), AND (D).

2. (S) DEPARTMENT (EUR/RUS, EB/TRA/MA) DELIVERED THE POINTS IN PARAGRAPH 3 TO RUSSIAN EMBASSY OFFICIALS
(MARITIME ATTACHE CHECHEKHIN AND BILATERAL AFFAIRS COUNSELOR SAKULKIN) ON JANUARY 31, 2001. THIS DEMARCHE
IS ONE COMPONENT OF A RECENTLY APPROVED INTERAGENCY MEMORANDUM OF AGREEMENT THAT PROVIDES FOR
INCREASED SCRUTINY OF ALL RUSSIAN FLAGGED VESSELS ENTERING PUGET SOUND PORTS IN WASHINGTON,
COMMENCING FEBRUARY 1, 2001.

ANOTHER COMPONENT OF THE MOU PROVIDES FOR THE IMPOSITION OF A UNIFORM THREE-DAY ADVANCE NOTICE REGIME
AT ALL 12 U.S. PORTS WHERE RESTRICTIONS ON RUSSIAN FLAGGED VESSELS CURRENTLY EXIST (A POSITION REFLECTED IN
THE AD REF

COMMERCIAL MARITIME AGREEMENT TEXT RECENTLY NEGOTIATED IN MOSCOW).

3. (S)

– THE UNITED STATES SHARES RUSSIA'S INTEREST IN SIGNING A NEW BILATERAL AGREEMENT ON MARITIME
TRANSPORTATION AS SOON AS POSSIBLE.

– WE ARE WELL AWARE OF YOUR GOVERNMENT'S CONCERNS ABOUT SHIP NOTIFICATION PROCEDURES THAT EXIST AT
CERTAIN U.S. PORTS.

– HOWEVER, IN THIS REGARD, WE REMAIN CONCERNED ABOUT CONTINUED PATTERNS OF UNACCEPTABLE ACTIVITY BY
RUSSIAN VESSELS BOUND TO OR FROM U.S. PORTS.

– CUSTOMARY INTERNATIONAL LAW, AS REFLECTED IN THE UN CONVENTION ON THE LAW OF THE SEA, STATES THAT
INNOCENT PASSAGE THROUGH THE TERRITORIAL SEA "SHALL BE CONTINUOUS AND EXPEDITIOUS. PASSAGE IS INNOCENT
SO LONG AS IT IS NOT PREJUDICIAL TO THE PEACE, GOOD ORDER OR SECURITY OF THE COASTAL STATE."

– AS YOUR GOVERNMENT IS FURTHER AWARE, CUSTOMARY INTERNATIONAL LAW RECOGNIZES THAT WITH REGARD TO
SHIPS PROCEEDING TO INTERNAL WATERS OR A CALL AT A PORT FACILITY OUTSIDE INTERNAL WATERS, THE COASTAL
STATE HAS THE RIGHT TO TAKE THE NECESSARY STEPS TO PREVENT ANY BREACH OF THE CONDITIONS TO WHICH
ADMISSION OF THOSE SHIPS TO INTERNAL WATERS OR SUCH CALL IS SUBJECT.

– IN THIS REGARD, THE GOVERNMENT OF THE UNITED STATES WOULD NOTE THAT IF RUSSIAN VESSELS CONTINUE TO
ENGAGE IN ACTIVITIES THAT ARE INCOMPATIBLE WITH INNOCENT PASSAGE, AS WELL AS SUCH ACTIVITIES WHILE BOUND TO
OR FROM U.S. PORTS, THE UNITED STATES MAY FIND IT NECESSARY TO TAKE APPROPRIATE NATIONAL SECURITY
MEASURES TO PREVENT SUCH ACTIVITIES. SUCH MEASURES MIGHT INCLUDE STRICTER CONTROL OVER THE MOVEMENT OF
INDIVIDUAL VESSELS BOUND FOR U.S

PORTS ON A CASE BY CASE BASIS, OR IN THE LIGHT OF FURTHER EXPERIENCE, A REVIEW OF THE GENERAL CONDITIONS
UNDER WHICH RUSSIAN SHIPS MAY ENTER U.S. INTERNAL WATERS OR CALL AT A PORT FACILITY.

4. (S) IN DELIVERING THESE POINTS, WE EMPHASIZED OUR CONTINUED INTENTION TO SIGN THE RECENTLY-NEGOTIATED
COMMERCIAL MARITIME AGREEMENT AS SOON AS POSSIBLE; WE NOTED THAT WE AWAITED A RESPONSE FROM THE GOR
TO OUR MOST

RECENT PROPOSED LANGUAGE TO ARTICLE 16. IN RESPONSE, SAKULKIN PROMISED TO CONVEY OUR MESSAGE TO
APPROPRIATE GOR

OFFICIALS. CHECHEKHIN WENT ON TO NOTE THAT OUR MESSAGE WOULD BE DELIVERED IN THE POSITIVE CONTEXT IN
WHICH IT WAS DELIVERED -- AS ONE COMPONENT IN A PROCESS THAT WOULD LEAD TO A NEW COMMERCIAL MARITIME
AGREEMENT, WHICH BOTH SIDES LOOKED FORWARD TO CONCLUDING SOON. CHECHEKHIN ADDED THAT

Russia remains a major intelligence threat, as the U.S. State Department secretly acknowledged in this diplomatic protest note sent in 2001. The note objects to intelligence-gathering by Russian merchant vessels in Washington State's Puget Sound, where U.S. nuclear submarines are based. *(pp. 262–263)*

THE GOR CONTINUED TO CONSIDER OUR LATEST PROPOSAL REGARDING THE TERMINATION CLAUSE OF THE PROPOSED AGREEMENT, AND THAT HE WOULD CONTINUE TO PRESS FOR AN ANSWER.

POWELL

BT

JOINT STAFF V1 2

ACTION (U)

INFO CMAS(*) CMAS(*) SHAPE LNO(1) JSAMS(1)

JSAMS UNCLAS DMS(*)

+USDP:ESC

SECDEF V2 1

ACTION (U)

INFO USSOCOMWO(1) CHAIRS(*) SECDEF-C(*)

SECDEF-C(*) USDAT:ICP(*) USDAT:STS(*) ASD:PA-SMTP(*)

USDAT-NCB-SMTP(*) DIR:PAE-RAM(*) DIR:PAE-PF(*)

USDAT-STS(*) USDP:TL(*)

DIA V3 0

ACTION (U,6)

INFO DOTE(*)

+SAFE

CINC/SVC CHF V5 0

ACTION (U)

INFO NMCC:CWO(*)

+OCSA WASHINGTON DC

+CNO WASHINGTON DC

TOTAL COPIES REQUIRED 3

#8478

NNNN

Secret *SI NOFORN*

CIA Worldwide National Intelligence Daily

14 July 2000 (Destroy any printed copies within 30 days of this date.)

PASS NID 00-163

Classified by: 2077863
Reason: 1.5 (b), (c), (d), and (e)
Declassified on: X1, X5, X6;
Derived from: Multiple Sources

Russia: Intelligence Gathering by Merchant Ship Confirmed (S SI NF)

Russia: Intelligence Gathering by Merchant Ship Confirmed (S NF)

Special intelligence provides the first solid evidence of long-suspected Russian merchant ship intelligence collection efforts against US nuclear submarine bases.
The cargo ship Kapitan Konev, while navigating the Strait of Juan de Fuca en route to Seattle last week, reported visual contact with a US submarine to a source in Vladivostok.

In this Worldwide National Intelligence Daily report, labeled "Secret," the CIA confirms that Russian merchant ships are spying on U.S. nuclear submarine bases.

TOP SECRET//COMINT//Releasable to
Canada//X1

DEFENSE INTELLIGENCE REPORT

RUSSIAN MILITARY SUBORDINATION OF COMMERCIAL SHIPPING:
Summary Report (U)

01 June 2000

                                                              this
project did surface SIGINT information that
conclusively indicates that Russian commercial
maritime vessels are reporting on U.S., allied, and
other naval units in the European theater.

The Office of Naval Intelligence produced this top-secret report, which provides important new information that "conclusively indicates" Russia's merchant ships are spying on U.S. vessels.

Secret

Special Operations Forces of the USSR, Eastern Europe, and Selected Third World Countries (U)

Defense Intelligence Reference Series

This is a Department of Defense Intelligence Document Prepared by the Soviet/East Europe Division, Directorate for Research, Defense Intelligence Agency

Product Manager:
Political-Military Affairs Branch,
Internal Affairs Section

Information Cutoff Date: 9 April 1991

Secret

Defense Intelligence Agency analyst Ana Montes, a longtime spy for Communist Cuba, was able to downplay the Cuban threat in U.S. intelligence reports, including this secret DIA report on Special Operations Forces. *(pp. 266–268)*

(S/WN) Though unparalleled political and
military changes have transpired in Poland, no
comparable effects have been discerned regarding Polish special purpose forces. This is in part
attributable to Polish concerns of a resurgent
Germany, and potential changes in Poland's
view of operations in the eastern sector of the
country. Currently there is one special purpose
regiment (actually battalion sized) subordinate
to the Intelligence Directorate of the General
Staff and a battalion in each of the three military districts. The total peacetime assessment
of the General Staff-subordinate regiment is
800 with a wartime strength of nearly 2,000.
The SPF regiment is at Lubliniec, 160 miles
southeast of Warsaw, where approximately 30
6- to 8-man teams are available for deployment
from the current 800-man force. There is also a
modest-sized naval SPF force targeted for operations in the Baltic Sea.

(S/WN) Romania's armed forces, primarily
configured for defensive operations, have a
limited SPF capability. Each of Romania's
four armies contains one airborne regiment,
with one long-range reconnaissance company.
Though they can deploy seven teams of six to
seven men each, these companies are oriented
primarily toward operations against invaders
within Romanian borders; as demonstrated in
the recent civil strife, they can be employed as
an internal security force.

LATIN AMERICA

Cuba

(S/WN) Special operations are the primary
responsibility of the Directorate of Special Operations (DGOE) of the Ministry of the Interior (MININT) and are not a responsibility of
the Cuban Ministry of the Armed Forces. At
least two SOF elements have been identified
in Cuba, the MININT's Special Troop Brigade
and the Revolutionary Navy's Special Destination Detachment. The Special Troops is a
highly motivated, well-trained, politically indoctrinated, rapid deployment light infantry
force of 2,500 to 3,000 personnel. Its members
are airborne-, airmobile-, and scuba-qualified
and are considered to be well trained in both

UNCLASSIFIED

**Figure 11. (U) Members of the DGOE
During Parachute Training.**

conventional and unconventional warfare (figure 11). It has the missions to support the Ministry of the Interior in internal security operations, provide training and support to foreign insurgents, act as a security force for selected VIPs both in Cuba and overseas, and deploy as a combat force at the direction of Fidel
Castro (e.g., MININT Special Troops personnel were among the first combat troops sent
to Angola in 1975). Among the most highly
skilled and disciplined units in the Cuban military, they are considered capable of carrying
out their assigned missions, which could include limited strikes against strategic targets
in the continental United States. Though not
a Soviet hybrid, the Special Troops might be
influenced by the Soviets through their advisers to the DGOE. The MININT Special Troops
is garrisoned at La Habana Airborne Training
Camp.

8

(S) The Special Destination Detachment, known as the DDE *(Destacamento de Destino Especial)*, is a unit similar to US Navy SEAL forces. Basic missions of the DDE are port security, naval mine clearing, underwater demolition, reconnaissance, and sabotage operations. In the past, the DDE was considered to be a small group of approximately 200 personnel; however, there are new indications that this organization might have between 500 and 1,000 personnel. Members of the DDE are assigned to naval bases and selected ports throughout Cuba. DDE headquarters is Punta Ballenatos Naval Facility. DDE personnel are well trained and equipped and are capable of conducting assigned missions.

(S/WN) Another organization linked to Cuban special purpose operations is the General Directorate of Intelligence. This organization, which is under the supervision of the Ministry of Interior, directs a variety of intelligence operations. Since there is a Soviet advisory body to the directorate, it most likely provides some guidance on development of special purpose-associated operations. Further, a sizable contingent of Soviet military advisers from the 10th Main Directorate (Foreign Military Assistance) of the General Staff serves as instructors to the Cuban Army and the Intelligence Directorate. Although their influence on Cuban special purpose forces has been noted, the Cubans should not be characterized as Soviet surrogate SPF forces. Cuban special purpose forces are organized in a manner that reflects the local military area of operations. The Soviet GRU maintains a presence in Cuba, both in an advisory and intelligence collection role. Additionally, evidence suggests that Soviet SPF may train with Cuban special forces personnel on a very limited scale. Finally, evidence also suggests that Cuban special troops may have been trained in the Soviet Union.

Nicaragua

(S/WN) Ms. Chamorro's assumption of the Nicaraguan presidency has had a profound effect on the Sandinista-designed military structure. This may have included SPF forces as well, but there has been very little report-

ing on this issue. The following is the status of Nicaraguan SPF as of May 1990. In the past, Nicaraguan special operations forces totaled approximately 750 personnel, in the Army, Navy, and Ministry of Interior. The primary mission of the Army's Small Unit Special Forces (PUFE) and Special Destination Companies was to provide intelligence on enemy insurgent locations to counterinsurgency battalions. These special forces units were also assigned combat missions, such as ambushes and raids, and were authorized to operate in Honduras and Costa Rica. The PUFE consists of 5 66-man units and is subordinate to the Military Intelligence Directorate of the armed forces General Staff. The Special Destination Companies consist of 2 77-man units, 1 each subordinate to the intelligence staffs of the headquarters of military regions II and IV. Many SOF personnel were trained in Cuba and all are parachute qualified. PUFE personnel are also scuba qualified and are trained to use surface-to-air missiles and sniper rifles. The Nicaraguan Navy possessed a 64-man amphibious special operations unit called the Special Destination Detachment. It is responsible for underwater demolition, reconnaissance, and operations, as well as removing underwater mines from vessels and ports. The unit was originally organized and trained by Cubans. The Ministry of Interior reportedly has a Special Troops Battalion of some 1,200 men. The battalion falls under the Ministry of Interior Special Operations Directorate, and its mission is to collect intelligence on and attack specific enemy insurgents. The troops were trained by Cubans and Vietnamese instructors. Personnel are parachute qualified and have operated inside Honduras.

ASIA

Afghanistan

(S/WN) Afghanistan's Ministry of State Security (WAD), the successor to the ubiquitous KHAD, is a Soviet-inspired intelligence and security unit that conducts a variety of operations, including national-level SPF-type sabotage and agent operations against targets in

9

Secret

DATE: 2 February 1998
FROM: DIRNSA
TO: NSA/SPECIAL-HCO
           EXCLUSIVE FOR:

INFO:

TOP SECRET UMBRA ORCON US ONLY

SERIAL:

TAGS: IQR MAGG PFOR IQ US

SUBJ: Iraq/Crisis: Iraqi Intelligence Officer Receives Information of Imminent U.S. Attack; Also Learns of Desire of U.S. Group to Meet with Him (TSC-OC-UO)

REQS: 2R1864 CFI CON DIP FPR

TEXT: Dissemination and Extraction of Information Controlled by Originator

An Iraqi Intelligence Officer in Baghdad learned on 29 January 1998 that the U.S. may stage an attack against Iraq within the next 10 days and that there are unidentified people in Chicago who wanted to meet with him within a week to pass on unspecified information.

DETAILS (U)

Salah al-Hadithi, head of the Americas Desk at the Iraqi Intelligence Service, reported on 29 January that he had learned from a U.S. person, identified only by last name, that the U.S. plans to attack Iraq within 10 days using smart bombs called the "smart" and

US ONLY
ORCON

This top-secret 1998 report shows that Saddam Hussein had agents in Chicago providing information to Iraq's intelligence services. It would take the FBI six years to identify one agent. Khaled Abdel-Latif Dumeisi, publisher of an Arabic-language newspaper in Illinois, was convicted of illegally working as an agent for Saddam.

IN THE UNITED STATES DISTRICT COURT FOR THE

EASTERN DISTRICT OF VIRGINIA

Alexandria Division

UNITED STATES OF AMERICA	)	
	)	
v.	)	CRIMINAL NO. 1:06cr257
	)	
RONALD N. MONTAPERTO,	)	
	)	
Defendant.	)	

STATEMENT OF FACTS

Should this matter proceed to trial, the United States would prove the following beyond a reasonable doubt:

1.   In October 1981, defendant RONALD N. MONTAPERTO began employment with the Defense Intelligence Agency (DIA) in Arlington, Virginia as an intelligence analyst on issues pertaining the People's Republic of China (PRC). He held a Top Secret security clearance. On October 2, 1981, MONTAPERTO signed a DIA Secrecy Agreement by which he acknowledged that he would never divulge any classified information relating to the national security without prior consent of the Director of the DIA or his designated representative. MONTAPERTO further acknowledged that he was responsible for ascertaining whether information was classified and who was authorized to receive it. MONTAPERTO acknowledged that he had read and understood the provisions of the Espionage Act, including Title 18, United States Code, Sections 793, 794 and 798.[1]

---

[1] The designation "Top Secret" applies to information, the unauthorized disclosure of which reasonably could be expected to cause exceptionally grave damage to the national security. The designation "Secret" applies to information, the unauthorized disclosure of which reasonably could be expected to cause serious damage to national security. The designation "Confidential" applies to information, the unauthorized disclosure of which reasonably could be expected to

In June 2006, former Defense Intelligence Agency analyst Ronald Montaperto pleaded guilty to unlawfully retaining classified documents. But as this statement of facts signed by Montaperto reveals, his betrayal went deeper: Montaperto disclosed top secret information to Chinese military intelligence officers. U.S. officials ignored numerous warning signs of Montaperto's spying. *(pp. 270–277)*

2.   In 1983, MONTAPERTO was reassigned by the DIA to work as Chief, Current

Intelligence, China Branch, at the Pentagon in Arlington. From July 1986 to February 1992, he

was assigned by the DIA to work at the Defense Intelligence Analysis Center (DIAC) at Bolling

Air Force Base in Washington, D.C.

3.   In February 1992, MONTAPERTO began working at the Institute of National

Strategic Studies at the National Defense University (NDU) in Washington, D.C. In March

2001, he was hired as the Dean of Academics at the Asia-Pacific Center for Security Studies

(APCSS), in Honolulu, Hawaii. APCSS is a Department of Defense (DOD) educational

institution in which civilian and military security professionals from the various nations of the

Asia-Pacific Region and the United States study issues and problems related to Asian security.

4.   As part of his responsibilities as a PRC analyst at the DIA, MONTAPERTO was

among five or six DIA analysts selected in 1982 to participate in a pilot program initiated by the

DIA to foster social and professional interaction between DIA's PRC experts and the PRC

military attachés assigned to the PRC Embassy in Washington, D.C. All contacts between DIA

participants and the PRC military attachés were to be documented. None of the DIA participants

was authorized to disseminate classified information to the PRC military attachés. By 1984,

when MONTAPERTO was working at the Pentagon, all the other participants in the pilot

program had either retired or transferred. MONTAPERTO continued to maintain contact with

the PRC military attachés as part of his official responsibilities, yet failed to execute contact

reports after each meeting as required by DIA regulations. He did file an official "assessment" of

---

could be expected to cause serious damage to national security. The designation "Confidential"
applies to information, the unauthorized disclosure of which reasonably could be expected to
cause damage to national security.

2

each of the two PRC military attachés with whom he was primarily meeting – one was filed in

October 1983, the other in May 1987. He only filed these two assessments after being directed to

do so by DIA security. He then submitted additional assessments in 1988. On occasion,

MONTAPERTO discussed with his superiors his meetings with the military attachés, and, by

early 1989, he was directed by his immediate supervisor to discontinue his meetings with the

military attachés altogether.

     5.   In 1988, MONTAPERTO applied for a position as a DIA analyst detailed to the

Central Intelligence Agency (CIA). During security processing in January 1989,

MONTAPERTO made the following admissions: a) in 1982, he separately showed both his

father and his wife (neither of whom held a security clearance) a classified document (level

unknown); b) in 1982, he removed a Confidential U.S. government document from its proper

place of storage and brought it home; c) in 1987, he invited into the DIAC, without authorization,

a private researcher (who, further investigation revealed, was uncleared and had been given

access to classified information by Montaperto); and d) in 1988, he removed and brought home a

Secret document. He also admitted to maintaining contact with PRC military attaché Yu Zenghe

and his predecessor. MONTAPERTO was not able to successfully complete security processing

at the CIA and was not offered the position he was seeking at that agency. However, his DIA

clearances remained in place and no effort was made to restrict his access to classified

information.

     6.   On January 29, February 6, February 13, and February 20, 1991, FBI agents

interviewed MONTAPERTO about his relationship with the PRC attachés. MONTAPERTO

stated that he had developed close relationships with at least two of the attachés – Senior

3

Colonels Yang Qiming and Yu Zenghe. Investigation by the FBI has determined that both men - were intelligence officers for the PRC during the time of MONTAPERTO's association with them. MONTAPERTO admitted to verbally providing these attachés a considerable amount of information that was useful to them, including classified information. However, MONTAPERTO stated he could not recall specifically what classified information he had disclosed to the attachés, and the investigation was closed by the FBI without referral for a prosecutive opinion.

7.   In August 2001, a joint Naval Criminal Investigative Service (NCIS) and FBI investigation was initiated on MONTAPERTO in Honolulu, Hawaii. As part of the investigation, a ruse was established in which a U.S. military representative approached MONTAPERTO in July 2003 and asked him whether he would be interested in working on a sensitive project on China. In accordance with the ruse, MONTAPERTO was told that he would have to submit to a counterintelligence polygraph examination administered by the NCIS as a prerequisite to working on this special project. MONTAPERTO volunteered to do so.

8.   In two pre-polygraph interviews conducted by NCIS agents in October 2003, MONTAPERTO admitted the following: a) he met with PRC military attachés Yang Qiming and Yu Zenghe, individually, from 1983 to 1990; b) he knew when he met with the two attachés that both were trained intelligence officers; c) he would often discuss classified issues with the attachés by talking "around" the information; and d) he had verbally disclosed to Yu Zenghe information classified by the U.S. government at the Secret and Top Secret levels (although he stated he could not recall specifically what classified information he had disclosed to Yu Zenghe). Additionally, MONTAPERTO stated that he might have a document either at his

4

residence or his office in Honolulu, Hawaii, or at his townhouse in Springfield, Virginia, which

MONTAPERTO had written based on a conversation he had had with Yang Qiming.

MONTAPERTO stated that this document pertained to relations between the United States

government and the PRC and that he believed he had placed the document in question in a book.

He provided the NCIS with consent to search his residence, vehicle, and office in Hawaii, as well

as his residence in Springfield. Consequently, after the October interviews were completed,

NCIS agents conducted searches of the locations in Honolulu. No document of the sort

described by MONTAPERTO was found.

     9.   When NCIS agents arrived at MONTAPERTO's Springfield, Virginia townhouse

on November 12, 2003 to conduct a search, MONTAPERTO's wife directed the agents to a large

bookshelf containing numerous books in a second floor office. The agents did not find any

document of the sort described by MONTAPERTO or any other related evidence during the

search of those books.

     10.   On November 19, 2003, NCIS agents conducted a third pre-polygraph

examination interview of MONTAPERTO in Honolulu. MONTAPERTO stated that during the

late 1980's, he had two discussions with Yu Zenghe involving Top Secret information. One

disclosure dealt with the sale of military equipment by the PRC to a Middle Eastern country.

MONTAPERTO identified the specific type of equipment and the country that purchased the

equipment. The second Top Secret discussion dealt with the sale of missiles from the PRC to

another Middle Eastern country. MONTAPERTO stated he could not recall specifically what he

had disclosed to Yu Zenghe with respect to these sales. Although some information about these

sales was officially available to the public, MONTAPERTO's knowledge on this topic was derived from highly classified sources and sensitive compartmented information. Pursuant to his secrecy agreement with the government, MONTAPERTO had a legal duty to confirm that any such derived information was releasable, yet he failed to do so.

      11.   On December 3, 2003, the FBI conducted a final interview of MONTAPERTO in Honolulu. During this interview, MONTAPERTO elaborated on admissions he had made in previous interviews about having disclosed classified information to PRC military attachés in the 1980's. He also stated that from 1989 to 2001 he continued to meet with PRC military attachés from the PRC Embassy. MONTAPERTO named several attachés, all of whom were determined by the FBI to be PRC intelligence officers who worked within the United States. MONTAPERTO admitted he may have orally disclosed classified information that he recollected from his previous position to PRC military attachés as late as 2001. However, during this interview, MONTAPERTO stated he could not recall specifically what classified information he had disclosed to the attachés.

      12.   On February 4, 2004, FBI agents executed a search warrant issued by the U.S. District Court for the Eastern District of Virginia at MONTAPERTO's residence at 7936 Birchtree Court, Springfield, Virginia. At this time, MONTAPERTO had stored within a file cabinet drawer in his basement a number of classified documents, six of which contained national defense information classified at the Secret level and clearly marked as such. These documents consisted of: three February 1984 DIA memoranda regarding "Future PRC Relationship," "Future DIA PRC Relationship," and "A Plan for DIA-PRC Relationship;" a February 1984 DOD cable regarding "The Maturing US/PRC Military Relationship;" and two July 1988 DIA memoranda regarding "Policy Regarding Contact with Chinese Nationals."

within the DOD. As MONTAPERTO well knew, he was not authorized to store or retain classified materials at his residence.

13.　　A July 2005 paragraph-by-paragraph analysis by the DIA of the previously-described Secret documents seized from MONTAPERTO's townhouse determined that all of these documents were properly classified at the time they were created and that all retained their Secret classification at the time of this analysis.

14.　　At all times during the above-described incidents, defendant MONTAPERTO acted unlawfully and knowingly and not by mistake or other innocent reason.

Respectfully submitted,

Chuck Rosenberg
United States Attorney

By:　W. Neil Hammerstrom, Jr.
Assistant United States Attorney

Stephen M. Campbell
Assistant United States Attorney

Renate D. Staley
Trial Attorney
U. S. Department of Justice

After consulting with my attorney and pursuant to the plea agreement entered into this day between the defendant, RONALD N. MONTAPERTO, and the United States, I hereby

After consulting with my attorney and pursuant to the plea agreement entered into this

day between the defendant, RONALD N. MONTAPERTO, and the United States, I hereby

stipulate that the above Statement of Facts is true and accurate, and that had the matter proceeded

to trial, the United States would have proved the same beyond a reasonable doubt.

Ronald N. Montaperto
Ronald N. Montaperto
Defendant

I am RONALD N. MONTAPERTO's attorney. I have carefully reviewed the above

Statement of Facts with him. To my knowledge, his decision to stipulate to these facts is an

informed and voluntary one.

Stephen P. Anthony
Stephen P. Anthony
Counsel for Defendant

Hope Hamilton
Hope Hamilton
Counsel for Defendant

8

Acknowledgments

This book is based on research and interviews with scores of intelligence, counterintelligence, and national security specialists in and out of government. Counterintelligence, the practice of identifying and exploiting the activities of foreign spies, is a very difficult but extremely important function within the often arcane world of intelligence. The material in this book draws on my experience as a newspaper reporter in Washington, D.C., for more than twenty years, and includes coverage of scores of spy cases and interviews with many U.S. intelligence and national security officials, as well as foreign intelligence officers who defected to the United States. I have been very fortunate to work with some tremendous people inside the U.S. government who were instrumental in helping with this project. To those officials, I offer my sincere thanks for their anonymous assistance.

I have presented information here that I believe to be accurate and true. Much of it is based on information that comes from inside the intelligence system, and I have tried to the best of my abilities to confirm the information with multiple sources. In light of the U.S. intelligence community's intelligence failures of September 11, 2001, and the 2002 Iraq weapons-of-mass-destruction errors, I have tried to be especially careful in using some of the important intelligence information that has come into my possession. As in the past, the classified information contained in this book has been checked and I have been careful in disclosing it.

Despite some criticism of me in the past for releasing such information, I have no apologies. I believe strongly that in an information age it is vital for the preservation of our democratic system for people to be empowered with knowledge. It is my hope that the information contained in this book, however flattering or unflattering it may be to the U.S. government, will spur public debate on the need for reforming our counterintelligence institutions in government, a reform that is urgently needed to protect the nation from a variety of threats and dangers.

Among the many people I want to thank are those at my employer, the *Washington Times*. The *Times* was founded in 1982 by the Reverend and Mrs. Sun Myung Moon and has been widely acknowledged as an authoritative source of political and national security news both in the nation's capital and worldwide. I also want to thank the three senior editors at the *Times* for their support: Editor in Chief Wesley Pruden, Managing Editor Francis B. Coombs Jr., and National Editor Ken Hanner. My colleagues Rowan Scarborough and Jerry Seper were helpful as well, as were many others. The editor of the *Times*'s National Weekly Edition, Robert Morton, was helpful in providing advice, too.

Thanks also to the private Centre for Counterintelligence and Security Studies in Alexandria, Virginia, for its excellent work. The Centre provided valuable reference material for the book. Thanks also to the George Bush School of Government and Public Service at Texas A&M University for hosting a conference on counterintelligence in March 2005.

I also want to thank my editor at Crown Forum, Jed Donahue, who provided great help and assistance.

Finally, my wife, Debra, provided wonderful support for this project.

index

About the Author

BILL GERTZ is the defense and national security reporter for the *Washington Times* and the author of the *New York Times* bestsellers *Treachery, Breakdown,* and *Betrayal.* An analyst for Fox News Channel, he has been interviewed on many television and radio programs, including *This Week with George Stephanopoulos,* John McLaughlin's *One on One, Hannity & Colmes, The O'Reilly Factor,* and *The Rush Limbaugh Show.* He has lectured at the FBI Academy and the National Defense University. Gertz lives with his family near Washington, D.C.